ROMMEL'S LAST BATTLE

Also by the author:

ROMMEL'S DESERT WAR: *The Life and Death of the Afrika Korps*
TRIUMPHANT FOX: *Erwin Rommel and the Rise of the Afrika Korps*
HITLER'S LEGIONS: *German Army Order of Battle, World War II*

ROMMEL'S LAST BATTLE

THE DESERT FOX
AND THE NORMANDY CAMPAIGN

SAMUEL W. MITCHAM, JR.

STEIN AND DAY / *Publishers* / New York

FIRST STEIN AND DAY PAPERBACK EDITION APRIL 1986
Rommel's Last Battle was originally published in hardcover
by Stein and Day/*Publishers*.
Copyright © 1983 by Samuel W. Mitcham, Jr.
All rights reserved, Stein and Day, Incorporated
Designed by Louis A. Ditizio
Printed in the United States of America
STEIN AND DAY/*Publishers*
Scarborough House
Briarcliff Manor, N.Y. 10510
ISBN 0-8128-8250-4

Contents

Tables

Maps

Photographs

A self-propelled gun knocked out in Normandy
"Ost" or Eastern Troops, captured in Normandy
Lieutenant General Karl Wilhelm von Schlieben
Field Marshal von Kluge
Field Marshal Gerd von Rundstedt with U.S. Lieutenant General
   Alexander M. Patch
Field Marshal Gerd von Rundstedt

Acknowledgments

I would like to thank Mrs. V. M. Destefano of the Defense Audiovisual Agency's Reference Library, Sharon Culley and Jim Trimble of the National Archives, and Dr. Trumpp of the Bundesarchiv for their kind help.

Thanks also goes to Mrs. Barbara Ware for assistance in translating; Robert Wyatt, Linda Bonner, and Bob Bass for comments and proofreading; and special thanks to Benton Arnovitz, my editor, for all of his hard work.

Also, thanks go to Drs. John C. Lewis and Lorraine Heartfield for all their help and encouragement along the way: "Was mich nicht umbringt, macht mich starker!"

1

The Atlantic Wall

It was November 21, 1943, and Field Marshal Erwin Rommel, the famous "Desert Fox," legendary panzer leader and military hero of the Third Reich, had just lost his job. Effective that day his rival, Luftwaffe Field Marshal Albert Kesselring, would be Commander-in-Chief of the Italian Front. It was a bitter disappointment for Rommel, made doubly so because Nazi dictator Adolf Hitler had promised the assignment to him just a few weeks before. In fact, the dispatch promulgating Rommel's appointment was being transmitted when Hitler changed his mind and revoked the order. "I'll take it as it comes," Rommel philosophically wrote to his wife, as he did almost every day. Perhaps a little more depressed than he admitted, he took a day off and drove to the tiny republic of San Marino near the Adriatic coast to engage in one of his favorite hobbies: stamp collecting. Shortly afterwards the choice of Kesselring for the job of defending Germany's southern flank was publicly announced. Rommel packed his bags, boarded an airplane at the Villafranca airfield, and left Italy forever.[1] It was the second time in nine months that Erwin Rommel had become a commander without a command.

Military commanders of Rommel's caliber were rare even in Nazi Germany, which was noted for its brilliant soldiers. Rommel's career had been meteoric. From 1939 to 1942 he had risen from colonel, commanding the obscure infantry school at Wiener Neustadt in the Austrian Alps, to field marshal, the highest rank in the German Army.* He had commanded the Fuehrer's bodyguard in Poland, the 7th Panzer Division in France, and then the vaunted Afrika Korps, Panzer Army Afrika, and Army Group Afrika in Libya, Egypt, and Tunisia. Time after time he had smashed numerically superior enemy armies at places like Sidi Rezegh, Sollum,

---

*For a comparison of German and U.S. ranks, see Appendix I.

Gazala, Benghazi, Tobruk, and the Kasserine Pass. Finally decisively defeated at El Alamein, Rommel correctly concluded that North Africa could not be held. He urged Hitler to abandon the unequal struggle, but this only earned him the label "defeatist," and, his health damaged by two years of warfare on the Sahara Desert, he was ordered home in semidisgrace in March 1943. His Army Group Afrika was taken over by Colonel General Jürgen von Arnim, a veteran of the Russian Front. Nine weeks later von Arnim was forced to surrender to the Allies. The 5th Panzer Army, the 1st German-Italian Panzer Army, and the elite Afrika Korps were all destroyed; 130,000 Axis soldiers, many of them Germany's best, were marched off to prison camps. Italy rapidly became destabilized after this disaster. Soon the British and Americans invaded Sicily, the 6th Italian Army collapsed on the first day of the battle, Mussolini fell from power, the new government in Rome prepared to defect to the Allies, and the Mediterranean became an enemy lake. All of these developments, plus the loss of 320,000 Axis soldiers at Stalingrad, temporarily shook Hitler's faith in his own infallibility. "I should have listened to you," the former house painter confessed to Rommel as German resistance in Tunisia disintegrated.[2] Hitler took him out of semiretirement and eventually gave him command of Army Group B in Italy, where he briefly shared hegemony with Kesselring. Rommel had charge of northern Italy, where he thought the Allies might land, while his competitor directed Axis forces in Sicily and the south.

It soon became obvious even to Hitler that his old political principle of "divide and rule" would not work in Italy. The military situation and both field marshals argued against it, when they were not arguing against each other. In the end Kesselring was picked for the top assignment because Rommel advocated abandoning all of Italy south of the northern Apennines, while Kesselring promised to hold the boot of Italy despite the Allies' amphibious capabilities. The Desert Fox was again employed.

Erwin Rommel had something other than military matters on his mind in November 1943, as he flew from Villafranca to Wiener Neustadt. The war had transformed his old post from a quiet, mountain city into an industrial center which specialized in the production of Messerschmitt fighter planes,[3] and Rommel wanted to get his family out before the Allies bombed the place. He told Lucie, his wife of 26 years, and his only child, 14-year-old Manfred, to pack their belongings. He shipped them off to the

village of Herrlingen, near Ulm, in his native Swabia, where they temporarily lived at the villa of Frau Laibinger, the widow of an Ulm brewer, until
Rommel's own new home could be made ready.[4] It was here that Field
Marshal and Frau Rommel celebrated what turned out to be their last
wedding anniversary on November 27. Erwin Rommel was a devoted
family man who had fallen hopelessly in love with his wife when he was an
officer candidate at Danzig in 1911. Time had not weakened his affection
one degree and he apparently never considered being unfaithful to her,
even though he was a hero of Nazi Germany and could have had his pick of
dozens of beautiful women if he had wished. In fact, the famous Desert Fox
was slightly henpecked! Now, in late November 1943, Germany's youngest
field marshal settled down to family life at the Laibinger villa. His vacation,
however, was destined to be very short. At the end of the month the High
Command called; Rommel had a new assignment.

Hitler was looking for something for him to do, although it is extremely
doubtful that he intended Rommel to be permanently assigned to the
Western Front when he ordered the Field Marshal to conduct an inspection
of the Atlantic Wall in late 1943. The Fuehrer no doubt intended to
eventually send his former desert commander to the Eastern Front, which
promised to take some very heavy blows in 1944. In the meantime,
Rommel could do a useful job by assessing the state of German defenses in
Denmark, the Netherlands, Belgium, and France. His skeleton staff from
Italy, designated Army Group B. z.v.B. ("for Special Purposes"), would
accompany him on the tour.

The reason Hitler gave Erwin Rommel this new task was obvious.
Everyone knew that the Western Allies would mount their cross-channel
invasion sometime in 1944, and that it would be the greatest amphibious
assault in history. This invasion represented both a great threat to and a
grand opportunity for Nazi Germany. If the Reich could repel it, the
Western Allies would be unable to launch another attempt for at least a
year. Dozens of divisions, including elite panzer units, would be released for
service on the Eastern Front. With these men, Russia could perhaps be
defeated, or at least halted short of the German border. If Germany could
not regain her military superiority in Europe, she could at least reestablish
the balance of power and perhaps force the Allies to accept a negotiated
peace. Even if this failed, German scientists would have another year to
perfect their "miracle weapons," which included new and more dangerous
U-boat models, guided rockets, remote-controlled tanks, jet airplanes, and

atomic bombs. On the other hand, if the invasion succeeded, Adolf Hitler's empire was doomed. This is why Hitler sent his best commander to evaluate the strength of this, his most critical sector.

The "Atlantic Wall" was an all-inclusive term for the German defensive network in Western Europe. Rommel was instructed to examine the dispositions, mobility, and combat readiness of all units in the zone, with particular emphasis on the reserves. He was authorized to prepare defense and counterattack studies and to make recommendations concerning the employment of panzer forces in the potential zone of operations.[5] Hitler promised to give him a tactical command when the battle started, but made no mention of this promise to Field Marshal Gerd von Rundstedt, who was in overall command of the Western Front.[6] The 69-year-old von Rundstedt was beside himself with anger anyway. A Prussian aristocrat who had entered the Kaiser's army in 1892—when Erwin Rommel was one year old—he was a patrician of the Old School, the direct opposite of the Desert Fox. To many, von Rundstedt represented the symbol of a better, bygone era, when it was possible for German officers to serve their country without running the risk of becoming criminals. Erwin Rommel, on the other hand, was perceived as the propaganda version of the National Socialist officer—tough, blunt, demanding, energetic, and, above all, fanatically loyal to the Fuehrer. Von Rundstedt, who had become a general while Rommel was a captain and who had commanded an army group before Rommel had led a division, suspected he was about to be replaced.[7] Bitterly he referred to his new rival as "Marschall Bubi"—roughly Marshal Laddie, and even asked Field Marshal Wilhelm Keitel, Chief of the Oberkommando der Wehrmacht (the High Command of the Armed Forces or OKW) if Rommel was being earmarked as his successor.[8]

Meanwhile, Erwin Rommel was driving down the North Sea coast and was not impressed by what he saw. He told his chief engineer officer, Lieutenant General Doctor Wilhelm Meise, "When the invasion begins, our own supply lines won't be able to bring forward any aircraft, gasoline, rockets, tanks, guns, or shells because of the enemy [air] attacks. That alone will rule out any sweeping land battles. Our only possible chance will be at the beaches—that's where the enemy is always weakest." Then Rommel got down to brass tacks. Meise listened in fascination as Rommel described his plans for the defense of the West. He would turn the Atlantic Wall into an El Alamein line, very much like the one he used to hold up Field Marshal Sir Bernard Law Montgomery's numerically superior British 8th Army for two terrifying weeks in North Africa. "I want anti-personnel mines, anti-tank mines, anti-paratroop mines," he said. "I want mines to sink ships and mines to sink landing craft. I want some minefields designed so that our infantry can cross them, but no enemy tanks. I want mines that detonate when a wire is tripped; mines that explode when a wire is cut; mines that can be remote controlled, and mines that will blow up when a beam of light is interrupted. Some of them must be encased in a nonferrous metal, so that the enemy's mine detectors won't register them. . . ." As he spoke, Rommel drew diagrams to illustrate what he had in mind.

"Quite apart from Rommel's greatness as a soldier," Meise wrote later, "in my view he was the greatest engineer of the Second World War. There was nothing I could teach him. He was my master."[9]

There was much that was still to be done and valuable time had been lost. The defense of occupied Western Europe had been of little interest to the Third Reich during its expansion period. When Field Marshal Erwin von Witzleben, the first German Commander-in-Chief, West, requested that the army begin work on permanent defensive fortifications, OKH (Oberkommando der Heer, or the High Command of the Army) refused to give him a single construction battalion.[10] Needless to say, no progress was made.

The High Command began taking notice of their vulnerable position in the West only after March 1942, when 600 British commandoes did irreparable damage to the Normandy Dock at St. Nazaire, at the mouth of the Loire River in France. Although fewer than half of the raiders returned and the U-boat pens were not damaged, Hitler was furious and the weaknesses of the Atlantic defenses were dramatically pointed out. The Chief of Staff to the Commander-in-Chief, West, Lieutenant General Karl Hilpert, was immediately sacked and replaced by the energetic Major General Kurt Zeitzler, the future Chief of the General Staff. Construction efforts were quickly intensified. Organization Todt (Hitler's construction and labor force) tripled the amount of concrete poured in Western Europe from 100,000 to 300,000 cubic meters per month.[11]

The same month as the St. Nazaire raid, Field Marshal von Witzleben somewhat reluctantly retired and was replaced by Field Marshal von Rundstedt. The distinguished but aging commander was not an advocate of the strong fortification theory and therefore did little to improve the overall situation along the coast. Hitler himself provided much of the added impetus to the construction program during 1942 and 1943. On August 13, 1942, he ordered that the western coast of Europe be turned into an impenetrable fortress. He wanted 15,000 permanent defensive positions constructed by the end of spring 1943. He wanted 20 positions constructed per kilometer of coastline, although he said that 10 per kilometer might be tolerable. The positions were to be manned by 300,000 combat troops, backed up by 150,000 reserves. He felt that 450,000 to 500,000 men could hold the Atlantic Wall against anything the Allies could muster.[12]

The leaders of Organization Todt were horrified. They estimated that they could have only 40 percent of Hitler's program completed by the deadline.[13] They were right: when the target date arrived, construction was not even close to half finished. Organization Todt simply lacked the resources and personnel to accomplish such an ambitious task. In addition, Hitler's own order of priorities for coastal defense work further distracted attention away from the beaches on which Eisenhower's men would eventually land. The protection of U-boat bases received top priority, followed by harbor defense for coastal traffic, harbor defense against enemy landings, and the defensive works on the Channel Islands. The defense of the open beaches was listed as the last priority.[14]

Hitler himself apparently never attached great importance to the Atlantic Wall, either. Although his propaganda machine made a big to-do over it and he boastfully described it as "the greatest line of fortifications in history,"[15] his remarks were apparently aimed at giving the German people a greater sense of security. Except for a triumphant trip to Paris in the summer of 1940, the Fuehrer did not return to France until after D-Day. He apparently never laid eyes on the Atlantic Wall in his life.

OB West (the German abbreviation for the Commander-in-Chief, West, or his headquarters) did not help matters by unevenly distributing the resources that were available. During 1942, for example, it allocated four times as much concrete to the left corps of the 15th Army (in northwestern France) as it did to the LXXXIV Corps of the 7th Army in Brittany and Normandy. By May 1943, the 15th Army had almost three times as many men as did the 7th Army to the south, in whose zone the Allies would eventually strike.[16]

The Atlantic Wall was further weakened by the demands of the Eastern Front. In September 1942, most of OB West's 28 infantry and seven panzer or panzer grenadier divisions had three regiments. By September 1943, von Rundstedt had 34 infantry and six mobile divisions, but only a handful of them had their full contingent of three regiments, because most of the third regiments had been sent to the Russian Front. In short, the number of divisions in the West had increased slightly, but their power had declined substantially.[17]

The prevalent attitude at von Rundstedt's headquarters did not improve the situation. In 1943, German Vice Admiral Friedrich Ruge found ". . . a fatalistic acceptance of the deteriorating situation, and a lack of alertness in looking for possible improvements."[18]

Erwin Rommel, who was in for an education, began his inspection at Copenhagen, Denmark, on December 11, 1943. He had believed the Propaganda Ministry's reports concerning the great strength of the Wall, but soon saw through the curtain of deception. Rommel then denounced the Atlantic Wall as a farce—a "figment of Hitler's Wolkenkuckucksheim (cloud cuckoo land)."[19] He called it an "enormous bluff . . . more for the German people than for the enemy . . . and the enemy, through his agents, knows more about it than we do."[20]

Rommel rapidly toured the front from the North Sea to the Pyrenees Mountains on the Spanish frontier. On December 14 he billeted at Fontainebleau, a château which once belonged to Madame de Pompadour. In keeping with his simple tastes, he did not like it. The next day he had a pleasant lunch with Field Marshal von Rundstedt.[21] Prior to this meeting, von Rundstedt had been warned about Rommel by Wilhelm Keitel. Hitler's chief military lackey told him: "You'll find Rommel a tiresome person because he doesn't like taking orders from anybody. In Africa, of course, he very much ran his own show. But the Fuehrer believes you are the one man to whom even a Rommel will show due respect."[22] Contrary to the expectations of the High Command, however, Rommel and von Rundstedt quickly developed an understanding and even a faint liking for one another. This was particularly surprising, considering their opposing attitudes and backgrounds. The elder marshal, however, recognized Rommel's leadership abilities and listened to his opinions, even if he did not always agree with them. Rommel, on the other hand, respected von Rundstedt's age and seniority although, as in North Africa, the opinions of others would have little influence on him once he made up his mind on a particular question. Neither of the men liked the terms of Rommel's current assignment. To von Rundstedt, it was like having a spy whom he could not control roaming freely about in his territory. To Rommel, it must have been an equally frustrating experience. He, the Desert Fox, always a man of action, had no forces under his command and could not influence the campaign which promised to be the decisive engagement of the Second World War. The two field marshals no doubt discussed this intolerable arrangement at their lunch, for von Rundstedt would forward a plan to remedy it about two weeks later.

First, however, Erwin Rommel had a report to write. He finished his whirlwind inspection in late December. In general, he was greatly displeased and disturbed by what he saw. He found the Army's forces "barely adequate" for a vigorous defense and the Navy and Luftwaffe were too weak to be of substantial help. There were no defense plans except for around major ports, and even here not all the necessary measures had been carried out. The Army was severely hindered by a lack of mobility and a shortage of land mines. Rommel concluded that almost every commander had a different idea for defending his own coastal sector and had no overall policy to guide him.[23] As to where the Allies would land, the Desert Fox reported to Hitler: "The focus of the enemy landing operation will probably be directed against the 15th Army's sector [the Pas de Calais area], largely because it is from this sector that much of our long-range attacks on England and central London will be launched. . . . "[24] In making this prediction, which he later retracted, Rommel underestimated Allied shipping capacity and overestimated the effect the V-1 and V-2 rockets would have on the Allied High Command. True, the rockets would cause great panic and destruction in England, but not enough to force them to change the target of their attack. They would eventually land on the Cotentin Peninsula in Normandy, far south of the Pas de Calais.

Rommel also predicted in this report that the enemy would launch his invasion with aerial bombings, naval bombardments, and airborne assaults, followed by the actual seaborne landings. He did not believe the coastal defenses would hold. Once the coast was penetrated, he felt that only a rapid counterattack by the mobile infantry and panzer divisions could defeat the Allies. These units would have to be moved close to the coast, he wrote, so they would be in position to deliver the decisive counterattack.[25] On this critical issue he disagreed with von Rundstedt, who felt that the decisive battle should be fought somewhere in the interior of France, well out of range of the heavy guns of the British and American battleships.

Despite their differences over how the decisive battle should be fought, von Rundstedt recommended that Rommel's Army Group B headquarters

Map 1—Rommel's General Area of Responsibility

be subordinated to OB West. On December 30 he proposed that the 7th and
15th armies, along with the German Armed Forces of the Netherlands, be
placed under Rommel's command. It is not known which of the field
marshals originated the idea, but it was clearly acceptable to both from the
beginning. Hitler did not seem terribly enthusiastic about the proposal, but
finally agreed to go along with it, although he reserved the right to transfer
the army group headquarters (i.e., Rommel and his immediate staff) to the
Russian Front if he deemed it necessary. Von Rundstedt agreed to this
provision and Erwin Rommel received his largest and last command. Map
1 shops Rommel's general area of responsibility.[26]

The Desert Fox had a formidable task ahead of him and he knew it. He
was shocked over the lethargy he found at von Rundstedt's headquarters
and indeed throughout the Western Front. "To me, things look black," he
commented.[27] The confidence of the front-line soldiers had to be restored
and, with that intangible gift he had for instilling fighting spirit in his men,
Rommel threw himself into his work. The arrival of the Desert Fox
immediately boosted the self-confidence of the men of the Western Front.
The U.S. Army's official history of the campaign recorded: ". . . Rommel's
reputation in combat was a stimulant and a dramatization of the new
importance assigned to the west."[28] The rank and file, it seemed, were eager
to serve under a leader of Rommel's caliber. Morale soared in both armies
as they looked upon their leadership with renewed confidence.

When Rommel assumed his new responsibilities, OB West had four
armies plus the Armed Forces Netherlands under its command. Rommel
took over the two strongest armies, plus the Dutch command. As C-in-C,
Army Group B, Field Marshal Rommel directed two armies with eight
corps, 24 infantry divisions, and five Luftwaffe field divisions. The
northernmost (Dutch) sector belonged to Luftwaffe General Friedrich
"Krischan" Christiansen, a bluff seaman who had distinguished himself as
a pioneer in the field of naval aviation, but who did not possess the
education or mental qualities to serve successfully as the Wehrmacht
commander of the Netherlands. He owed his appointment and continued
tenure solely to his friendship with Reichsmarschall Hermann Goering.
Lieutenant General Heinz Helmut von Wuehlisch, a former cavalryman
and long-time General Staff officer now in the Luftwaffe, served as Christiansen's Chief of Staff and did much to offset the deficiencies of his boss.[29]

In early 1944 Christiansen's command consisted of one corps: the
LXXXVIII. It had three weak divisions: the 347th Infantry Division, the
719th Infantry Division, and the 16th Luftwaffe Field Division.[30]

The 15th Army under Colonel General Hans von Salmuth held the center of Rommel's coastal line and was where most of the German leaders expected the Allies to strike, for it defended the West European coastline nearest to the British Isles and covered the Ruhr, Germany's industrial heartland. On a clear day, German soldiers could actually see England at its closest point to the continent. The 15th Army leader was no stranger to responsibility, for he had already held a number of tough commands. Von Salmuth had been Chief of Staff to Field Marshal Fedor von Bock in the Dutch and French campaigns of 1940, and later commanded the XXX Corps in the Crimea and the 2nd Army on the Russian Front, until he was unjustly relieved of his command following the German defeat at Kursk in July 1943. The Nazis eventually realized their mistake and returned von Salmuth to active duty; nevertheless, they had incurred his undying hatred.[31]

The LXXXIX, LXXXII, LXVII, and LXXXI Corps were under the 15th Army. They had six infantry divisions along the coast: the 70th, 47th, 49th, 344th, 348th, and 711th, along with the unreliable 17th and 18th Luftwaffe field divisions. Eight Army infantry divisions (the 64th, 712th, 182nd Reserve, 326th, 331st, 85th, 89th, and 346th) backed up the front. The 19th Luftwaffe Field Division was also part of the infantry reserve.[32]

The 7th Army held the western and southernmost sectors of Rommel's zone of operations and formed his left flank, which included the Brittany and Cotentin peninsulas. Rommel did not expect the Allied landings to come in this sector, but he eventually changed his mind and poured men and resources into the area, as we shall see.

Colonel General Friedrich Dollmann, an experienced General Staff officer who had been promoted beyond his capabilities, directed the 7th Army. He possessed little field experience, was in poor health, and had trouble with his conscience, as he was deeply disturbed by the methods of the Nazi regime. He really should not have been in command of the 7th Army at that time.[33]

Dollmann's army included the LXXXIV, LXXIV, and LXX corps. Its coastal or front-line units included the 716th, 352nd, 243rd, 319th, 266th, 343rd, and 265th Infantry divisions, with the 84th Infantry, 353rd Infantry, and 91st Air Landing divisions in reserve. The II Parachute Corps, with the 3rd Parachute Division and elements of the 5th Parachute Division, later joined the 7th Army.[34]

Rommel's Army Group was not assigned a single panzer division when it became operational. These units were under the command of Panzer

Group West, a headquarters created in November 1943 by von Rundstedt. The elder field marshal believed that the Allies could best be defeated by a massive armored counterattack; so he formed the Panzer Group to direct this stroke, as well as to train panzer soldiers and advise him on all matters pertaining to armored employment. He chose General Baron Leo Geyr von Schweppenburg, a veteran armored corps commander from the Eastern Front, to lead this special force.[35] Rommel had no authority over von Schweppenburg or any of his men.

General von Schweppenburg had two corps in his Group: the I SS Panzer and the LXIII Panzer. Five panzer divisions were camped in the I SS area, north of the River Loire: the 1st SS Panzer "Leibstandarte Adolf Hitler," the 12th SS Panzer "Hitler Jugend," and the Army's 2nd, 21st, and 116th panzer divisions. South of the river lay the LXIII Panzer Corps with the 9th and 11th panzer divisions. The 2nd SS Panzer "Das Reich" and 17th SS Panzer Grenadier "Gotz von Berlichingen" divisions were also south of the Loire, but not assigned to a specific corps.[36]

The total Atlantic coast frontage of OB West was 2,500 miles. Fifty-eight divisions manned this huge frontage. Most of these divisions were semi-mobile or practically immobile and were made up of men from the older age groups who were by and large unfit for service on the Eastern Front. They were poorly equipped with foreign or obsolete material and weapons, and lacking in all forms of transportation, including horses and donkeys. Rommel pointed out to Hitler that such units would be useless in modern warfare until they were provided with a proper number of vehicles. Hitler curtly rejected Rommel's conclusions and stated that it was a soldier's duty "to stand and die in his defenses," not to be "mobile."[37] It is highly unlikely that Germany could have manufactured enough vehicles to supply these formations anyway and still meet its requirements on the Eastern Front. In any event, petroleum resources were too limited to have made mobile divisions of much value, even if they had been equipped as Rommel demanded.

Most of Rommel's divisions, though by no means all, had been reduced from normal 1939 strength of nine battalions to six understrength battalions by 1944. The authorized full establishment of the average German infantry division (called Table of Organization and Equipment or TOE in the U.S. Army) had been steadily reduced from 17,200 men in 1939-type divisions to 13,656 in 1943. The 1944-type divisions had a strength of

12,769 at full establishment, but very few were at 100 percent strength and many were well below that.[38] Many units had so few transport vehicles that they were classified as "static," and relied on horses and ox carts to haul supplies and even their artillery.

The number of troops, size of area of responsibility, equipment, nationality, and organization of these static units varied remarkably. The 709th Infantry Division, for example, had eleven battalions under three regimental headquarters, while the 716th had six battalions and only one regimental HQ.[39] Some of these divisions were composed of men who had special disorders which prevented them from serving or returning to the Eastern Front. The 70th Infantry Division, for example, was composed largely of soldiers with stomach ailments and was nicknamed the "Whipped Cream" or "White Beard Division" because of its special diet. It fought extremely well, nev...neless, single-handedly holding up Montgomery's Army Group for nine days in the Battle of the Scheldt in November, but that is another story.

The Third Reich was nearing the end of its manpower reserves as it entered 1944—the fifth year of the war. In the West it faced a serious shortage of first-rate combat troops. Of the 4,270,000 men in the German Army in December, 1943, more than 1,500,000 were over 34 years of age. Many of those below 34 were very young (17 to 19), or victims of third degree frostbite, or were ethnic Germans (Volksdeutsche), or were "Eastern Troops" (i.e., non-Germans recruited in occupied countries). The average age in the whole Nazi Army was 31.5 years, or four years older than the average age of the Kaiser's army in 1917, the year before the Second Reich lost World War I. It was more than six years older than the age of the average American soldier in 1943.[40]

The problem of age was more pronounced in some units than in others. The average age in the 709th Division, for instance, was 36. Gun-crew ages averaged as high as 45 and some of the men were over 55.[41]

Many of Rommel's men were not Germans or Volksdeutsche at all, but Russians. Most of them volunteered from POW camps when it looked as if Germany would win the war in the East. By 1943 the Soviets were advancing on all fronts and these men were reconsidering their decisions. To preserve their "loyalty" to the Reich, the High Command transferred most of them to France, where their arrival released German units for the Russian Front. By May 1944, the 7th Army had 23 Osten (Eastern) infantry battalions, which represented about one sixth of all the infantry battalions in that army. In the LXXXIV Corps, which defended Normandy, eight of 42 rifle battalions were made up of Osttruppen.[42]

The Eastern Front was taxing Hitler's empire almost to the breaking point, so little could be spared for the defense of the West prior to 1944. In 1943 German losses in Russia reached 2,086,000, of which 677,000 were permanent (killed, missing, captured, or permanently incapacitated). Of the 151 German divisions fighting on this front, 10 panzer and 50 infantry divisions were classified as "fought out." To meet this drain of manpower, plus the demands of the new Italian Front, Adolf Hitler called on units stationed in France, Belgium, and the Netherlands. By October 1943, 36 infantry and 17 mobile divisions had been transferred from OB West to other fronts. Almost all these units ended up in Russia.[43] Despite these reinforcements, the Third Reich's strategic situation in the U.S.S.R. verged on the critical. In the spring of 1944, despite astronomical losses, Russia still fielded over 5,000,000 troops in 300 field divisions, as opposed to Germany's 2,000,000 soldiers in less than 200 divisions.[44] Table 1 shows the dispositions of Germany's divisions by theater on June 1, 1944, and clearly indicates the drain caused by the Eastern Front.

Table 1

GERMAN DISPOSITIONS OF DIVISIONS BY THEATER
June 1, 1944

Theater	Army	Luftwaffe Field	SS	Total
Eastern	149	—	8	157
Finland	6	—	1	7
Norway-Denmark	15	—	—	15
Western	47	3	4	54
Italy	23	3	1	27
Balkans	18	—	7	25
	258	6	21	285

Source: Seaton: 458

Rommel found that many of his new units were formations previously mauled in the East. They were in France primarily to recuperate from their exhausting campaigns and in many cases needed to be refitted or completely rebuilt. Unfortunately for Germany, Army Group B simply did not have the resources to carry out a project of this magnitude.

If the manpower drain to the East was serious in itself, it became catastrophic when coupled with the material requirements of that theater. First priority of equipment was to the East until January 1944, and with good reason, for tank losses in Russia were tremendous. Between October and December 1943, 979 Panzer Mark IIIs and IVs were lost, along with 444 assault guns and tons of other equipment.* In the last six months of 1943 Germany lost 2,235 field guns and 1,692 antitank guns on the Russian Front alone.[45]

Hitler's industrial program emphasized massive output of new panzers instead of a balanced program of production. As a result, a critical spare parts shortage developed which nullified all the gains of the German war industries. In June 1943 the German Army had 3,032 tanks. Only 463 of these, or 15 percent, were nonoperational. By February 1944, the Reich had 3,053 tanks, but 1,534, or more than 50 percent, were in need of major repair. This meant that over half of the tanks of an army which depended on its mobility for its survival were inoperable because of a lack of spare parts! In that month, only 145 damaged tanks were repaired and sent back into combat. Colonel General Heinz Guderian, Inspector-General of Panzer Troops, estimated that tanks and assault guns awaiting repair in early 1944 equalled about nine months of new production. By the end of March the situation had not improved. The number of employable panzers in Hitler's armies continued to decline, despite increasing industrial productivity.[46]

By February 1944 the threat in the West became real enough for the High Command to warrant an increase in tank delivery to von Rundstedt and his subordinates. Although new Panzer Mark VI (PzKw VI or "Tiger") production still went east, PzKw V ("Panther") output was largely sent to France. By the end of April, OB West had 1,608 German-made tanks and assault guns, of which 674 were PzKw IVs and 514 were Panthers.[47] This still fell far short of the great concentrations in Russia. At the Battle of Kursk in July 1943, for example, Hitler's forces lost almost 3,000 tanks. In

---

*For a description of German and Allied armor, see Appendix II.

1944, OB West never could muster more than 2,900 tanks against the Allies at its peak strength.[48]

Rommel established his headquarters at Château La Roche-Guyon, a beautiful residence 40 miles downstream from Paris. The château had been the seat of the dukes de la Rochefoucauld for centuries.[49] It's not known who selected the site, but it certainly was not Rommel, who had a well-deserved reputation from indifference to physical comfort. The Field Marshal allowed the ducal family to remain and chose for his own quarters a small apartment on the ground floor, adjacent to a rose terrace. His office had a high ceiling with a faded Gobelin tapestry on one wall and an ancient portrait of Duke François de la Rochefoucauld on the other. Nothing in the room belonged to Rommel. He brought in no photographs of his family, no souvenirs, no mementos from his Afrika Korps days—nothing. He could have walked out of the place at any moment and there would have been no evidence that he had ever been there.[50] From these pleasant but impersonal surroundings, Erwin Rommel went about the business of expanding his skeleton staff.

The Desert Fox initially appointed Lieutenant General Alfred Gause chief of staff, but had a personal falling-out with him and replaced him with Lieutenant General Doctor Hans Speidel.[51] Like his commander, Dr. Speidel was a Swabian from the Württemberg district of southwestern Germany. The two had met in the Argonne Forest battles of 1915 and had later served together in the 13th Württemberg Infantry Regiment.[52] Also, both men were the sons of teachers. Here the similarity ended, however, for Hans Speidel was a career staff officer. Before the war he had been chief of Section "West" of the General Staff's Foreign Armies Department. From July 1940 until March 1942 he had been Chief of Staff to the German Military Governor of France, before spending two years on the Russian Front as Chief of Staff, 8th Army. He joined Rommel in April 1944.[53] Speidel was an anti-Nazi and much more politically adroit than his chief, who was naive about such matters. He undoubtedly helped influence Rommel to support the conspiracy against Hitler, which was now growing into a full-blown resistance group, unofficially led by the dynamic Colonel Count Claus von Stauffenberg. The count had served briefly with the 10th Panzer Division on the North African Front and lacked an arm and an eye as a result. Nevertheless he soldiered on, and by 1944 was Chief of Staff to the Commander-in-Chief of the Replacement Army, headquartered in Berlin. This human dynamo spun a web of intrigue and began hatching a plot to remove Adolf Hitler and save Germany from occupation, complete brutalization, or both.[54] Among the men whom he needed on his side was Erwin Rommel—so General Speidel quietly went to work convincing his boss to act against the leader the Desert Fox had once admired.

Rommel picked Vice Admiral Friedrich Ruge as his naval advisor. Prior to being assigned to Rommel's staff (on the recommendation of General Gause), Ruge had been commander of the German naval forces in Italy, such as they were. He and the Field Marshal became good friends and were to have many long walks and private conversations together in the rose garden.

The remaining members of Rommel's staff were also talented, capable professionals. The handsome Colonel Hans-Georg von Tempelhoff was operations officer; Colonel Anton Staubwasser, intelligence chief; and Colonel Freyberg, adjutant. Rommel's technical staff was small but also capable and included Colonel Hans Lattmann (artillery advisor), Lieutenant General Meise (engineer advisor), Lieutenant General Gehrke (signal advisor), a Luftwaffe General Staff officer, several clerks, and a few war historians. The Army Group's Quartermaster Department was abolished before the invasion and its responsibilities were assumed by the Quartermaster General of France. Despite regulations requiring one, Rommel refused to appoint a National Socialist Political Officer. The result of these appointments, according to Speidel, was "outer and inner harmony and mental balance; the officers were free, in so far as possible, to use their own initiative."[55]

Rommel's entourage grew by two more members on January 21, 1944, when members of the Todt Organization presented him with two dachshunds, one a year old and one a three-month-old puppy. The puppy was quite affectionate and Rommel fell in love with it almost immediately. He had always been fond of dogs, but seems to have become particularly attached to this one. He named it Elbo and it was soon sleeping in his room, underneath his luggage stand. Rommel later sent the older, less energetic dog home to Germany, where it was killed by a car. The Todt people must have heard about its death, because they replaced it with a big, brown, smooth-haired hunting dog.[56]

It was good that Rommel could enjoy at least one aspect of domestic life,

for elsewhere the war closed in. On January 6, 1944, his fourteen-year-old
son was drafted.[57] His family was now completely broken up and Germany
looked to him to defeat the invasion, which promised to strike soon, and in
overwhelming force. Despite his growing distaste for the Nazi dictatorship, Erwin Rommel threw his entire being into the task.

The Desert Fox was not the sort of man to admit defeat easily. The
ordinary mortal might shrink in the face of odds weighted so heavily
against him; Rommel's reaction was the opposite: the greater the odds, the
more energetic and ingenious his response became. Rather than trying to
share or shirk his huge responsibilities, Rommel assumed more and
insisted on everyone else doing the same. His job was to defeat the enemy
and that was precisely what he intended to do, despite their huge margin of
superiority in every conceivable material category. Soon Rommel was
shouldering a greater burden than anyone on the Western Front. The U.S.
Army's official history reports:

> The evidence indicates that Rommel had an energy and strength of conviction
> that often enabled him to secure Hitler's backing, whereas [von] Rundstedt,
> who was disposed whenever possible to compromise and allow arguments to go
> by default, seems to have relaxed command prerogatives that undoubtedly
> remained formally his. It is possible, of course, that he too came under Rommel's
> influence and because he was content to allow Rommel to assume the main
> burden of responsibility. In any case the clear fact is that after January, 1944,
> Rommel was the dominant personality in the west with an influence dispropor-
> tionate to his formal command authority.[58]

David Irving, the noted British historian, seems to agree. He writes:

> Rommel's activity changed the whole face of the Atlantic defenses. With his
> Party backing and influence on Hitler, he was able to start fresh divisions
> moving west. He demanded millions of mines per month, to lay along the coast.
> He prepared to flood or swamp low-lying areas. He conferred with the Todt
> Organization's chief, Xaver Dorsch, on an ingenious arsenal of deadly gadgets to
> meet the invaders: submerged barriers of massive spikes designed to gash open
> the hulls of landing boats, and nutcracker mines supported on iron girders,
> staggered and echeloned along the beaches, some visible, some below the water's
> surface. Tempted by cash rewards, the male French population willingly

assisted, while their womenfolk made rush-matting for sand traps or helped to erect antiparatroop defenses.[59]

The Atlantic Wall was little more than a joke when Rommel took over in early 1944. The length of the coast permitted only the erection of a system of strong points, not a continuous line of fortifications. However, not even that had been accomplished by January 1944. France had become a giant recuperation center for the wounded and frostbitten veterans limping back from the Russian Front. Rommel immediately cleared the air and made his position known beyond any possible misunderstanding. Preparation for Eisenhower's invasion, not recuperation from the winter war, was the mission of Army Group B. The men had rested long enough; now the work would begin in earnest.

Colonel General Hans von Salmuth was among the first to feel Rommel's famous temper. The Desert Fox first inspected the 15th Army in December 1943 and told von Salmuth that he wanted hundreds of thousands of mines laid all along the Atlantic coast. Less than a month later Rommel paid another visit to the coast of northern France and Belgium and was not satisfied with the progress being made. He visited von Salmuth at the latter's headquarters, a luxurious château near Tourcoing, and ordered him to increase the amount of time each soldier spent laying mines, even if training time had to be sacrificed. The 15th Army commander protested. "When the battle begins, I want fresh, well-trained soldiers— not physical wrecks," he told Rommel.

The Desert Fox accepted the challenge. "Evidently you don't intend to carry out my orders," he snapped.

Von Salmuth scoffed and advised Rommel to "stick around a bit and you'll soon see that you can't do everything at once. Your program is going to take at least a year to put into effect. If anybody tells you different, then he's either just trying to flatter you or he's a pig idiot."

Rommel was not the type to be patronized by anybody. As soon as his staff officers were in their cars, he gave the colonel general the dressing down of his life. Rommel screamed at him until it seemed he would burst his lungs. As he drove away, Rommel laughed to Admiral Ruge: "He's quite a roughneck, that one. That's the only language he understands."[60]

Rommel got his message across to the commander of the 15th Army. Mine field and obstacle construction in von Salmuth's zone picked up considerably after this outburst. Word soon got around that Rommel meant business. It was as if a cold wind had blown through the comfortable headquarters throughout France. The staffs didn't like it, but there was little they could do about it. Work and anti-invasion preparations picked up with a vengeance.

Rommel found that the coast of Normandy had been particularly neglected, but things were almost as bad elsewhere. Between Dieppe and St. Nazaire, a distance of 600 miles of coastline, only 11 batteries existed, with a total combined strength of 37 guns. Only the Channel Islands, the Cape Gris Nez, and Brest were properly fortified. The entire defensive system lacked matériel, leadership, and an overall plan.[61] Rommel now provided two of the three essential elements.

The Atlantic Wall was short not only of fortifications and mine fields; it was short of defenders as well. The average defensive sector of a division on the Western Front ranged from 50 miles of frontage in the 15th Army to 120 miles in the 7th Army's sector. This compared to an average corps frontage of 32.5 miles (for three divisions) on the Russian Front.[62] Lieutenant General Karl Wilhelm von Schlieben's 709th Infantry Division, which would be decisively engaged on D-Day, had to defend a 40-mile front with only two regiments. A division could hope to defend successfully only six miles of frontage against a determined assault.[63]

Rommel's solution to von Schlieben's problem was the answer he had to everybody's problem: obstacles and minefields. His defense of France would be his defense of El Alamein on a larger scale. At El Alamein he had held up the enemy for two weeks, despite their overwhelming ground, air, and naval superiority. If he could delay them on the French coast for just a few hours, and simultaneously inflict heavy casualties on them, the panzer reserves might be able to counterattack and push them back into the sea. This was Germany's only remaining chance to avoid losing the war. Admiral Ruge wrote: "He [Rommel] knew that there was no hope of winning [the war], but hoped that the war could be brought to a tolerable end. . . . So he looked for a way to defeat the landing on the beach, and to win a respite which could be exploited politically."[64]

The Desert Fox had several ideas for strengthening the Atlantic Wall. First, the depth of the mined and fortified zone had to be extended five to six miles inland, to provide depth to the defense. The number of strong points at and near the coast must be increased, along with the number of antitank guns and heavy machine guns in the forward sectors. Finally, the principal mobile reserves must be brought up from far inland so they would be close enough to launch a major counterattack on the first or second day of the invasion.[65]

Rommel believed the battle would be decided at the water's edge. He said: "The enemy is at his weakest just after landing. The troops are unsure, and possibly even seasick. They are unfamiliar with the terrain. Heavy weapons are not yet available in sufficient quantity. That is the moment to strike at them and defeat them."[66]

The Desert Fox was quick to put his talent for improvisation to work in his new environment. There was much to be done. Since von Rundstedt believed that the decisive battle would be fought well inland, he had not put the French coast into shape for the defense. Not even the existing strong points were protected by mines. In three years only 1,700,000 mines had been laid.[67] The beach obstacles were extremely primitive, and useless against tanks. Since Organization Todt was almost fully committed with port fortifications and railroad repair and maintenance, the Desert Fox realized that he would have to put the soldiers themselves to work on laying barriers, obstacles, antitank devices and mine fields.[68] On January 13 Rommel made his initial request for mines to the visiting Colonel General Alfred Jodl. He wanted 2,000,000 mines per month,[69] which means he intended to lay more mines every 30 days than his predecessors had laid in 3½ years. Shortly afterward he increased this figure when he wrote Lieutenant General Dr. Meise and told him that he wanted a mine laid every 10 yards, for a 1,000-yard-wide stretch all along the French coast. This would require 20,000,000 mines. Then phase two could begin. This would involve laying a mine every 10 yards for a distance of 8,000 yards inland, and at other strategic spots, requiring another 20,000,000 mines.[70]

Rommel was seldom happy with the progress of his subordinates' mine-laying efforts. Four years had been wasted, and Rommel was feverishly trying to make up for lost time. In mid-January, when the commander of LXXXI Corps informed him that General von Salmuth was requiring each sapper to lay ten mines a day, Rommel tersely replied, "Make that twenty."[71] This was one of the orders that led to the famous chewing out of the 15th Army commander a few days later.

Up to May 20, 1944, 4,193,167 mines had been laid along the channel, most of them since the end of March. Numerous obstacles had been laid under the surface of the water, to act as artificial reefs to destroy shore-bound ships and personnel carriers. Some of these were stakes carrying an antitank mine at the tip; others were concrete tetrahedrons, equipped with either steel blades or antitank mines. Various other devices were employed, such as Rommel's "nutcracker mine," which consisted of a stake protruding from a concrete housing containing a heavy shell. A landing craft striking the stake would cause the shell to detonate.[72]

Rommel envisioned four belts of underwater obstacles. They were: 1) a belt in six feet of water at mean high tide; 2) a belt in six feet of water at half tide of a 12-foot tide; 3) a belt in six feet of water at low tide; and 4) a belt in 12 feet of water at low tide.[73]

Rommel felt that the Allies would come at high tide, to minimize the distance of open beach over which their soldiers would have to run for cover. By D-Day, only the first two belts had been completed in most sectors. Up to May 13, a total of 517,000 foreshore obstacles were laid, of which 31,000 were armed with mines.[74]

The Field Marshal also emphasized the construction of antiaircraft obstacles. "... The important thing," he write, "is to ensure that all territory which might conceivably be used for landing airborne troops is treated in such a manner that enemy aircraft and gliders will break up while landing, and the enemy as a result suffer severe losses in men and material. . . ."[75]

These obstacles, nicknamed "Rommel asparagus," consisted of stakes approximately 10 feet high driven into the ground at 100-foot spacings. Shells were to be attached to them with interconnecting wires. Troops aboard any glider landing in these areas would suffer heavy casualties. However, owing to the inefficiency of the Nazi bureaucracy, Rommel only received the shells in early June: too late to install them before D-Day.[76] Nevertheless the stakes were dangerous, and caused a number of gliders to pile up on June 6.

The Desert Fox also emphasized the construction of dummy positions. "Dummy batteries attracted a great many Allied air attacks and helped the real guns to survive," Admiral Ruge wrote. By nightfall of June 5, the U.S. and Royal air forces had only destroyed 16 German guns —eight in the Pas-de-Calais area, five in the Seine-Somme region, and three in Normandy.[77]

Rommel's program also called for the construction of naval mine fields in the English Channel. The German Navy, however, proved unequal to the task and uncooperative as well. It had done very little to infest the Channel with mines in the previous five years and did little to improve its poor performance in 1944, despite Rommel's strong protests.

The U.S. Army's official history summed up Rommel's efforts well when it reported: "In all these ways Rommel sought to make the expected invasion physically impossible. The Allied force entangled in the spider web of obstacles would be given the paralyzing sting by the German Army waiting at the water's edge."[78]

"About all that was missing from Rommel's medieval arsenal of weapons were crucibles of molten lead to pour down on the attackers," Cornelius Ryan wrote, "—and in a way he had the modern equivalent: automatic flame throwers."[79] He even concealed kerosene tanks along approaches leading off the beaches. The push of a button would engulf advancing troops in flame.[80]

Under Rommel, the 7th and 15th armies laid three times as many mines in France in six months as all the German armies had buried in almost four years. Still it did not satisfy him. He ordered: "I hereby forbid all training, and demand that every minute be used for work on the beach obstacles. It is on the beaches that the fate of the invasion will be decided, and, what is more, during the first 24 hours."[81]

Rommel spent his days inspecting and monitoring the progress of his program. "I have only one real enemy now and that is time," Rommel told his aide, Captain Hellmuth Lang. The two of them were usually on the road by 4:30 A.M., heading for an inspection which might be in Holland or in Brittany.[82] After the war, Admiral Ruge described a typical day with Rommel to Brigadier Desmond Young. "He got up early, traveled fast, saw things very quickly and seemed to have an instinct for places where something was wrong," Ruge said. "On one typical winter inspection we arrived at Perpignan late one night. We left at 6:00 A.M. next morning, without breakfast. Driving through snow and rain, we reached Bayonne at 2:00 P.M. An hour later, having received the report of the local commanding general, we left, without luncheon, for St. Jean-de-Luz, on the Spanish frontier. There we inspected batteries. We arrived at Bordeaux at 7:00 P.M. and conferred with [Colonel] General von Blaskowitz. At 8:00 P.M. we had an hour off for supper, the first meal of the day. We settled down to work again at 9:00 P.M., but fortunately the engineer-general fell asleep over the table."[83]

General Doctor Speidel recorded similar experiences. On a typical day, he wrote, Rommel ate an early breakfast with his chief of staff. Then, between 5:00 A.M. and 6:00 A.M., he left on his inspection tours, accompanied only by Captain Lang and sometimes Vice Admiral Ruge. During these inspections, he would frequently insist that his men obey the laws of humanity to the letter. This antagonized Hitler, who regarded these demands as a sign of weakness. Rommel was usually gone from La Roche-

Guyon until evening. The headquarters conferences would begin immediately upon his return.[84]

Rommel still ate a simple supper, as he had always done, but instead of eating alone (as in Africa), he dined with the 10 to 12 officers who worked most closely with him. He would discuss any subject brought up during the meal. After dinner, Rommel would go on an evening walk with Ruge and Speidel. Then further conferences occupied his night until bedtime, which was usually early.[85]

Rommel's physical ailments, most of which he had acquired in North Africa, continued to plague him in the winter of 1943–44, and were no doubt aggravated by the demands that he made upon himself. The Desert Fox, after all, was no longer a young man; he was 52 years old and had recently spent two years in the brutal environment of the Sahara Desert. In January, for instance, lumbago attacks caused him severe pain, but he continued his inspection of the Normandy coast as if nothing were wrong.[86] At least his desert sores, which caused him such agony in early 1943, were gone now.

The Desert Fox never slowed down. He spent December 20–24 inspecting parts of the 15th Army's zone. Christmas Day was spent catching up on paperwork. The last week in December was devoted to more planning sessions and inspections, except for a December 27 conference with von Rundstedt. He celebrated New Year's Eve in his typical puritan fashion: he consumed two small glasses of claret.[87]

Early January was spent in the same manner. Rommel inspected the coastal defenses of the Netherlands and Belgium from January 2 to 5. He did not really expect the Allies to land here, because of the swampy nature of the terrain and the innumerable streams, rivers, and canals that marked the countryside, but then one never knew. He was in a bitter mood when he examined the interior of these two occupied countries. "Everywhere the deepest peace," he wrote on January 3. "They are well paid, they don't have the crippling taxation that we do, and they just can't wait to be liberated from us. Their towns are beautiful and are spared by the enemy. It makes you sick, when you think how hard our people are having to fight to defend our existence against all comers."[88]

Despite his contempt for the French, Dutch, and Belgian civilians, Rommel never inconvenienced or punished them, except out of military necessity. He continued to work even harder. From February 7 to 11 he drove 1,400 miles and inspected the 1st and 19th armies from the Bay of

Biscay to the Mediterranean Sea, apparently in an attempt to confuse Allied intelligence as to what his area of responsibility really was. A few days later he attended a major war game, conducted by General von Schweppenburg in Paris. All the inspecting and planning took its toll, however, and on February 22 an exhausted Rommel left France for a ten-day rest. The brief furlough seems to have recharged Rommel's batteries. As soon as he returned to Army Group B he made another inspection of Normandy with General Erich Marcks, whose LXXXIV Corps included the 709th and 243rd Infantry and 91st Air Landing divisions.[89] Marcks's opinions of the Swabian were mixed. He wrote his son: "Rommel's the same age as [I am] but looks older—perhaps because Africa and its many trials have left their mark on him. He's very frank and earnest. He's not just a flash in the pan, he's a real warlord. It's a good thing that A.H. [Hitler] thinks a lot of him, for all his bluntness, and gives him these important jobs."[90] However, after a March inspection he grew more critical, and wrote: "These visits are very strenuous because Rommel is a fanatic and it's impossible to do too much on the schemes he's thought up, like the gigantic mine field." In April he added other thoughts. "Rommel is cantankerous and frequently blows his top—he scares the daylights out of his commanders. The first one who reports to him each morning gets eaten for breakfast; the next ones after that get off lighter."[91] It seems Marcks himself must have received a "counseling session" with Rommel. Things had not changed very much since Africa, after all.

Not even Rommel's energy and personal supervision could entirely make up for all the deficiencies in the German defensive system. The worst problem, which was never really solved, was that of command fragmentation. Adolf Hitler never allowed a unified command to develop on either major front, a system which violated every dictate of military science and common sense. By 1944, the command system was fouled up beyond belief. At the top, OKH under Colonel General Kurt Zeitzler, the Chief of the General Staff, directed the war on the Eastern Front, while OKW—which was mainly supervised by its operations officer, Colonel General Jodl—was responsible for all other theaters. These included France, Belgium, the Netherlands, Denmark, North Africa (until von Arnim surrendered), Italy, the Balkans, and Scandinavia. "This division in the Supreme Command led to daily friction and seriously damaged the conduct of the whole war," Rommel's chief of staff wrote later.[92] It got to the point where, when Jodl or his deputy, General Walther Warlimont, began discussing "OKW fronts," such as Norway or Italy, Zeitzler and his staff would get up and walk out.[93] The interests of the Navy, the Luftwaffe, and the SS conflicting with the Army and with each other only added fuel to the flames.

In the West, von Rundstedt had no control over the Luftwaffe or the Navy in his area. He might ask Field Marshal Hugo Sperrle, the commander of the 3rd Air Fleet, for his cooperation, but Sperrle was subordinate only to Hermann Goering's OKL (the High Command of the Luftwaffe), and likely as not would ignore OB West's requests. Admiral Theodor Krancke, the commander of Naval Group West, was also independent of von Rundstedt and reported directly to Grand Admiral Karl Doenitz and the OKM (High Command of the Navy).[94] The military governors of France (General Heinrich Karl von Stuelpnagel), northern France and Belgium (General Alexander von Falkenhausen), and the Netherlands (General Christiansen) were subordinate to OB West in tactical matters, but not in administrative matters nor in the internal affairs of their territories, for which they were responsible directly to OKW. In addition, SS forces received orders from Reichsfuehrer Heinrich Himmler, and the Todt Organization worked directly for Albert Speer, the Reichsminister of Arms and Munitions.[95]

The fragmentation of command debilitated the German armed forces right down to the tactical level. The naval coastal guns, for example, would remain under naval control even while the Anglo-American amphibious vessels were on their approach runs to the coast. The moment they landed, however, command of the coastal batteries reverted to the Army. If there was ever an order changing horses in midstream, this was it.

Hitler, in short, exercised the political principle of divide and rule, just as he had in his election campaigns prior to the establishment of the Nazi regime. It may have worked well there, but it proved disastrous in the military arena.

The main question the chain of command had to answer was the issue of how to employ the strategic reserves. Von Rundstedt's concept was that of the old school. He wanted to hold his reserves southeast of Paris and use them against the Allies as they approached the French capital, long after the landings. He believed that in this way he could bring the German tank superiority to bear against Eisenhower's forces and decisively defeat them in open battle. What he failed to notice was that German armored superiority no longer existed. True, the Panther might be superior to the Allies'

Sherman tank, but it was not superior to the fighter-bomber or the heavy bomber. Von Rundstedt had not yet learned the value of the Allied tactical air forces, as Rommel had in North Africa. He was in for an education.

Rommel's concept was diametrically opposite to von Rundstedt's. He wanted to group the reserves near the expected points of invasion and deal the attackers a crushing defeat on the beaches. He said, "If we cannot get at the enemy immediately after he lands, we will never be able to make another move, because of his vastly superior air forces.... If we are not able to repulse the enemy at sea or throw him off the mainland in the first 48 hours, then the invasion will have succeeded and the war will be lost...."⁹⁶

Although Rommel was the dominant personality in the western armies, he was not unchallenged on the issue of the strategic reserves. In fact, he stood almost alone, for of all the major commanders only he had experienced firsthand the awesome effect of Allied aerial domination. He also realized that Eisenhower's air armada would vastly exceed anything that supported the 8th Army when it virtually annihilated his Panzer Army Afrika in late 1942.⁹⁷ He also realized that, if the Wehrmacht allowed the Americans and the British to secure themselves on the beaches of France, nothing would ever be able to dislodge them. Rommel argued, but his contemporaries did not really believe him, because they had not shared the experiences of El Alamein, Alma Halfa, and Tunisia. They simply could not grasp what Rommel was telling them.

General von Schweppenburg led the opposition to Rommel's theories, insisting that the decisive engagement must be fought inland. Like many other German commanders, he didn't realize that the days of the blitzkrieg were over. He also seems to have underestimated the ability of the British and Americans to wage mobile warfare. The Americans were particularly suspect, for it was not yet clear to most German generals how well they had learned the lessons of Kasserine Pass, where the Desert Fox had dealt them a major defeat the year before.

The more Rommel insisted that his mine fields and obstacles were not only the best defense for the Reich, but its only defense, the more opposition he inspired. Even Colonel General Heinz Guderian joined those supporting the von Rundstedt-von Schweppenburg school of thought. He visited Rommel on April 27, 1944. The inventor of the blitzkrieg had a healthy respect for the Desert Fox, with whom he had maintained friendly contacts since before the war. He called Rommel "... an open, upright man and a brave soldier ... [who] possessed energy and subtlety of appreciation; he had great understanding of his men and, in fact, thoroughly deserved the

reputation that he had won for himself."[98] Guderian tried to intercede on
behalf of von Schweppenburg and convert the Swabian marshal to their
way of thinking. "I was . . . not surprised by Rommel's highly tempera-
mental and strongly expressed refusal when I suggested that our armor be
withdrawn from the coastal areas," he wrote later. "He turned down my
suggestion at once, pointing out that as a man from the Eastern Front I
lacked his experiences of Africa and Italy; that he knew, in fact, far more
about the matter in hand than I did and that he was fully convinced that his
system was right." The colonel general seems to have known his friend
quite well, for he continued: "In view of this attitude of his, an argument
with Rommel . . . promised to be quite fruitless. . . ."[99] Hence he dropped the
subject. The conference ended without achieving any tangible results.

Colonel General Georg von Sodenstern, the commander of the 19th
Army (in southern France) caustically, though privately, expressed his
fears that German generalship would exhaust itself building masses of
concrete. "As no man in his senses would put his head on an anvil over
which the smith's hammer is swung, so no general should mass his troops
at the point where the enemy is certain to bring the first powerful blow of
his superior material," he commented.[100]

Of remarks of this nature, Rommel said, "Our friends from the East
cannot imagine what they're in for here. It's not a matter of fanatical hordes
to be driven forward in masses against our line, with no regard for
casualties and little recourse to tactical craft; here we are facing an enemy
who applies all his native intelligence to the use of his many technical
resources, who spares no expenditure of material and whose every operation goes its course as though it had been the subject of repeated
rehearsal."[101]

General Marcks, commander of the LXXXIV Corps, had a composite
idea. He wanted to construct a number of small fortifications to give depth
to the German line. The object of these strong points would not be to stop
the attackers, but to split up their attacks to give the German reserves time
to come up for the decisive counterattack. He felt that this would be better
than putting all his strength forward, because even by doubling his manpower, LXXXIV Corps would only be able to provide a thin coastal screen
across its huge area of responsibility.[102] Although next to nothing came of
the idea it is interesting, because it was in Marcks's sector that Eisenhower
struck on D-Day.

Hitler should have been the one to choose between Rommel's concept of
operations and those of von Rundstedt, Guderian, and von Schweppen-

burg. Unfortunately for the German war effort, he was far too preoccupied with the war in Russia to even visit the Western Front. As a result, a sort of defense by compromise was adopted, without the total consent of any of the major commanders involved. Without an overall policy, Rommel and von Rundstedt had to depend on mutual agreement, despite their divergent theories. This resulted in the moving forward of some of the panzer units, but not nearly as many as Rommel demanded. The U.S. Army's official history put it this way:

> In summary, the conflict between Rommel's and [von] Rundstedt's theories of defense was never resolved definitely in favor of one or the other and led to compromise troop dispositions which on D-Day were not suitable for the practice of either theory. The pool of mobile reserves had been cut down below what would be needed for an effective counterattack in mass; it had been removed from OB West's control, and, as though to insure finally that it would not be employed in force, it had been divided among three commands. While the possibility of seeking a decision by counterattack had thus been whittled away, considerable forces were still held far enough from the coast so that, if Rommel's theories were correct, they would be unable to reach the battlefield in time to influence the action. In short, operational flexibility had been curtailed without achieving a decisive thickening of the coastal defense.[103]

In mid-March 1944, it appeared that Hitler had finally made up his mind to adopt a single strategy and philosophy of defense in the West. On March 20 he addressed the commanders-in-chief of the three services in France (Sperrle, Krancke, and von Rundstedt), along with their top subordinates, and told them that he believed the most suitable places for the invasion were the two west coast peninsulas (Brittany and Cotentin). The Allies' initial strategic objective would probably be the port cities of Cherbourg or Brest. Then he said: "The destruction of the enemy's landing attempt means more than a purely local decision on the Western Front. It is the sole decisive factor in the whole conduct of the war and hence in its final result."[104] He also said, "The enemy's entire invasion operation must not, under any circumstances, be allowed to survive longer than hours, or at the most days, taking Dieppe as an ideal example. Once defeated, the enemy will never again try to invade. Quite apart from their heavy losses, they would need months to organize a fresh attempt. And an invasion failure would also deliver a crushing blow to British and American morale. For one thing, it would prevent Roosevelt from being reelected—with any luck he'd finish up in jail somewhere! For another, war weariness would grip Britain even faster and Churchill, already a sick old man with his influence waning, wouldn't be able to carry through a new invasion operation." According to Hitler, the defeat of the Allied invasion would win the war for Nazi Germany. "The forty-five divisions that we now hold in Europe ... are vital to the Eastern Front," he said, "and we shall then transfer them there to revolutionize the situation there as soon as we have forced the decision in the west. So the whole outcome of the war depends on each man fighting in the west, and that means the fate of the Reich as well!"[105]

Rommel found the speech one of "marvelous clarity and sovereign composure,"[106] and why not? It clearly indicated that Hitler was leaning toward Rommel's concept of operations. As in battle, the Desert Fox lost no time in pressing his advantage. As a field marshal, he had the right to appeal directly to Hitler any time he saw fit. He met with the Fuehrer the next day and the former corporal agreed with Rommel's opinion on the necessity of stationing strong reserves, including panzer and motorized divisions, near the coast. Rommel had won the great strategic political battle for the panzer reserves. Unfortunately for him, his victory lasted only 24 hours. Members of Hitler's entourage, led by Jodl and backed by a written protest from von Rundstedt, convinced the Nazi dictator that he should again reverse himself. The policy would remain as it was before, which was—no policy. Of Hitler at this time, Rommel snapped: "The last [person] out of his door is always right."[107]

At least Rommel did win some new units as a result of this encounter, for Hitler now felt compelled to compromise with him. The 2nd, 21st, and 116th Panzer divisions were transferred from the control of Panzer Group West to Army Group B. Three other panzer divisions (9th and 11th and 2nd SS) were earmarked for soon-to-be activated Army Group G (1st and 19th armies) under Colonel General Johannes Blaskowitz. General von Schweppenburg was allowed to keep only four of his original 10 mobile divisions: the 1st SS and 12th SS panzers, 17th SS Panzer Grenadier, and Panzer Lehr.[108] This compromise satisfied no one.[109] Of decisions like this one, Field Marshal von Rundstedt later bitterly remarked to a Canadian interrogator after the war: "As Commander-in-Chief West my one authority was to change the guard in front of my gate."[110] Nevertheless, Rommel kept his three panzer divisions, but even their areas of operations were dictated by OKW. Second Panzer Division was sent to the Somme area; 116th Panzer was posted north of the lower Seine; and 21st Panzer

Division was assigned to the Orne River area near Falaise in Normandy. Rommel, who had come to believe the Allies would land in Normandy, objected, but was overridden by OKW. "As a result," Admiral Ruge wrote later, "only the 21st Panzer Division was in the area where Rommel expected the blow to fall. He pleaded in vain. . . ."[111]

Finally, on March 29, Rommel and von Schweppenburg had a bitter (and probably inevitable) personal confrontation at La Roche-Guyon. "Listen," the Desert Fox snapped, "I am an experienced tank commander. You and I do not see eye to eye on anything. I refuse to work with you anymore. I propose to draw the appropriate conclusions." No doubt Rommel would have fired him on the spot if he had had the authority. Von Schweppenburg said nothing; he simply saluted and walked out, resolving never again to speak to Rommel unless he simply had to. The deadlock continued.[112]

Throughout the six months of his command of Army Group B before D-Day, Erwin Rommel bombarded the High Command with requests for aid, particularly in the Normandy sector, which he felt was far too weak. Rommel proposed that the Luftwaffe be used to lay mines along possible Allied approach routes, but his request was denied. He also requested that naval vessels be used for the same mission. They were, but off the coast of southern France, not off the northern coast, where Rommel wanted them.[113]

At the beginning of May, Rommel demanded that the III Flak Corps (which had 24 batteries grouped into four regiments) be concentrated in Normandy. At that moment, it was scattered all over France. Goering, as usual, refused to cooperate, and the III Flak remained present everywhere but with no strength anywhere.[114]

Rommel also begged Hitler for a panzer division to place near St. Lo in Normandy. His request was turned down.[115]

On April 23, the former Afrika Korps commander tried to convert his old enemy, Alfred Jodl, to his concept of coastal defense. He wrote to the Bavarian: "If, in spite of the enemy's air superiority, we succeed in getting a large part of our mobile force into action in the threatened coast defense sectors in the first few hours, I am convinced that the enemy will collapse completely on the first day . . . failing the early engagement of all our mobile forces in the battle for the coast, victory will be in grave doubt."[116] Again, however, he gained no converts.

Several days later Rommel demanded that the High Command send an entire antiaircraft corps, a Nebelwerfer (Rocket Launcher) Brigade, the 12th SS Panzer Division, and the Panzer Lehr Division to Normandy. Again, OKW turned down his "request."[117]

In May, Rommel again tried to draw the remaining panzer and panzer grenadier divisions of Panzer Group West closer to the coast. Von Rundstedt protested immediately, informing OKW that this move would be tantamount to committing the reserves prior to the beginning of the battle.[118] Again Rommel's ideas were rejected. "He [Rommel] pleaded in vain to move Panzerlehr [Division] and 3rd AA Corps up between the Orne and the Vire, the 12th SS Panzer to straddle the Vire, and to have a rocket-launching brigade stationed west of the Orne," the naval advisor to Army Group B recalled. "They would have been exactly in the right places to counter the invasion. . . .[119]

All this was very frustrating to a professional of Rommel's caliber. Here he was, trying to save Germany from defeat, but found himself blocked at every turn.

One reason for all the opposition to Rommel's concept of operations was the fact that no one on the German side had anything but the vaguest idea of where the enemy would land. By this, the fifth year of the war, the German intelligence network in England had been badly damaged. Many of its best agents had been picked up, killed, or forced to hurriedly leave the country. Allied security measures were most thorough. Their total domination in the air made long-range reconnaissance flights almost suicidal, and information from neutral countries was often contradictory. German intelligence estimates were based on logic, rather than real facts; they amounted to little more than educated guesses.

Most of the High Command believed that the Allies would land on the English Channel near Cape Gris Nez. Rommel, however, didn't believe that the Allies would attack the strongest point in the German defensive network just to have a short supply line. He also disagreed with those members of the High Command who believed that Eisenhower would attack at the mouth of the Scheldt on the coast of Belgium. Rommel believed that the Western Allies had one primary strategic objective: Paris. Therefore, they would have to come somewhere along the northern coast of France. This proved to be correct. He also felt that a secondary invasion force would land on the Mediterranean coast of France and push up the Rhone River Valley to take the Atlantic Wall in the rear.[120] Again his basic ideas were right, but again his views were largely ignored.

It would be impossible to expect even a top military power to be strong everywhere along the entire coast from the Spanish border to Norway. It was the common consensus that the sector of the 15th Army from the Scheldt to the Seine was most gravely threatened because of its short distance to England, and its nearness to the Ruhr, Germany's industrial heart. Rommel initially agreed with the consensus and concentrated his primary effort on the left flank of the 15th Army, but later he concluded that the invasion probably would come in Normandy and gave top consideration to the right flank of the 7th Army (i.e., the LXXXIV Corps sector), where the Allies actually landed. Adolf Hitler at various times picked the Gironde, Brittany, the Cotentin, the Pas-de-Calais, and Norway as the site of the invasion.[121] In March, for some unexplained reason, he changed his mind again. Normandy, he declared, would be the target. Perhaps it was merely his intuition, but he nevertheless demanded that this sector be strengthened. The Fuehrer "sent his generals repeated warnings about the possibility of a landing between Caen and Cherbourg," B. H. Liddell Hart wrote. "Rommel," he continued, ". . . came round to the same view as Hitler. In the last few months he made feverish efforts to hasten the construction of underwater obstacles, bomb proof bunkers, and mine fields . . ." in the Normandy sector.[122]

Rommel's reasons for picking Normandy were more scientific than Hitler's. The Desert Fox noted that Allied airplanes were bombing all the bridges into Normandy, as if they were trying to isolate it. He also noted that the Seine Bight area off the Normandy coast was left unmined by the U.S. and Royal navies, while the English Channel waters were heavily mined. Also, Rommel discounted the Scheldt area of Holland—which at first seemed a good site for an invasion—because it was also heavily mined and its hinterland was completely ignored by the Allied air forces.[123] The Field Marshal began to shift whatever units he could muster into the Normandy zone. In the month of May alone he dispatched the 91st Air Landing Division, the 6th Parachute Regiment, the 206th Panzer Battalion, the 7th Army Sturm Battalion, the 101st Stellungswerfer (Rocket-Launcher) Regiment, the 17th Machine Gun Battalion, and the 100th Panzer Replacement Battalion to Normandy.[124]

These units varied greatly in quality. The 6th Parachute Regiment under Lieutenant Colonel von der Heydte was an elite, veteran formation. It was placed under the operational control of Major General Wilhelm Falley's 91st Air Landing Division, which was also an experienced and reliable combat force. The 206th Panzer Battalion was of less value, because it was equipped with miscellaneous French, Russian, and obsolete German light tanks (PzKw I's, PzKw II's, and probably some old Czech tanks). The Sturm Battalion was an irregular force of 1,100 infantrymen, designed for use as a shock unit. The Stellungswerfer Regiment consisted of three mobile rocket-launcher battalions, armed with 210mm, 280mm, and 320mm launchers. The 100th Panzer Replacement Battalion was equipped with a few light French and Russian tanks and therefore was of very little value. Most of these units were initially assigned antiparatrooper missions.[125]

In the months prior to D-Day, several excellent combat divisions were withdrawn from OB West's control and sent to the Eastern Front because of the deteriorating military situation there. In February 1943, after an epic siege, the 6th Army surrendered at Stalingrad, and Germany lost 320,000 of her best soldiers. Field Marshal Erich von Manstein temporarily restored the situation in the following months. Despite odds of 5 to 1 he counterattacked, retook Kharkov on March 14, and brought the Russian winter offensive to a halt. Unfortunately, Hitler did not leave the direction of the Eastern Front to von Manstein or any other commander. In July 1943, the Nazi dictator launched a major offensive at Kursk, despite the objections of von Manstein, Guderian, and others. It was a disaster. Germany lost more panzers in this single battle than she was ever able to commit on the Western Front at any single time.[126] Hitler had exhausted his capabilities and resources in the East: the initiative had passed forever to the Soviets. Defeat after defeat followed; Kharkov fell, the siege of Leningrad was broken, German armies were beaten at Demyansk, Mius, and Bukrin; the Dnieper line was breached and the Zaporozhye bridgehead was wiped out. At Cherkassy two German corps were surrounded. They broke out, but their losses were ruinous just the same. Kiev was threatened, as was Minsk in Belorussia. The 17th German Army was cut off in the Crimea and eventually destroyed at Sevastopol. In Galicia, the 1st Panzer Army was encircled. In March 1944, Hitler dismissed two of his best "Eastern" marshals: Ewald von Kleist, who commanded Army Group A, and von Manstein, then commander of Army Group South. He replaced them with two rabid Nazis who could be relied on to obey orders from the Fuehrer despite the costs. It did not take a mental giant to see that the situation on the Eastern Front would grow even darker in the near future.

The political situation was equally bleak. At the Casablanca conference in January 1943, Roosevelt and Churchill agreed to demand an unconditional surrender. Gone forever was the chance of a negotiated peace. In September 1943, Italy defected, and Hitler's other allies (Hungary, Rumania, Finland, and Bulgaria) grew exceedingly nervous as the Red Army neared their borders. They could no longer be counted on to remain loyal.[127] The only really dependable ally the Nazis had left were the Japanese. Both were in full retreat, each too weak to help the other.

On the Western Front, the Allies introduced a second subtheater in Italy with an amphibious landing at Anzio on January 22, 1944. Von Rundstedt transferred the motorized 715th Infantry Division to Kesselring in Italy, to help contain the beachhead.[128] Two months later the Russian spring offensive resulted in the collapse of large sections of the Eastern Front. The German Army could no longer contain the Russians, even in good campaigning weather. Panzer Lehr Division, the 361st Infantry Division, and the 349th Infantry Division were all hurried east, to help stem the tide. At the same time the 326th, 346th, and 348th Infantry divisions and 19th Luftwaffe Field Division were ordered to give up all their assault guns for use on the Russian Front. On March 26 the big blow fell, as far as OB West was concerned: the entire II Panzer Corps (9th and 10th SS Panzer divisions) was withdrawn from Panzer Group West and sent to Galicia, with orders to help rescue the trapped 1st Panzer Army. This mission was accomplished, but its transfer and that of a number of other panzer divisions left OB West with only one fully mobile armored division (the 21st), and the Allied invasion was less than three months away. The OKW historian went so far as to suggest that, had the Allies struck at this moment, von Rundstedt could not have offered effective resistance.[129]

During the next six weeks the shuttling of units from the Western Front, plus the skill and courage of the German defenders in the East, temporarily stabilized the situation in Russia. Hitler was able to begin rebuilding the mobile reserves of OB West for the invasion he knew must come soon. Panzer Lehr Division, now under former Afrika Korps Chief of Staff Lieutenant General Fritz Bayerlein, returned from Hungary, and the old fighters of the 1st SS and 2nd SS Panzer divisions returned from Russia to rebuild their battered regiments in France. At the same time the XXXXVII Panzer Corps Headquarters of General Baron Hans von Funk was transferred from Russia to OB West. Funk and his staff represented one of the most experienced armored leadership teams in all the Third Reich.[130] Even the II SS Panzer Corps would eventually return to the West, although not before the Allies had landed on the shores of France.

Despite the return of these and other panzer units, Rommel did not face D-Day with any degree of optimism. Of the three modes of warfare—land, sea, and air—Germany could compete only on the ground. At sea the German Navy was a broken reed, and what little power it had left was destroyed soon after the invasion. On June 14 a low-level air attack at Le Havre destroyed 38 surface vessels, including nearly all remaining torpedo and patrol boats. It was almost the final blow for Naval Group West. On June 29 Admiral Krancke had only one torpedo boat, a dozen patrol boats, and eight schnorkel-equipped U-boats left. The Navy was operationally bankrupt.[131] More importantly, the Luftwaffe had reached approximately the same straits.

To tell the story of the final decline of the Luftwaffe, we must regress a bit. On August 17, 1943, the Allies launched two major bombing raids. One target was the ball-bearing plants at Schweinfurt, and the other was the Messerschmitt aircraft factory at Regensburg, where the Me 109's were built. Both targets were located deep inside the Reich.

Of the 474 aircraft involved, 60 were shot down, a very heavy loss for the British and American bomber commands, particularly in view of the fact that little damage was done to the targets. On October 14 the Americans tried again, this time only against Schweinfurt. The result was an unmitigated disaster. Casualties exceeded 25 percent, and again little damage was done. These aerial defeats demonstrated clearly that the Allied Air Forces possessed air superiority only over the fringe areas of German air space.[132]

Following the debacle at Schweinfurt, Allied planners reevaluated their strategic position, and increased their numbers and use of long-range fighters. By February 1944, the U.S. 8th Air Force under Lieutenant General James H. Doolittle felt strong enough to plan bombing missions designed to deliberately provoke air battles with the Luftwaffe. Although the German fighter pilots, led by Lieutenant General Adolf Galland, put up quite a battle, they were unable to overcome the huge swarms of U.S.A.A.F. and R.A.F. Spitfires, Hurricanes, and Mosquitoes which protected the Allied bombers. Despite heavier Allied casualties, the Luftwaffe was driven from the sky. The losses the German Air Force suffered in these battles could never be replaced. By June, so many planes and pilots had been lost that Allied aircraft flew virtually unchallenged (except by AA guns) over the skies of Berlin, even in broad daylight. Experienced fighter pilots were in particularly short supply. The pilot training program of the Luftwaffe was reduced from 260 hours of flight time per student in 1940 to as little as 50 in 1944, and even then it could not keep up with losses. The new, green German pilots were no match for the superbly trained British and American aviators; many of them could not even land properly. In May, for example, the Luftwaffe lost 712 aircraft to hostile action and 656 in flying accidents.[133] It was the loss of its veteran fliers, not the loss of aircraft, that finally broke the back of the misused German Luftwaffe.

In the West, Rommel had to deal with Luftwaffe Air Marshal Sperrle, a man of dynamic energy. The two marshals got along well together, despite Sperrle's frequent outbursts of bitter sarcasm. They also agreed politically, which eventually led to Sperrle's dismissal in August 1944.[134]

Unfortunately for Rommel, Sperrle did not have the resources to help him, except on very rare occasions. On June 1, according to General Speidel, Sperrle had only 90 bombers and 70 fighter aircraft in his entire 3rd Air Fleet.[135] On D-Day, Eisenhower's pilots flew 25,000 sorties,[136] against approximately 100 for the Germans.[137] Almost all of these were intercepted miles from the actual landing sites. It was a complete rout in the sky.

Hitler, Goering, and their staffs played right into the Allies' hands by dissipating the remaining air power they had on strategically senseless raids on civilian targets in England. In January 1944, the England Attack Command ("Angriffsfuehrer England") launched the so-called "Baby Blitz" on England. From January 21 until May 29 the United Kingdom was struck by 29 separate raids with an average strength of 200 aircraft per raid. Despite Rommel's pleas that the Allied embarkation ports (especially Portsmouth and Southampton) be bombed, the attacks centered on heavily defended London. When the Baby Blitz began, the England Attack Command had 462 operational aircraft; by the end of May it could put only 107 planes into the air. Conditions were so bad that the Luftwaffe had to abandon its airfields on the French coast and retreat to the interior.[138]

Eisenhower finally gained control of the Allied strategic air forces in April and he used them with devastating effect against two primary targets: the French rail network and the German fuel industry.[139] Since it was common knowledge that OB West did not have enough motor transport or gasoline to make up for the loss of the railroads, the aerial offensive was a sure tip-off that D-Day was near.

Goering's Luftwaffe was powerless to prevent the wholesale destruction of the French rail network. The scattered III Flak Corps was as ineffective as 3rd Air Fleet against these attacks. Six hundred locomotives were shot up by American and British fighters and fighter-bombers,[140] and attacks against railroad bridges were even more successful. The destruction of the Brussels-Paris-Orleans line made it impossible to organize a railroad supply line, and by the middle of May the German supply network was in chaos. All the bridges on the Seine below Paris and all those on the Loire below Orleans were knocked out.[141] By the end of April, 600 army supply trains were backlogged in France alone.[142]

To meet this crisis, von Rundstedt canceled all military leaves. In April, 18,000 construction workers were taken off the Atlantic Wall and put to work on the railroads. Another 10,000 were transferred in May, but it was all in vain: repairs simply could not keep pace with the destruction.[143] Allied bomber experts selected 80 railroad depots as primary targets and by D-Day over 50 of these were either heavily damaged or virtually obliterated.[144] The attacks against the locomotives also continued at an accelerated pace. On May 21 alone, U.S. and British aircraft destroyed 113 railroad engines, 50 of which were claimed in the 7th Army's sector.[145] Before the antirail offensive began, the German transportation staff was running over 100 supply trains a day in France. By the end of April this figure was reduced to 48; by the end of May, only 20 trains per day were operating throughout France.[146] After D-Day it would drop even lower. By the end of May traffic over the Seine, Oise, and Meuse rivers was at a virtual standstill.[147] General Esposito was right when he wrote: "Allied air attacks had weakened the railroad transportation system in France to the point of collapse."[148] Although not as hard-hit as the railroads, the French highway system was by no means neglected.

By June 6, Normandy was, for all practical purposes, a strategic island. German reinforcements to the invaded sector would now have to march there overland over damaged roads, which would increase their travel time by days when hours counted. They would also be exposed to repeated aerial attacks from strong fighter-bomber squadrons reserved specifically for that purpose. Eisenhower had won a major, perhaps decisive victory on the very eve of the invasion; what is more, he knew it.

The Allied bomber offensive against German fuel installations was carried out by American pilots on pinpoint, daylight raids, and was only slightly less successful than the offensive against the French rail network. The fuel industry was always one of Nazi Germany's critical weaknesses and any decline in fuel production severely damaged the German war effort. By early May 1944, production had fallen from 5,850 to 4,820 metric tons per day, causing Munitions Minister Albert Speer to bluntly tell Hitler: "The enemy has struck us at one of our weakest points. If they persist this time, we will soon no longer have any fuel production worth mentioning. Our one hope is that the other side has an air force General Staff as scatterbrained as ours!"[149] They did not.

As the bombing offensive heightened and the season for the invasion grew near, Rommel redoubled his efforts to meet it. On April 29 he set out for the Bay of Biscay, Pyrenees, and Mediterranean zones, again trying to deceive Allied intelligence into thinking his area of responsibility was greater than it actually was. Five days later he was back at La Roche-Guyon, but on May 9 he was off once more, back to LXXXIV Corps in Normandy. He found work in Marcks's zone proceeding to his satisfaction, although a great deal more needed to be done. Things were less satisfactory in the 21st Panzer Division area, where Nazi Major General Edgar Feuchtinger held command. Feuchtinger had organized the annual Nuremberg party rallies in the 1930s, and held his command for political reasons. Rommel appeared at the division's 22nd Panzer Regiment headquarters at Falaise at 8:00 A.M. one morning, and found nobody of any rank there. Half an hour later the regimental commander, Colonel von Oppeln-Bronikowski, showed up, drunk at 8:30 in the morning! Rommel asked him what would happen if the Allies landed before 8:30 A.M. "Catastrophe!" replied the colonel, who then fell into a chair. Remarkably enough, Rommel overlooked the incident and left Oppeln-Bronikowski in command of the regiment.[150]

From mid-May, there was little Rommel could do but wait. "My inventions are coming into action," he wrote on May 6. "Thus I am looking forward to the battle with profoundest confidence. . . ."[151] Much remained to be done, but much had been accomplished. Many mines had been laid, obstacles constructed, booby traps set, and reinforcements acquired. Most importantly, the German people and particularly the soldiers of the Western Front no longer feared the invasion, as secret Gestapo reports indicated. "People see it as our last chance to turn the tide," one of them read. "There is virtually no fear of the invasion discernible."[152]

"No fear of the invasion discernible." This is a tremendous tribute to Rommel, who had achieved all he could have been expected to achieve, given the enemy's resources, the lack of cooperation from his superiors and his own staggering material deficiencies. However, on June 4 he threw much of this advantage away, and made the greatest mistake of his military career: he decided to return to Germany and personally ask Adolf Hitler for more reinforcements. When the invasion finally came, the one man who might have repulsed it was away from his post.

2

D-Day

On the eve of its greatest battle, OB West was weaker than German planners had hoped it would be, but nevertheless it represented a formidable military force. Field Marshal von Rundstedt had 58 combat divisions, of which 33 were either static or reserve, suitable only for defensive or limited offensive missions. Of the 24 divisions classified as fit for duty in the East, 13 were mobile infantry, two were parachute, four were panzer, four were SS panzer and one (the 17th) was an SS panzer grenadier division. One Army panzer division (the 21st) was classified as unfit for duty on the Eastern Front, because it was largely equipped with inferior, captured material.[1] The U.S. Army's official history assessed OB West's condition this way: "... the steady drain of the Eastern Front left to [von] Rundstedt on the eve of his great battle two kinds of units: old divisions which had lost much of their best personnel and equipment, and new divisions, some of excellent combat value, some only partially equipped and partially trained."[2] Map 2, page 56, shows German dispositions on the Western Front on June 6, 1944.

The panzer divisions varied as greatly in numbers and strengths as did the infantry divisions. They ranged from 12,768 men in the 9th Panzer to 21,386 in the recently rebuilt 1st SS Panzer. All the panzer divisions were larger than their American and British counterparts, with the 1st SS Panzer (Leibstandarte Adolf Hitler) being more than twice as large. On the other hand, they all had fewer tanks than the Allied armored divisions. All the SS panzer divisions had six panzer grenadier (i.e., mechanized infantry) battalions per regiment, as opposed to four in the Wehrmacht's armored divisions. Therefore, all SS panzer divisions were larger than their Army counterparts, at least insofar as was reflected in their tables of organization.[3]

If authorized strength and equipment varied somewhat, actual differ-

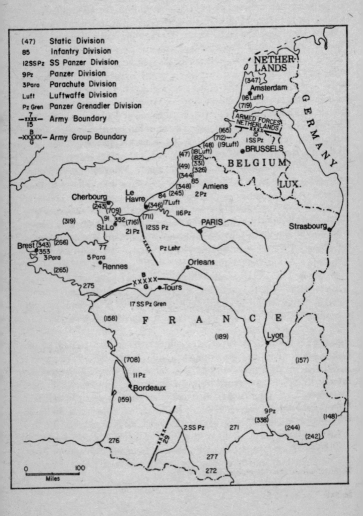

ences within divisions fluctuated remarkably. Although both Army and SS
divisions each were to have a panzer regiment with one battalion of PzKw
IVs and one battalion of PzKw Vs, their actual equipment figures differed
in almost every case. The 1st SS Panzer, for example, was authorized 101
PzKw IV and 81 PzKw V Panther tanks, but had only 88 tanks in all (50
PzKw IVs and 38 PzKw Vs), which means it had only 48 percent of its
authorized armored strength at the time of the invasion.[4] Like so many
other German divisions, this unit was well below its assigned strength
because of losses suffered on the Russian Front. Every German panzer
division was understrength in terms of tanks except Panzer Lehr, which
had 183. Second Panzer Division was close to full strength, having 161
panzers (94 PzKw IVs and 67 PzKw Vs). However, five of the panzer
divisions in the West had fewer than 100 tanks. The figures for the 2nd SS
"Das Reich" Division, shown in Table 2, are typical. Note that this unit was
particularly deficient in heavy tanks (i.e., PzKw Vs and PzKw VIs, or
Tigers).[5]

The Allied armies suffered from few of the difficulties and deficiencies
under which Rommel and von Rundstedt labored, and certainly not to the
same degree. Rommel's Chief of Staff estimated that the Western Allies
had about 75 divisions on June 6, of which 65 were at full strength and fully

Table 2

ACTUAL VS. AUTHORIZED STRENGTH
2nd SS PANZER DIVISION
June 6, 1944

Item of Equipment	Number Authorized	Number on Hand
Assault Guns	75	33
PzKw IIIs	7	0
PzKw IVs	57	44
PzKw Vs (Panthers)	99	25
PzKw VIs (Tigers)	0	0
TOTAL NUMBER OF PANZERS	163	69

% of authorized tank strength on hand: 42.3%

Source: Harrison: 240

trained.[6] Actually, they had 2,876,000 men in 45 full-strength divisions.[7] All were either armored, mechanized, airborne, or motorized, and all were fully mobile. They were supported by 17,000 aircraft, which opposed 160 in the entire 3rd Air Fleet, and the Allies had an overwhelming naval superiority, an excellent intelligence network, and a chain of command which functioned much better than that of Nazi Germany.[8] Table 3 shows their basic organization on D-Day.

The actual landings took place in the zone of the LXXXIV Corps of the 7th Army. Rommel (in his capacity as Commander-in-Chief of Army Group B) first inspected this corps sector in February 1944 and was not satisfied with what he saw; specifically, he felt that the 352nd Division at St. Lo was positioned too far inland. As a result of his objections, Colonel General Dollmann ordered this unit forward to the coast, where it took over the left flank of the 716th Infantry Division in March.[9] This move was routinely reported to Allied intelligence by the French Underground via the usual method: carrier pigeon. The procedure was to dispatch each message twice, just in case German soldiers armed with shotguns killed one of the birds. This time, however, the specially assigned pigeon hunters got lucky and shot down both pigeons. As a result, the Americans didn't learn of the strengthening of the sector until the men of the 352nd started firing on them. It provided General Omar Bradley with a nasty shock on D-Day, as we shall see, and it almost cost the Americans one of their beachheads.[10]

Rommel's comments also led to the stationing of two "Eastern" battalions (the 795th Georgian and the 642nd Ost of the 709th and 716th Infantry divisions, respectively) closer to the coast. One reinforced regiment of the 352nd Division was held in corps reserve at Bayeux. Marcks periodically rotated his reserve forces to give the soldiers in all three of the 352nd's regiments occasional rest periods from mine laying, obstacle building, and the like. On D-Day, the 915th Infantry Regiment held Bayeux.

As elsewhere in his army group's area, Rommel's construction program had greatly improved the defenses, but work was far from complete. LXXXIV Corps suffered from shortages of transport and cement, a problem that became especially critical in late May, after the cement plant at Cherbourg was shut down owing to a lack of coal. On May 25 General Marcks estimated that the construction program in his area was only half finished.[11] Between the Orne and Vire rivers, where the British and Americans landed, strong points and machine-gun nests were still an

SUPREME COMMANDER, ALLIED EXPEDITIONARY FORCE:
General Dwight D. Eisenhower

ALLIED NAVAL EXPEDITIONARY FORCE:
Admiral Sir Bertram Ramsay

ALLIED EXPEDITIONARY AIR FORCE:
Air Chief Marshal Sir Trafford
Leigh-Mallory

Br. 21st Army Group:
Field Marshal Sir Bernard L. Montgomery
U.S. 1st Army: Lt. Gen. Omar Bradley
Br. 2nd Army: Lt. Gen. Miles Dempsey

Table 3—Allied Organization, June 6, 1944

average of 875 yards apart.[12] Rommel's overall antiseaborne landing system, with its four belts of obstacles, had shown significant progress only in belts 1 and 2 (see chapter 1). As a result, the obstacles would be deadly if the Allies came at high tide as Rommel expected, but would be left high and dry, and therefore useless, if they struck at low tide. If the Allies did come at low tide, however, they would have to cross a greatly enlarged strip of beach, and this would drastically increase the effectiveness of any German machine gunners who survived the naval bombardment.

In other aspects of the defense, Rommel was not satisfied with the progress of his antiairborne obstacles, although he complimented Marcks for doing all that he could do. As a result of the inexcusable slowness of response from OKW, he received the major shipment of captured French mines only in early June. It was with these mines that he intended to arm his antiglider obstacles in the rear of LXXXIV Corps. Now it would be too late.[13]

Rommel inspected the 21st Panzer Division again in late May, and seems to have been satisfied with the antitank hedgehogs at Cairon, halfway between Caen and the sea, which later held up the Canadian 3rd Infantry Division for eight days. This was all he was happy with, however. He found a divisional transport composed mainly of captured French vehicles, mine fields still surrounded by barbed wire and labeled as such, and, worst of all, French civilians still wandering freely about the area, despite orders he had given to the contrary. Erwin Rommel was quite angry about this state of affairs and, as usual, made no secret of the fact. Unfortunately for the German Army, however, he did not relieve Major General Feuchtinger of his command. This decision would have serious consequences for the Third Reich in the very near future.

One final factor must again be mentioned before the picture of the LXXXIV Corps on the eve of D-Day can be considered complete, and this is the intangible factor of morale. As the German soldiers faced their greatest test, this vital element was very high indeed. Since Rommel's arrival, the West Wall soldiers had gained a new sense of self-value. Germany's greatest general had been chosen to command them! No longer was duty in France looked upon as a soft job for used-up men who were not fit for duty on the Eastern Front; now they counted for something! Feverishly they prepared to meet the challenge, and their self-confidence rose accordingly.

The Americans unwittingly aided Hitler and his propaganda minister in their efforts to stir the private soldier into a white heat. In May 1944, the details of the Morgenthau Plan were leaked to the news media and the public. This notion, named for Roosevelt's favorite advisor and Secretary of the Treasury, called for the systematic dismantling of Germany's industry and the purposeful crippling of her agriculture as soon as the Allies won the war. Germany would become a conquered province, to be kept forever at the subsistence and poverty levels, much like it had existed during the Dark Ages. The German people and the Nazis were viewed as one and the same by people like Morgenthau. The public airing of this scheme, however, was a piece of stupidity on the part of the American government. It weakened the hand of Colonel Count Claus von Stauffenberg and his coconspirators (including Rommel), for its harsh terms allowed Germany no reward for an early capitulation. No matter what, her people would be reduced to virtual serfdom. Roosevelt, now in deteriorating health, allowed himself to be carried along by Morgenthau, the only member of his cabinet who was allowed to call the President by his first name. The cunning Churchill, of course, would have nothing to do with it. "You can't punish a whole people," he remarked. Even Eisenhower, who carefully avoided political divisions in Allied circles, denounced the Morgenthau Plan as "silly" and "criminal." Unfortunately for his men, the damage had already been done. Goebbels, always the evil genius, played up the plan for its full propaganda value, which was immense. Even many of the anti-Nazi or non-Nazi officers and men in the Wehrmacht now felt that they had to resist to the utmost, not for Hitler and his regime, but in defense of the Fatherland and generations to come. A typical comment on Allied propaganda broadcasts at this time was an ominous "They're coming." To this, the German soldiers frequently replied: "Let them come." The entire incident materially strengthened German resistance on the mainland at the very moment Eisenhower and his forces could least afford it.[14]

For months Erwin Rommel had been laboring against incredible odds. As Harrison wrote: "To stake everything on a battle whose place and timing would be entirely of the enemy's choosing was to put an all but impossible burden on the defense, demanding of it a mobility it did not have and a sure knowledge of enemy intentions it had no means of acquiring."[15]

The strain of labor and uncertainty took its toll on the Desert Fox. In early June he needed a rest. He also wanted to see Adolf Hitler again, to ask for more reinforcements, so he planned a trip to Berchtesgaden, where he intended to again ask that two additional panzer divisions and a mortar brigade be sent to Normandy. "The most urgent problem is to win the Fuehrer over by personal conversation," he wrote in his diary.[16] He decided to take June 4–7 off. June 6 was his wife's 50th birthday, and he wanted to spend it with her at Herrlingen before continuing on to Hitler's Bavarian residence in the Alpine region.

Before departing, Rommel checked the weather reports, which were encouraging. Colonel Professor Walter Stoebe, the chief Luftwaffe weather forecaster in Paris, predicted increasing cloudiness, high winds, and rain. It was already drizzling in some locations, and Channel winds were 20 to 30 miles per hour at 6:00 A.M. on June 4. The weather forecasts from Poland were equally encouraging. The Allies were not expected to invade until the Red Army could launch their summer offensive, and the late thaw of 1944 would not dry up until the latter part of June. Thus reassured, the Desert Fox left his headquarters at La Roche-Guyon at 6:00 A.M., convinced that the British and Americans would not land in the immediate future.[17] Little did he realize that, the next day and hundreds of miles away, Dwight D. Eisenhower would make the decision he was born to make. Despite the bad weather, he unleashed his forces for the long-awaited invasion. With tears in his eyes he watched the airplanes take off, loaded with paratroopers. This courageous decision marked the beginning of the end for the Third Reich. It also meant that Erwin Rommel would not be on hand for what many consider the most important battle of his career.

Colonel General Dollmann, the 7th Army commander, was also convinced that the invasion would not be launched in such miserable weather. To keep his subordinates on their toes, he ordered a map exercise to be conducted at Rennes. All divisional commanders plus two regimental commanders per division were ordered to attend. He left his headquarters at Le Mans to observe the war game in person. As a result, the 7th Army would be without many of its important leaders on June 6. Major General Max Pemsel, Dollmann's chief of staff, would act as de facto commander of the 7th Army on D-Day, just as Dr. Speidel did at Army Group B Headquarters.

Eisenhower's decision also took Admiral Krancke by surprise. He canceled the sea patrols scheduled for the night of June 5/6, because he was sure that the enemy would not attempt any significant naval operations in such foul weather. The huge Allied naval armada had the English Channel to itself: it approached the European mainland undetected. In fact, British Admiral Ramsay reported that the Allied passage had an "air of unreality" because of the complete absence of any kind of German reaction.[18]

The Luftwaffe was also unlucky. As a result of the bad weather, it chose this moment to rotate its fighter units. For reasons known only to Reichsmarschal Goering, the 26th Fighter Wing (which contained 124 of the 3rd Air Fleet's 160 operational aircraft) was sent from Lille (within range of Normandy) to Metz in eastern France.[19] No replacements were available, because Goering had moved the other fighter squadrons from France to Germany a few days before. "I can't keep my fighters in France waiting for an invasion," he said. "I need them for the defense of the Reich."[20] Colonel Josef Priller, the outspoken commander of the 26th Fighter who had personally shot down 96 enemy aircraft, denounced the order as "crazy." On June 6, Priller could bring only two airplanes to bear against the huge Allied air armada; these had been left behind as a sort of rear guard when the rest of the wing moved to the French-German border.[21] The Luftwaffe was debilitated before the battle began.

Shortly after nightfall on June 5, the bombs began to fall all over northwestern France, with particular concentration in and behind the 7th Army's sector. Although this was not unusual in itself, the aerial attacks continued well into the night, and soon reached an unprecedented level of fury.

The French Resistance was also out in full force on the night of June 5/6. Since France had surrendered in 1940, this heterogeneous force had grown to a strength of 200,000 men, women, and children. Under the nominal command of General Joseph P. Koenig, they were informed of the imminence of the invasion only 48 hours beforehand. The Allied planners felt that they would be of highly dubious value in this battle and were worried that the messages to the Underground would alert the Germans. The Resistance (known as the FFI, or Free Forces of the Interior) proved to be surprisingly effective. During June, they cut German rail lines a total of 486 times. By June 7 twenty-six trunk lines were unusable, including the vital arteries to Normandy. The Avranches-St. Lô, St. Lô-Cherbourg, and St. Lô-Caen rail lines were all sabotaged by multiple cuts. These and other critical rail lines were useless for some time, significantly slowing the speed with which reinforcements arrived in Normandy.[22] At the same time telephone systems were sabotaged, telegraph wires cut, road bridges blown up, and communications generally disrupted throughout the rear of Army Group B.

The Allies feared that the alerting of the FFI would tip off Rommel that the invasion was imminent. It should have, but it did not. On June 1–2, Gestapo agents who had penetrated the Resistance picked up at least 28 coded messages signaling the underground to stand by for orders to begin executing their sabotage missions. The SS intelligence agency quickly reported this development to Admiral Doenitz, with the comment that the invasion could be expected within two weeks. Undoubtedly they also informed Himmler, but neither he nor Doenitz took the warning seriously. Thinking an exercise was in progress, the Grand Admiral did not see fit to inform Rommel's headquarters of the Gestapo's message.[23]

Fifteenth Army's Intelligence Officer, Lieutenant Colonel Helmut Meyer, also intercepted a signal, this one telling the FFI that the invasion would come within 48 hours. He relayed the news to von Salmuth's chief of staff, Major General Rudolf Hofmann, who immediately put 15th Army on alert. Colonel Meyer telephoned Army Group B and OB West and sent a teletyped message to OKW. Colonel General Jodl, however, did not order an alert, assuming that von Rundstedt would do so. Von Rundstedt did not give the order either, assuming Army Group B would do so. Army Group B, whose commander had already left for Germany, did nothing; apparently General Speidel dismissed the message as just another rumor. As a result, 7th Army was not put on alert, and the invasion was only hours away.[24] General Dollmann's HQ actually canceled an alert planned for that night! No information at all was passed down to LXXXIV Corps, which was about to be struck by the greatest amphibious assault in history.

General of Artillery Marcks proved to be quicker of decision than his superiors. Scattered and fragmentary reports came in to his headquarters with disturbing frequency. At 12:40 A.M. on June 6 elements of the 919th Panzer Grenadier Regiment clashed with enemy paratroopers east of Montebourg. The enemy units were identified as part of the U.S. 82nd Airborne Division. A few minutes later British parachute units seized the Caen Canal crossing at Benouville and blew up the Dives bridge on the Varaville-Grangues road. More importantly, glider forces blew up the Dives River bridge at Troarn. This explosion cut the road which connected Caen with the Seine River cities of Rouen, Le Havre, and Paris, and did much to isolate LXXXIV Corps from the rest of OB West. Meanwhile, at

711th Infantry Division headquarters on the far left flank of 15th Army (near the LXXXIV Corps boundary) Major General Josef Reichert was playing cards with members of his staff when two British paratroopers landed on his lawn and were taken prisoner by his intelligence officer. Reichert informed von Salmuth's headquarters immediately. The message was relayed to General Marcks about 1:45 A.M.[25] At the same time, Marcks received a report from Colonel Hamann, the acting commander of the 709th Infantry Division (whose leader was en route to the famous map exercise at Rennes). The dispatch stated that his men had captured prisoners from the U.S. 101st Airborne Division. Twenty-one minutes later Major General Wilhelm Richter, who commanded the 716th Infantry Division on the LXXXIV Corps' right flank, reported to Marcks that enemy paratroopers had landed east of the Orne. This news convinced Marcks, who put his corps and the nearby 21st Panzer Division on immediate top alert. Then he telephoned Major General Pemsel, 7th Army's Chief of Staff, and told him the invasion was definitely in progress.[26] It was a little after 2:00 A.M.

In the absence of his commander, Pemsel put 7th Army on the highest state of alert and telephoned General Speidel at La Roche-Guyon. Speidel did not believe the invasion had come in such miserable weather. He told Pemsel that it was merely a diversion and that he should sit tight. Then he hung up. About the same time, von Salmuth phoned for Rommel and was put through to Speidel. The 15th Army commander had just talked to General Reichert. Over the wires, the sound of machine-gun fire had been clearly audible; the men of the 711th Infantry were clashing with enemy paratroopers very near divisional HQ. Speidel listened, but still refused to believe—even now—that the invasion might really have come.[27] Miles away, in Germany, Erwin Rommel, the one man who might have saved the situation, was sound asleep.

While General Speidel did nothing, the American 82nd and 101st Airborne divisions landed in the left rear of the 352nd Division and the British 6th Airborne dropped down on both sides of the Orne River. Their objectives were obvious from the very beginning: cut off the flow of supplies to LXXXIV Corps and seal off the coastal areas from any possible reinforcements. Meanwhile, a huge Allied air force destroyed airfields, supply depots, and bridges far into the French interior. The rear echelons of LXXXIV Corps were pulverized. Meanwhile, all the railroad bridges over the Seine between Paris and the ocean were knocked out by fighter-bombers. Thirteen highway bridges between the French capital and the coast were destroyed, as were the five main highway bridges between Orleans and Nantes.[28] The LXXXIV Corps sector was virtually a strategic island on the morning of June 6.

Field Marshals von Rundstedt and Sperrle, Admiral Krancke, and Lieutenant General Speidel all felt that the airborne attack was a diversion designed to attract attention away from the 15th Army's sector. To pacify Marcks, who was hotly insisting that the invasion was imminent and would come in his sector, they took the 91st Air Landing Division and the mobile elements of the 709th Infantry Division out of reserve and gave them to Marcks. These units, located in the western Cotentin, were ordered to counterattack the American paratroopers. Little else could be done to directly assist the LXXXIV Corps at this stage of the operation.[29]

On the enemy's side, the plan was this: both U.S. airborne divisions (a total of over 13,000 men in 822 planes) were to drop in the eastern half of the Cotentin Peninsula between Ste.-Mère-Église and Carentan, establish a bridgehead, and wait for the U.S. VII Corps, which would form the right flank of the Allied landing forces. It was to link up with the paratroopers, build up forces and supplies for a few days, and then cut the peninsula at its neck and divide the German army in the Cotentin. Eventually, VII Corps would have the goal of taking the port-city of Cherbourg, the strategic objective of the landings.

Immediately to the left of the VII Corps, U.S. V Corps would land. Its job was to link up with the VII Corps 15 miles to its right, and the British XXX Corps to its left.

The British Army landed with two corps on three beaches. On the British right flank (i.e., the Allied center), the XXX Corps had the objectives of linking up with the Americans and capturing the important town of Bayeux on the Caen-Cherbourg highway. To the left of the XXX, British I Corps formed the Allies' left flank. It was to land on two beaches and was thus the only corps on D-Day to be responsible for more than one beach. Its objectives were to join up with the British 6th Airborne Division on the Orne and to capture Caen, the only really strategic objective in the British sector. South of this university city was country fit for armored operations. North of it, the Germans would have the advantage of excellent defensive terrain. It was therefore critical that Caen fall on the first day of the invasion, before Rommel could build up a defensive front and place the entire invasion in a stalemate.

Each of the corps had a code-named landing site assigned to it. U.S. VII Corps landed at Utah Beach, while U.S. V Corps went ashore at Omaha Beach. British XXX Corps landed at Gold Beach, while British I Corps entered the continent at Juno and Sword beaches. Map 3 shows these landings, as well as the divisions which spearheaded them and the airborne drops which screened and supported them.

Although the British 6th Airborne Division "dropped precisely on its objectives along the estuary of the Orne" and secured Montgomery's left flank,[30] the American paratroopers were unlucky as a whole. Their formations were broken up by low clouds and sporadic antiaircraft fire. The 101st lost 30 percent of its men and 70 percent of its equipment in the landing.[31] By the end of the day the division could rally only 2,500 of the 6,600 men it dropped more than 22 hours before. It also failed to effectively link up with the 82nd Airborne to its west. The "Screaming Eagles" did, however, secure the southern exits to Utah Beach, thus covering it from German counterattack.[32] The U.S. 82nd Airborne was even less successful than its sister division, for most of its units jumped into the wrong target areas. Most of the 82nd's men landed on the edges of the 91st Air Landing Division's assembly areas and were immediately heavily engaged by aggressive German junior officers and their battalions, companies, and platoons. The drop of the 82nd was even more scattered than that of the 101st. Many of its men landed in swamps, or in areas recently flooded on Rommel's orders, and were drowned before they could shed their heavy equipment. Brigadier General James Gavin, the assistant division commander, tried to establish a bridgehead over the small Merderet River with the men he could find, but was soon defeated. Other elements of the division took the crossing at La Fière, but could not hold it. The 82nd, in fact, accomplished only one of its divisional missions, but it was the most important: elements of the 505th Parachute Infantry Regiment seized and held the vital crossroads town of Ste.-Mère-Église.[33] This victory very effectively screened Utah Beach from German counterattacks. The tough paratroopers flocked to the town in small groups, formed a perimeter defense under whatever officers and N.C.O.'s were present, and dug in. They would have to be ousted before any attempt could be made to overrun Omaha Beach while it was still vulnerable. Considering the high level of spirit and training of the paratroopers,

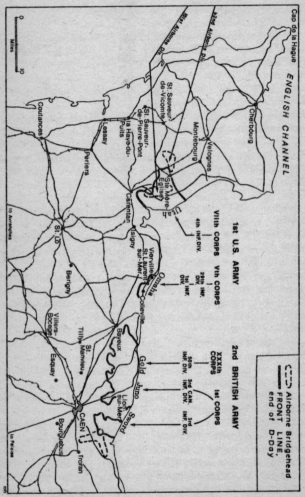

**Map 3—The Allied Landings on D-Day
and the Situation at the End of June 6, 1944**

plus the tremendous blows it was absorbing elsewhere, this would be a tall order indeed for the understrength LXXXIV Corps.

An isolated and anonymous band of lost American paratroopers also scored a major victory in the early morning hours of June 6, although they didn't know it at the time. Major General Wilhelm Falley, the commander of the 91st Air Landing Division, was on his way to the map exercise at Rennes when the air raids began. He soon became alarmed about their intensity, and decided they might well be the start of the invasion. He ordered his driver to return to base. Near the château which served as his headquarters, Falley heard the rattle of automatic weapons fire. He drew his pistol and went to investigate. A few minutes later he lay dead, the victim of an enemy paratrooper. The Battle of Normandy had claimed its first general.[34] The 91st Air Landing Division would be without a leader on the most important day of its existence.

Elsewhere, the British and American navies and air forces were paving the way for the actual troop landings. They had at their disposal 3,467 heavy bombers and 1,645 medium bombers, light bombers, and torpedo planes, protected by 5,409 fighters and fighter-bombers. The Luftwaffe was utterly incapable of penetrating the Allied fighter screen, except for one isolated case. Two German fighters, flown by incredibly brave pilots (one of whom was Colonel Priller), broke through the wall, did whatever damage they could do by strafing one of the beaches, and then miraculously escaped to tell the tale. All other German aircraft were either shot down or forced to turn back.[35]

Isolated flak batteries provided all the antiaircraft protection 7th Army had on D-Day, and it wasn't much. These batteries shot down the bulk of the 113 aircraft the Allies lost that day,[36] but there simply weren't enough guns available to reduce the enemy's aerial effectiveness. If Rommel's pleas to concentrate the entire III Flak Corps in Normandy had been heeded, the story might have been much different. As it was, Allied aircraft bombed, strafed, and generally shot up German positions almost at will. The heavy battery at St. Marcouf was a prime target, because its four 210mm long-barreled guns and single 150mm gun represented a major threat to Allied shipping. The enemy airmen attacked it with more than 100 aircraft, and the battery's six 75mm antiaircraft guns were quickly knocked out. Over 600 tons of bombs struck in and around the battery. All its guns were destroyed.[37]

Two and a half miles further inland, the battery at Azeville was overrun by American paratroopers, and its four 122mm guns were captured.[38] Two of the largest coastal batteries in Normandy had been neutralized before they could fire on a single Allied ship.

The Royal and U.S. air forces flew thousands of sorties on D-Day, and dropped 11,912 tons of bombs. Within a few hours more bombs were dropped on Normandy than on Hamburg, the most heavily bombed city of 1943.[39] Many of these Allied bombs were destroyed to blast sideways, to wipe out German positions without making deep craters which might delay the Allied tanks when they advanced. In towns and villages this side-blast effect increased casualties and collapsed houses. The rubble thus created clogged Nazi supply lines, particularly those which passed through St. Lo and Caen. Between obliterated roads and the ever-present fighter-bombers, German supply vehicles were unable to reach the coast, and the front-line soldiers could not be resupplied.[40] Many were soon running short of ammunition.

The Allies did make one critical mistake, and it involved the 329 heavy bombers they sent to destroy German positions dominating Omaha Beach. General Doolittle, the 8th U.S. Air Force commander, informed General Eisenhower that, owing to poor weather conditions, the B-24s would have to drop their bombs by instruments. Doolittle wanted to delay the bomb release for several seconds, to be sure that the bombs didn't fall on the naval and amphibious forces gathering off the beach. It was a tough decision, for delay might mean missing the target. An early drop, however, would mean a catastrophe, because it would land on the assault vessels, which were now full of troops. The delayed release was approved. As a result, the bombs fell as much as three miles inland, missing the 352nd Infantry Division's coastal positions entirely.[41] The defenses would be very much intact when the American infantry landed.

On Utah Beach the story was considerably different. Here, the U.S. Army Air Force employed medium bombers at lower altitudes. They blasted some, but by no means all, of the German positions. Still, Utah Beach would prove to be a much safer place for the average American soldier than Omaha Beach on June 6.

Eisenhower came with 5,000 ships and 130,000 men. He had achieved three elements of surprise: he was expected at Pas de Calais, not Normandy; he was coming at low tide, not high tide as predicted by Rommel; and he was expected to come in calm weather, not in near-gale conditions.

At 5:30 A.M. the Allied Fleet attacked the surviving German shore batteries with six battleships, 23 cruisers, and 104 destroyers. Meanwhile, Allied special service teams began to demolish the beach obstacles, left exposed by the low tide. If Rommel had been allowed time to complete his preparations this would have been impossible. German riflemen and machine gunners made it difficult enough as it was.[42]

On Utah Beach, the Americans faced a 709th Division strong point named W-5. Erwin Rommel had personally inspected this position on May 11, just 26 days before. That day he had been in a very foul mood, which was quite usual for him when he was dissatisfied with the performances or preparations of his underlings. This day he was in a particularly ill temper, and he "sent rockets" after Major General von Schlieben and his regimental and company commanders. Only Second Lieutenant Jahnke, the strong point commander, refused to be intimidated. This young officer was no new hand, as his rank might imply. He had won the Knight's Cross on the Russian Front, and was even courageous enough to face the wrath of Field Marshal Rommel. He informed his C-in-C that, at this particular point, the tide washed up the Czech hedgehogs, mined stakes, and other obstacles as quickly as they were planted.

Rommel listened, unconvinced. Suddenly he snapped: "Let me see your hands for a minute, Lieutenant!" The surprised Jahnke presented a pair of hands covered with scratches and calluses, proving that he had personally helped his men lay the obstacles in question.

The Desert Fox nodded with satisfaction, his anger melting. "Well done, Lieutenant. The blood on an officer's hands from fortification work is worth every bit as much as that shed in battle." Thus appeased, and convinced that sufficient effort was being made, the Field Marshal departed.[43]

Now, covered by naval gunfire and at low tide, the enemy came. Most of the light guns and automatic weapons of Strongpoint W-5 were already knocked out before the first landing craft unloaded. Rommel's cunning obstacles were left high and dry. Second Lieutenant Jahnke vainly called for artillery support from the 901st Artillery Regiment, but the guns assigned to support him were already scrap iron. The young officer sent a messenger to a nearby battery of Colonel Triepel's 1261st Artillery Regiment, desperately calling for help. The messenger never made it, however; he was shot to death by a fighter-bomber. No help was forthcoming.[44]

Meanwhile, the efforts of the 7th Army to send reinforcements to the coast were just beginning. Colonel General Dollman ordered Lieutenant General Schlieben to break through to the ocean. This meant that Ste.-Mère-Église would have to be taken. To do the job, von Schlieben was given the 1057th and 1058th regiments (of the 91st Air Landing Division), the 6th Parachute Regiment, and the 100th Panzer Replacement Battalion. Later, Dollmann also sent up the 7th Army Sturm Battalion.[45]

Von Schlieben's counterattack never really got off the ground for a number of reasons. First, the 91st Air Landing Division had no real leadership since the death of General Falley. Second, von Schlieben himself was absent much of the morning, because he was still on his way to his headquarters from the 7th Army map exercise at Rennes. Third, all the units were delayed and harassed by scattered bands of lost American paratroopers, who were quite good at setting up ambushes. Fourth, the Allied air forces continually disrupted all German efforts to establish order out of the confusion. Finally, the 6th Parachute Regiment was in the vicinity of Carentan, too far away to take part in the Battle of Ste.-Mère-Église, at least on June 6.[46]

Von Schlieben finally reached his HQ at noon, almost the exact time the 101st Airborne Division and the U.S. VII Corps linked up south of Utah Beach. The lieutenant general recognized what was happening, but he did not have the forces to do much about it. He did launch an evening attack on Ste.-Mère-Église, using his heavy artillery batteries and a few obsolete tanks, but they were beaten back by the paratroopers. Meanwhile, at Strongpoint W-5, time had run out.[47]

The U.S. 4th Infantry Division under Major General Raymond O. Barton spearheaded the U.S. VII Corps landings on Utah Beach. They quickly overwhelmed W-5, captured Jahnke, and killed or captured almost all of his men. Personally led by the Assistant Division Commander, Brigadier General Theodore Roosevelt (the son of the former U.S. President of the same name), the men of this division surged forward in an attack reminiscent of San Juan Hill. Roosevelt won the Congressional Medal of Honor for his courage on this day.[48] Unfortunately, his luck would not hold: he was killed in action before the fall of Hitler's empire. Nevertheless, June 6 was his day. Utah Beach was secure, and the Allies had their first toehold in "Fortress Europe."

Fifteen miles east of Utah Beach lay the defensive positions of Lieutenant General Krauss's 352nd Infantry Division. It occupied a thinly held coastal line from the Vire Estuary to Port-en-Bessin. Unlike most static divisions at the time, it had three regiments: the 726th Grenadier (under Colonel Korfes) and the 916th Grenadier (under Colonel Ernst Goth) were forward, and Major Meyer's 915th Grenadier held Bayeux. Unlike the defenders of Utah Beach, these men had been missed by the bombings; even their interregimental telephone systems were operative. Rather than smashing the defenders as planned, Doolittle's bombers only alerted the German soldiers that something serious was afoot. When the first assault wave came, they were ready.[49]

Brigadier General Esposito later referred to the 352nd as "an elite German infantry division."[50] It was not. It had been created only seven months before, when the remnants of the 268th and 321st Infantry divisions had been withdrawn from Army Group Center on the Russian Front and consolidated.[51] Although not elite, the 352nd was a tough, skilled, and disciplined collection of veterans. They were entrenched in eight concrete bunkers with guns of 75mm or higher; 35 pillboxes with various types of artillery and/or automatic weapons; six mortar pits; 35 rocket-launching sites; and 85 machine-gun nests.[52] Survivors of the first wave of American infantry later reported that they could hear the bullets striking against their amphibious vessels even before they were grounded and their ramps dropped. The U.S. 16th Infantry Regiment, spearhead of the 1st Division, was slaughtered.

The U.S. 1st Infantry Division, nicknamed "The Big Red One" from its emblem, led the U.S. V Corps onto Omaha Beach and came in at two points: "Fox Green" (16th Regiment) in the vicinity of Colleville, and "Dog Green" (116th Regiment) in the Vierville area, west of Colleville. They committed 32 amphibious Sherman tanks for "Dog Green," but released them too far offshore, and almost all of them sank. Those that did reach the beach were immediately knocked out by German antitank gunners.[53]

At "Dog Green" the American naval gunfire overshot the mark, and their rocket fire fell short. Unaware that their support fire had been a complete fiasco, the first six American landing craft approached the beach. They met a hail of antitank gunfire, and two of them went down in the ocean. The remaining four reached the first sandbar and dropped their ramps. The American infantrymen ran into a hail of bullets. One of the few survivors later wrote: "Within ten minutes of the ramps being lowered, A Company had become inert, leaderless, and almost incapable of action.

Every officer or sergeant had been killed or wounded. . . ."[54] Other assault waves rushed ashore with similar results. The 1st Infantry Division bogged down on "Bloody Omaha." By midmorning, U.S. casualties were tremendous, particularly among their artillery units. All but one of the 111th Field Artillery Battalion's howitzers were sunk or destroyed. The 58th Armored Field Artillery Battalion suffered a similar fate: all their amphibious tanks were gone, their crews killed, drowned, or pinned down with the infantry on the far edge of the beach. On the right flank of Omaha Beach, 16 more Shermans were brought in, but not launched. The naval officer in charge obviously felt that the sea was too rough, so he courageously disregarded both his original orders and German shellfire and carried the tanks right on to the beach. Half of these tanks were soon knocked out by German antitank gunners.[55] This left a total of eight Allied tanks intact on Omaha Beach.

On the far right flank of the U.S. 1st Division, American Rangers tried to capture the heavy gun emplacements on the west end of Omaha. They fired ropes with grappling hooks attached and used ladders borrowed from the London Fire Department in attempts to scale the cliffs. The German defenders tipped over the ladders and rolled boulders on top of the exposed Rangers. More conventionally, they fired machine guns and threw hand grenades at them. The Rangers, who had almost no cover, were checked and decimated.[56]

At 8 A.M. the battle for Omaha Beach had been in progress for less than three hours. The first assault was over, and there were 3,000 casualties on the sand, or a body for every six feet of beach.[57] U.S. Intelligence reported to General Bradley aboard his flagship *Augusta* that the 352nd Division, as well as the 716th, were defending the heights above the beaches. Bradley was shocked by this report, for it represented a gross intelligence failure. An entire division had been moved from St. Lô to the forward area without being detected: an entire division! Unlike most German divisions in France, this one had three grenadier regiments, which made things even worse. Bradley must have wondered what other unpleasant surprises would be in store for him that day. Already German resistance was twice as strong as expected.[58]

At approximately 8:20 A.M. Colonel Talley, the Deputy Chief of Staff of the U.S. V Corps, signaled General Bradley: "Such vehicles and armor as have reached the beach cannot advance any further while the German guns remain intact. They have got to be silenced at any cost."[59] This dispatch made up Bradley's mind: he ordered the fleet to bombard the coast, regardless of the casualties it caused to his own men. The U.S. Navy trained their huge 15-inch and 16-inch guns on the coast, and began to blast the strong points of the 352nd and 716th divisions.[60]

Individual courage and leadership by the American infantrymen kept hope alive on Omaha Beach when it looked as if the beachhead would have to be written off. German pressure finally weakened in the face of Bradley's persistence, and because Colonel Ocker's 352nd Artillery Regiment was running out of ammunition.[61] The Allied aircraft prevented any resupply of the gunners. Any attempt to drive an ammunition truck to the forward gun positions would be pure suicide.

The combination of naval gunfire and desperate courage of the isolated Americans led to the fall of WN-62, the first strong point on Omaha to be taken by the Allies. The defenders fought furiously, but were finally overwhelmed. Lieutenant Grass, the strong point commander, was killed, along with most of his men. The Americans now had a tenuous foothold on "Bloody Omaha."[62]

The 916th Grenadier Regiment, which held the center of the 352nd Division's line, called desperately for reinforcements. They were not forthcoming, however, because the few German reserves were even more urgently needed elsewhere.[63] After three hours of violent combat, the German front began to waver, even on Omaha Beach.

On the right flank of the beachhead, the Ranger companies also made a penetration. They finally scaled the cliffs and began to move inland, across ground pockmarked with craters dug by the Navy's superheavy guns. They found the German 155mm battery, which had caused so much trouble on Omaha, lying deserted. Apparently the gunners had abandoned the guns during the naval bombardment, or else they had run out of ammunition. The Rangers quickly destroyed the 155s and continued to move inland, until they were stopped by a counterattack from elements of the 914th Grenadier Regiment. The specially trained American shock troops held on, but lost most of their men in a battle which lasted, off and on, for two days. When it ended, only 90 Rangers were left standing, but they won the battle just the same.[64]

Omaha Beach was established at a tremendous cost. However, German resistance still continued in three zones near the beach: at Vierville, at St. Laurent, and at Colleville. At 11:00 A.M. the U.S. 116th Infantry Regiment and the 5th Ranger Battalion cleared Vierville. A whole series of confused firefights broke out in and around the other two villages, but the Germans continued to hold out.[65] Omaha Beach was still far from secure when D-Day ended, and the survivors of the 352nd were still putting up a fierce resistance. As a result of the time lost in making the initial breakouts, the obstacles off the coast were not cleared by the American engineers when the tide came in. About half of the engineers sent to do this job were killed or badly wounded, and most of their equipment was wrecked. The initial losses to the armor and artillery could not be made good for some time. As D-Day ended, the Americans on Omaha still had almost no heavy weapons. The confusion incurred in the first assault waves was compounded by each succeeding wave, and organization ceased to exist in many units. Although hundreds of individual soldiers continued to wage their private wars against Nazi Germany, the situation on Omaha Beach was still a fine mess as the sun set. Of the five beaches the Allies attacked on June 6, it was the only one still in serious jeopardy the next day.

Meanwhile, the German High Command was making one of those decisions (or, more precisely, nondecisions) which cost the Third Reich the war. Just before 5:00 A.M. on D-Day, Field Marshal von Rundstedt alerted the 12th SS Panzer and Panzer Lehr divisions and ordered them to form up, rush to the coast, and repel the invaders. He took this step even though he was not convinced the main blow had come and even though he had formerly advocated fighting the decisive battle in the interior of France, not on the water's edge. This order, more than anything else, indicates how much von Rundstedt had come under Rommel's dynamic influence, for these units were not supposed to be committed without Hitler's personal approval. Nevertheless, realizing not a moment could be wasted if the invasion had come, the old Prussian gave the command anyway; then he put in a formal request for approval to OKW.

About 7:00 A.M. Jodl's deputy, General Walter Warlimont, telephoned his chief at his temporary headquarters near Obersalzberg in the mountains of southern Germany, near Hitler's own temporary HQ. When Warlimont informed the OKW Operations Officer of von Rundstedt's request, Jodl replied: "According to the reports I have received it could be a diversionary attack.... OB West has sufficient reserves.... OB West should endeavor to clean up the attack with the forces at their disposal.... I do not think that this is the time to release the OKW reserves...."[66] The question of committing the panzers should have been referred to Hitler immediately; however, he was in a drugged sleep and everybody at Fuehrer

Headquarters was afraid to wake him! Warlimont was shocked by Jodl's refusal but knew better than to argue with his boss; instead, he telephoned von Rundstedt's Chief of Staff, Major General Gunther Blumentritt, and told him of Jodl's decision.

By 7:30 A.M. "shock and incredulity" reigned at OB West. Lieutenant Colonel Bodo Zimmermann, von Rundstedt's Chief of Operations, remembers that the old man "was fuming with rage, red in the face, and his anger made his speech unintelligible." Zimmermann himself tried to have the decision reversed and got himself chewed out for his troubles. "These divisions are under the direct control of OKW!" Major General Baron Horst von Buttlar-Brandenfels of the Army's operations staff yelled at him. "You had no right to alert them without our prior approval. You are to halt the panzers immediately—nothing is to be done before the Fuehrer makes his decision!" Zimmermann tried to argue, but was cut off. "Do as you are told!" von Buttlar-Brandenfels snapped.[67]

It was at this point that von Rundstedt should have phoned Hitler himself and insisted on being put through—as a field marshal he had that right; however, the proud commander-in-chief refused to plead with the man he habitually referred to as "that Bohemian corporal."[68]

Sir Basil H. Liddell Hart speculates that, had Rommel been at his post, he might well have telephoned Hitler personally and secured the release of the panzer divisions. Rommel "still had more influence with him than any other general," Hart writes.[69] The accuracy of this last comment is subject to debate, for Rommel had lost much of his influence by mid-1944. It is almost certain, however, that the Desert Fox would have made the attempt, for he never hesitated to personally contact Hitler when he wanted something or didn't like something. Such speculation is academic, however, for Rommel was not at his post and didn't even learn that the invasion was in progress until 3 hours and 45 minutes after the landings began.

Command paralysis had reigned at La Roche-Guyon for over eight critical hours when General Speidel finally telephoned Erwin Rommel at his home in Herrlingen, Germany at 10:15 A.M. Rommel listened to his chief of staff calmly and then muttered quietly, as if to himself, "How stupid of me. How stupid of me."[70] "The call had changed him . . . ," his wife recalled. "There was a terrible tension."[71]

Within the next 45 minutes the Field Marshal twice telephoned his aide, Captain Hellmuth Lang, at his home in Strasbourg. Rommel kept changing the time for their departure to what was now truly the Western Front.

The captain was worried: it was not like Rommel to be so indecisive. "He sounded terribly depressed on the phone," Lang remembered, "and that was not like him either."[72]

Meanwhile, at Berchtesgaden, Adolf Hitler was also being told of the landings. OB West had notified Fuehrer Headquarters of major Allied parachute and glider attacks in Normandy as early as 3:00 A.M.[73] Nevertheless, until 9:33 A.M., Hitler's entourage refused to believe the invasion might have come, when Eisenhower's press aide announced to the world that the Allies had landed in France.[74] At 10:00 A.M. Hitler's naval aide, Admiral Karl Jesko von Puttkamer, phoned Jodl and was told that there were "definite indications" that a landing had taken place. Immediately after the call General Rudolf Schmundt—Army Personnel Officer and Rommel's only friend at Fuehrer Headquarters—woke Hitler up. The dictator took the news calmly at first and ordered Schmundt to have Keitel and Jodl report to him at once.[75] The calm had evaporated by the time they arrived. "Well, is it or isn't it the invasion?" Hitler shouted as they entered.[76] Nevertheless, it would be more than five hours before he gave the vitally important Panzer Lehr and 12th SS Panzer divisions to Army Group B.

While Erwin Rommel's car sped across southwestern Germany and eastern France, and Hitler, Speidel, Jodl, and the others vacillated or did nothing, elements of the LXXXIV Corps were being cut to ribbons by the British 2nd Army.

The paratroopers of the British 6th Airborne Division had several prelanding objectives, including seizing and holding the Orne River and Caen Canal bridges at Benouville, eliminating the coastal battery at Merville, destroying the Dives River bridges at Troarn, and covering the left flank of the entire Allied invasion front.[77] Unlike the American paratroopers, the 6th Airborne accomplished most of its objectives, despite a scattered jump and heavy casualties. Many of the British troops landed in one of the areas Rommel had flooded, and a large number of the British 5th Parachute Brigade's soldiers were drowned. Brigadier Hill, the brigade commander, was wounded by an R.A.F. fighter-bomber which mistook him for a German. Nevertheless, the brigade managed to take the Benouville bridge by glider assault and attack the battery at Merville. Taking the battery was a critical mission, for it was in a position to shell Sword Beach if it could not be neutralized. It fell prior to 5:00 A.M., with severe losses on both sides. The bridges on the Dives were both destroyed by 5:20 A.M.; now the Germans would not be able to threaten the beachheads from the west. The 21st Panzer Division to the south, however, was still in a position to attack and overrun the lightly armed paratroopers.[78]

Meanwhile, the main British assault forces were "hitting the beach." The overall plan for their amphibious landings was as follows: the British 2nd Army under General Dempsey was to land on the western part of the Calvados coast, north of Caen, on a 19-mile strip of beach. His three beachheads, running west to east, were code-named Gold, Juno, and Sword. The script called for a rapid armored breakthrough of the German front, the seizing of the vital road junctions at Bayeux and Caen, a quick linkup with the paratroopers east of the Orne River, and a rapid joining of the individual beachheads. Monty planned to be 32 miles inland by nightfall.[79]

The naval bombardment began 40 minutes before dawn. At half-light the airplanes appeared to cover the infantrymen. Then came the amphibious assault forces. The British landings at Gold Beach, immediately east of Omaha, posed the greatest threat to the LXXXIV Corps on D-Day. Here, as on all his beaches, Montgomery had much more tank and heavy artillery support than did the Americans. When Montgomery heard that Rommel would be in command at Normandy, he decided to weight his initial waves with armor, because he knew from experience what type of defense to expect.[80] The American generals did not listen to his advice, and suffered heavier casualties as a result.

The British faced Lieutenant General Richter's badly overextended 716th Infantry Division, which held a front 21 miles long. They were also opposed by elements of the 352nd Infantry Division. At Gold Beach the British 8th Armored Brigade ripped through Richter's thin line—which had already been smashed by fighter-bombers and naval gunfire—and reached dry ground by 8:00 A.M. Bayeux was threatened almost at once. On the center and left flanks of the British landings the story was the same, except it was the British 27th Armoured and Canadian 2nd brigades breaking through. The Germans were simply not able to halt the British, and the 726th and 736th Grenadier regiments were cut to ribbons.[81]

The major gap in the 716th Division's line was in the sector of the 441st Ost Battalion, or at least where that unit was supposed to be. These former Russian POWs simply ran away, confirming the validity of a remark Lieutenant General von Schlieben had made some time earlier: "We are asking rather a lot if we expect Russians to fight in France for Germany against Americans."[82]

On Gold Beach the British 50th Infantry Division quickly overcame the initial resistance and pushed inland five miles. On Juno Beach the Canadian 3rd Division met stiff resistance on the coast, but once the thin outer shell was broken it advanced rapidly inland and cut the Caen-Bayeux highway by nightfall. On the British left the British 3rd Infantry Division also met initial resistance, but was soon moving rapidly inland and linked up with the 6th Airborne.[83]

In the morning it looked as if Montgomery might get his 32-mile penetration. However, he had not counted on the stubbornness of the individual German infantryman. Far too many of these men did not surrender but hid, let the tanks roll by, rallied, and attacked the flanks and rear of succeeding British assault waves. This maneuver, a common tactic on the Eastern Front whence many of Richter's men had come, surprised more than a few of the Allied commanders. Major Lehman of the 2nd Battalion, 726th Grenadier Regiment, made a determined stand against the Canadian 3rd Division at the hill of St. Croix, near Juno Beach. The Canadians had to recall their armor to take the position. At 3:48 P.M. the 2nd Battalion radioed in its final message: "Hand to hand fighting inside command post." Then there was silence. Major Lehman was dead, his battalion smashed. However, they had bought important time. The 2nd Battalion of the 736th Grenadier held Tailleville with the same determination as the 2nd of the 726th had shown at St. Croix. They were still fighting at 4:00 P.M. The 3rd Battalion of the 736th Grenadier, supported by a surviving battery of 150mm guns from the decimated 1716th Artillery Regiment, also allowed the first Allied assault wave to pass; then they counterattacked in the rear of the British 3rd Infantry Division and retook the village of Lion-sur-Mer, on the very edge of Sword Beach. They were finally cut off and bled white, but all this took irreplaceable time. A number of strong Allied units which had surged inland had to be recalled to deal with the stubborn, bypassed members of the 716th Division, which they had written off too quickly. Montgomery did not get his 32-mile penetration.[84] He could not even cover the 10 miles to Caen. These delays gave Rommel, Marcks, and Dollmann 24 hours to establish a loose front. This was not much time, but it was enough: Monty would still be fighting for Caen six weeks later.

Many small German units ambushed and fought the British and

Canadians in the coastal sector all day long. When darkness fell they faded away and escaped to the south, alone or in small groups, and helped form the new front which was already beginning to solidify.

Despite the gallant stands of its various units, most of the 716th Division was destroyed by nightfall. One by one the strong points signed off. That evening Colonel Krug, the commander of the 736th Grenadier Regiment, rang his division headquarters. "Herr General," he said to Richter, "the enemy are on top of my bunker. They are demanding my surrender. I have no means of resisting, and no contact with my own men. What am I to do?"

"Herr Oberst, I can no longer give you any orders," General Richter replied. "You must act upon your own judgment." Then he added "Auf Wiedersehen," and slowly replaced the receiver.

Present in Richter's HQ at the time were Major General Feuchtinger of the 21st Panzer and SS Colonel Kurt Meyer of the 25th SS Panzer Grenadier Regiment, 12th SS Panzer Division. No one said a word. The silence was oppressive.[85]

Colonel Krug continued fighting until 6:45 A.M. the following morning. In doing so, he tied down important Allied forces. When he finally surrendered, he had only three officers and 70 men left alive.[86]

As night fell on D-Day, the British bridgehead had a length of 20 miles, but a depth of only three to six miles. They had reached the outskirts of Bayeux, but were miles short of Caen. Bayeux fell the next day, but Caen had to be placed under siege. The German front had contained, but not repulsed, the Great Invasion.

And what had happened in the 21st Panzer Division's zone while all of this was going on? The surprising answer is very little, because the command paralysis which seemed to dominate the Western Front on June 6 was particularly severe at General Feuchtinger's headquarters.

Rommel had recognized the possibility of an Allied invasion at this very point, so he had positioned the 21st Panzer to counterattack against it. This division included a large number of veterans of the Afrika Korps who had escaped the disaster in Tunisia. Many of them had been in Europe at the time, recovering from wounds or illness. Other members of the 21st were veterans of the Eastern Front.[87]

The unit's weakness lay not in its men, but in its equipment. The division's panzers bore little resemblance to the old 21st that General von Ravenstein had commanded so successfully in Libya three years before. Its panzer regiment (the 22nd) under Colonel von Oppeln-Bronikowski had only two tank battalions: the 1st, under Captain von Gottberg, and the 2nd, under Major Vierzig. Gottberg had 80 tanks, but none was of German manufacture. Vierzig's battalion was outfitted with 40 PzKw IVs, but they were older models and were fitted with obsolete, short-barrel guns, so their range was far too short.[88] Certainly they were no match for the up-to-date weaponry of the invaders.

The division's two panzer grenadier regiments, the 125th and the 192nd, had the same poor quality equipment as the 22nd Panzer Regiment, except they did have the new German-made antitank weapon, the Panzerfaust. This shoulder-fired weapon could destroy any Allied tank that advanced too close, and would cause Eisenhower severe armored losses in the bitter days ahead.

On D-Day, Major General Feuchtinger was headquartered at St. Pierre-sur-Dives, too far from the coast to be of immediate help to the infantry. Colonel von Oppeln-Bronikowski was camped at Falaise, but his regiment was widely scattered along a line from Tours to Le Mans, so it would take him some time to assemble it.[89]

The 21st Panzer Division was mishandled all day long on June 6. Its activities were somewhat confusing and absolutely uncoordinated, owing partially to the divided command system established under Adolf Hitler and his cronies, but mainly to the hesitancy and ineffectiveness of its division commander.

Lieutenant General Richter had the authority to issue orders to the panzer grenadier regiments, but not to the 22nd Panzer Regiment. Initially he felt that the main threat to his sector was from the British paratroopers, who landed east of the Orne River. Shortly after 2:00 A.M. on June 6 he committed the 2nd Battalion of the 192nd Panzer Grenadier Regiment to the fighting at Benouville, along with reserve elements of his own 716th Division. This force, named Combat Group Zippe after its commander, Major Zippe, retook Benouville and its bridge by 3:30 A.M. The isolation of the 716th was now somewhat mitigated. General Richter ordered Zippe to stay put and hold the bridge, no matter what.[90]

Richter also tried to get Feuchtinger to commit the rest of his division against the British 6th Airborne. At 1:20 A.M. he phoned the panzer commander, but Feuchtinger did not feel that he had the authority to employ his unit without approval from OKW.[91]

At 2:00 A.M. Richter—who outranked Feuchtinger—gave him a direct order to attack the vulnerable paratroopers, but Feuchtinger again refused.

Several angry conversations took place in the next four-and-a-half hours, but the panzer leader refused to budge. More time was lost.[92]

Feuchtinger finally decided to move against the parachutists at 6:30 A.M. If he had attacked the 6th Airborne at 2:00 A.M. as Richter had ordered, he might have done the Allies a great deal of damage. Now, however, his attack was to Montgomery's advantage, for it tied down vital German reserves against relatively insignificant British forces. It was 8:00 A.M. before the 22nd Panzer Regiment was assembled and could start its advance. By this time, it should have been growing clear to Feuchtinger that the airborne troops did not constitute the main threat. Even so, he continued on against the paratroopers. It was a little after noon before Feuchtinger received orders from General Marcks, who did not bother appealing to him but went directly over his head, to Berlin. The one-legged corps commander informed him that 21st Panzer Division was now part of LXXXIV Corps. Marcks ordered Feuchtinger to leave a single company from the 22nd Panzer Regiment to deal with the paratroopers, and send the rest toward Caen, on which the British and Canadians were now advancing. The major general had no choice but to obey Marcks's order, but besides leaving the single panzer company he also left Lieutenant Colonel Baron von Luck's 125th Panzer Grenadier Regiment behind to contain the airborne bridgehead.[93]

Finally, early in the afternoon, the 22nd Panzer Regiment was moving in the right direction. Unfortunately for them, movement was not quite as easy as it would have been earlier, for it was now full daylight, the cloud cover had lifted somewhat, and swarming Allied aircraft took a heavy toll of the panzer troops. The 22nd finally reached Caen, but found the city in ruins and Colonel Oppeln had to order a long detour. It was 2:30 P.M. before he got his unit—which was accompanied by Colonel Rauch's 192nd Panzer Grenadier Regiment—into position south of the British I Corps. He sent 35 tanks under Captain Wilhelm von Gottberg to take Périers Ridge, four miles from the coast. Oppeln-Bronikowski decided to assume personal command of the remaining 25 tanks and attack the British on the ridge at Bieville. As he prepared to move out, he was joined by Generals Marcks and Feuchtinger. "Oppeln, the future of Germany may very well rest on your shoulders," the corps commander told him. "If you don't push the British back into the sea, we shall have lost the war."[94]

Oppeln must have been shocked. The future of Germany depended on a single motorized infantry regiment and a motley collection of 60 foreign-made tanks that had been obsolete for years. Nevertheless he saluted and

promised to attack at once. As he deployed, von Oppeln was hailed by
another German general. This one was Wilhelm Richter, the commander
of the 716th Infantry Division. He "was almost demented with grief," the
colonel remembered. "My troops are lost," Richter said, with tears in his
eyes. "My whole division is finished."[95]

Colonel von Oppeln and Captain von Gottberg struck as quickly as was
humanly possible, but they never had a chance. Their inferior tanks were
simply outgunned by the superbly equipped defenders on Périers and
Bieville Ridges. Oppeln's own tank was knocked out before it could get
close enough to fire a shot, so he called off the attack. He had lost six tanks
in 15 minutes. Von Gottberg did no better, losing 10 tanks in a matter of
minutes; he was repulsed before he could even get within range of the
British positions.[96] The 22nd Panzer Regiment was shattered. The defeat
also broke its spirit: its morale was gone, never to be recovered.[97]

Meanwhile, General Marcks personally led the 192nd Panzer Grenadier
Regiment into the attack. Its 1st Battalion was lucky enough to strike
exactly between Sword and Juno Beaches and penetrate to the coast, which
it reached at 8:00 P.M. However, its position was isolated at best. Marcks
wanted the battalion reinforced, but at 11:00 P.M. a misdirected glider lift for
the British 6th Airborne Division was mistaken for an attempt to cut it off,
and General Feuchtinger ordered the unit to abandon its position and
withdraw immediately. The chance to keep the British 2nd Army split was
thus forfeited. Lieutenant Colonel Zimmermann of the OB West staff
accused Feuchtinger of taking to his heels,[98] which seems to be fairly
accurate.

Meanwhile, von Oppeln and von Gottberg dug in to await the British
attack on Caen which, incredibly, did not come that day. "Caen and the
whole area could be taken within a few hours," the colonel said later. He
watched "German officers with 20 to 30 men apiece, marching back from
the front, retreating toward Caen." The remnants of Richter's infantry
division were coming home. "The war is lost," von Oppeln said aloud.[99]

Lost it was. Map 3, page 68, shows the situation at the end of June 6. The
next day the Canadian 3rd Division from Juno Beach and the British 3rd
from Sword Beach linked up to form a solid British front, but the Battle of
Normandy was far from over: Erwin Rommel would see to that.

While Colonel von Oppeln was working his way around Caen, Rommel
met Captain Lang at Freudenstadt and raced across France toward La

Roche-Guyon and Normandy. It was 1:00 P.M. when Lang got into the car. Rommel spoke hardly a word the whole trip, except to urge his driver, Private Daniel, to drive faster. Captain Lang had never seen his chief so depressed as he was now. Once, about 3:00 P.M., the Field Marshal looked at Lang and said: "I was right all along . . . all along."[100] This thought did not seem to comfort him very much, however.

About 6:00 P.M. Rommel's automobile reached Rheims. He phoned Speidel at La Roche-Guyon and talked for more than 15 minutes; then he silently climbed back into the car. Obviously the news had been bad. Sometime later he struck his palm with his fist and said bitterly: "My friendly enemy, Montgomery." Still later he added: "My God! If the 21st Panzer can make it, we might just be able to drive them back in three days!"[101] After night fell, Germany's youngest marshal became more realistic. "Do you know, Lang," he muttered thoughtfully, "if I was commander of the Allied forces right now, I could finish the war in 14 days."[102]

He reached headquarters at 10:00 P.M. and immediately requested that all regimental combat teams from 15th Army be sent to Normandy, to be followed by all divisions of the second line at Pas de Calais. OKW turned down all his requests, except one: it gave him the 346th Infantry Division.[103]

Meanwhile, Captain Lang had also become very depressed. He approached his commander in the hall of the Château of the Dukes de la Rochefoucauld. "Sir," he asked, "do you think we can drive them back?"

"Lang, I hope we can," came the answer. "I've nearly always succeeded up to now." Then, patting his aide on the shoulder, he said, "You look tired. Why don't you go to bed? It's been a long day." Rommel turned away, headed for his office and shut the door.[104]

As a result of Eisenhower's gamble on the weather, Rommel had literally missed one of the most important battles, if not the most important battle, of his career. By day's end the Western Allies had lost over 10,000 men, but had put 145,000 on shore and were threatening to shatter the thin German defense and burst into the interior of France.[105] The Allied beachhead was established. Somehow it had to be wiped out, or the Third Reich was doomed. The burden of destroying it fell onto the shoulders of Erwin Rommel. Before he could even consider this task, however, he had to somehow gain control of the battle that was already in progress.

3

Holding Fast

By nightfall on June 6 the German situation was quite precarious. The left flank of the LXXXIV Corps (i.e., Utah Beach/Ste.-Mère-Église sector) had collapsed; indeed, the Americans had lost fewer than 200 men on Utah Beach, which was the shortest casualty list on any of the beaches.[1] The Americans at Omaha Beach had gained two to three miles, primarily because of Bradley's ruthless determination to succeed. He had sent in wave after wave of infantry and had shelled his own beaches until the 352nd Division could no longer hold. The American casualty list had been enormous. Of the 6,603 U.S. casualties reported on D-Day (1,465 killed, 3,184 wounded and 1,954 captured or missing), the airborne divisions had lost 2,499. Almost all the remainder had been lost by the U.S. 1st and 29th infantry divisions on Omaha Beach. As June 6 ended, Omaha Beach was the only landing point not secure. Of the 2,400 tons of supplies the U.S. planners had scheduled to put on the beach on D-Day, only 100 tons actually reached shore. Omaha was short about 45 percent of its men, 50 percent of its vehicles, and over 70 percent of its matériel and heavy equipment.[2] On both American beaches, Bradley had planned to land 107,000 men, 14,000 vehicles, and 14,500 tons of supplies; he had landed 87,000 men, 7,000 vehicles, and less than 4,000 tons of supplies.[3] The U.S. position on Utah Beach might well have been untenable had Rommel been allowed to position the panzer reserves where he wanted them; there is little doubt that Omaha Beach could have been wiped out under those circumstances.

Conditions were better in the British zone, where only 3,500 to 4,000 casualties had been suffered (946 of which were Canadian). Second British Army had four divisions and three armored brigades on shore by the dawn of June 7.[4]

In the center of Marcks's line, Bayeux, defended by the small 915th

Grenadier Regiment under Major Meyer, was about to fall. The right flank, which defended the approaches to Caen, was also on the verge of collapse, but still held on, thanks primarily to the commitment of the 21st Panzer Division.

The commander of the LXXXIV Corps was ordinarily an easygoing man. A brilliant officer of the old school, General Marcks had always been disliked by the Nazis because of his connections with the former chancellor, General Kurt von Schleicher, whom Hitler had had murdered in 1934. On the other hand they recognized his abilities, for he had been one of the architects of the 1941 invasion of the Soviet Union. Marcks was also quite popular with his men. He wore an artificial limb in place of the leg he had lost while serving on the Russian Front.[5]

On June 6, Erich Marcks's customary calm was gone, not because of the invasion, but because he could not get anyone to believe it had arrived. Since early morning he had been in almost constant contact with 7th Army, Army Group B, and Fuehrer HQ. "I need every available armored unit for a counterattack," he exclaimed, but the panzer reserves remained uncommitted. Field Marshal von Rundstedt, even though he tried to help, still believed the landings were a diversion; Erwin Rommel was in a car, speeding back to the front, so no one could reach him; finally, Adolf Hitler was asleep and his subordinates were afraid to awaken him. "It's a disgrace!" Marcks snapped in disgust.[6]

Major Hayn, the corps intelligence officer, reported to the 7th Army that he had identified three Allied airborne divisions, which represented three-quarters of the paratroopers known to be in the United Kingdom. Also, other important units were spotted: elements of the U.S. 1st and 4th Armored divisions, the British 3rd and 50th Infantry divisions, and the Canadian 3rd Infantry Division, as well as the British 7th Armoured Division. That left only the 51st Highlander and the 1st British Armoured Division unaccounted for from the British elements of the 8th Army in North Africa. Clearly the Allies would not commit the bulk of their veterans of North Africa and Sicily to a diversionary operation. Major Hayn's report concluded: "If this isn't the invasion—then what units are they going to use for it?"[7]

Lieutenant Colonel Vorwerk, the 7th Army's Intelligence Officer, endorsed this report and immediately forwarded it to Paris, where even Lieutenant Colonel Meyer-Detring, the Intelligence Officer for OB West, signaled, "I agree with you entirely." However his chief, von Rundstedt, remained skeptical.[8]

One of the strangest aspects of the invasion was the metamorphosis that went on in Adolf Hitler's mind on June 6. The Fuehrer, who had correctly guessed the location and strategic objective of the invasion months in advance, now decided the landings were in fact a diversion. He became obsessed with the notion that Eisenhower's real thrust would come *east* of the Seine, in the Pas-de-Calais area. He clung to this idea for weeks, and steadfastly refused to weaken the 15th Army.[9]

As a result of the wishful thinking in Berlin and Berchtesgaden, few reinforcements were dispatched to Normandy in the first, decisive weeks of the invasion. The units OKW did send were armored, although the terrain was ideally suited for nonmotorized infantry. Rommel's front was and would remain extremely short of ground troops throughout his active tenure as commander of Army Group B. Conversely, when the front finally did break, the Germans were forced to wage mobile warfare at a time when most of their panzer divisions were burnt out. Unable to wage a war of maneuver, they had no alternative but to retreat to the frontiers of the Reich. The Battle of France was thus lost with the Battle of Normandy.

It was 3:40 P.M. on D-Day when Major General Blumentritt, Chief of Staff of OB West, phoned General Speidel and informed him that SS Lieutenant General Witt's 12th SS Panzer Division and Lieutenant General Bayerlein's Panzer Lehr Division finally had been released to 7th Army.[10] Eleven hours had been wasted, but the waste would not end here. While his division assembled, Fritz Bayerlein drove to 7th Army headquarters, where Colonel General Dollmann ordered him to move out for Caen at 5:00 P.M.—in broad daylight! Bayerlein had shared Rommel's experiences against Allied fighter-bombers in North Africa and had been pinned down beside the Desert Fox on more than one occasion, so he understood the danger posed by enemy domination of the air. A night move was dangerous enough, but a daylight move positively invited disaster. Panzer Lehr, assembling 75 miles southwest of Paris, would have to travel 90 miles to reach Caen. Bayerlein objected strongly, saying it would be better to advance cautiously and arrive on June 8, but Dollman refused to budge. As a result, the best division in the whole theater of operations was decimated before it even reached the front.[11]

The next day, June 7, Bayerlein met with SS General Josef "Sepp" Dietrich, the commander of the I SS Panzer Corps, at his headquarters north of Harcourt. Dietrich informed him that Panzer Lehr and 12th SS Panzer would launch a counterattack on the morning of June 8, to push the Allies back into the sea. Bayerlein probably did not think much of this idea, in view of Allied strength on shore and aerial domination, but he apparently did not object very strenuously, either. Dietrich was not always the type of man to listen to reason. In the last days of the war, for example, he was commanding the 6th SS Panzer Army when a group of Viennese politicians came to him and proposed that he declare the old capital of Austria an open city. Dietrich hanged them all without further ado. After receiving his orders from the SS chief, Bayerlein returned to his unit. On the way back Allied fighter-bombers attacked his car. Bayerlein and his aide escaped with a few minor shrapnel wounds, but his driver was killed.[12] Incidents of this nature would occur with alarming frequency for the rest of the campaign.

The 12th SS "Hitler Jugend" Division also had problems reaching the area of operations. It moved out at 4:00 P.M. on D-Day, after the cloud cover which had initially hampered Allied air activities had lifted. Promptly jumped by fighter-bombers, the young SS men suffered heavy casualties and soon went to ground. Further attempts to use the road network were suspended until after dark, and the division would not reach the Caen area in strength until June 8.[13]

The III Flak Corps also accomplished very little on D-Day. The corps commander, General Wolfgang Pickert, left his headquarters south of Amiens for a tour of inspection early that morning and did not learn of the landings until after noon. Although he started his three regiments (of two battalions each) to the threatened sector immediately, the vital antiaircraft guns did not reach the front until June 8–9.[14]

Meanwhile, during the night of June 6/7, Field Marshal Erwin Rommel finally took charge of the German combat effort. It was already too late to repulse the invasion on the beaches, but the determined Swabian began to reestablish some degree of control over the battlefield. He found that the British under General Dempsey had secured a beachhead 20 miles long and up to six miles deep, while the Americans under General Bradley had a second beachhead nine to two miles deep, although the Americans at Utah and Omaha Beaches had not yet linked up. All along the front the 716th and

352nd divisions were resisting stubbornly, but were gradually being crushed by elements of nine enemy divisions.

Rommel ordered a counterattack by the 21st and 12th SS Panzer divisions for June 7, but Feuchtinger had only about 70 tanks left in running order, and the 12th SS—as we have seen—was badly delayed by the Allied air forces. Also, Dietrich's I SS Panzer Corps HQ, which had just come up to direct the counterattack, was having a hard time getting itself organized, because fighting the Western Allies turned out to be much more difficult than fighting Russians. Despite a personal visit from Rommel, Dietrich's staff could not get control of its sector, and the counterattack never materialized.[15]

On June 7 the American and British forces continued their unrelenting attacks, while Rommel desperately called for reinforcements. The 30th Mobile Infantry Brigade was sent to the aid of General Krauss's 352nd Infantry Division, but its inexperienced soldiers, equipped mainly with bicycles, were subjected to constant aerial attacks. It was cut to ribbons and badly demoralized by nightfall,[16] and was never of much combat value after that.

The mobile infantry brigade was supposed to have reinforced Meyer at Bayeux, in the center of the German line. It was so badly scattered, however, that those who did arrive were too disorganized to be of effective help; thus, early on June 7, Meyer faced the bulk of the powerful British 50th Infantry Division with two understrength battalions of his 915th Grenadier Regiment. By noon the battle was lost. The Caen-St. Lô road was cut and Bayeux was soon cleared, while Combat Group Meyer was being pushed back toward Caen. By nightfall the 915th Grenadier had virtually ceased to exist. Major Meyer was among the dead.[17]

On the German left flank the U.S. 82nd Airborne Division linked up with the U.S. VII Corps, advancing inland from Utah Beach. The 795th Georgian Battalion collapsed and Turqueville fell. Lieutenant General von Schlieben realized that the situation was deteriorating rapidly, and that only a determined counterattack could restore it. His 709th Infantry Division, supported by three artillery battalions and the Sturm Battalion, attacked again. They pushed the paratroopers back to the outskirts of Ste.-Mère-Église, but at that moment the U.S. 4th Infantry Division arrived, along with about 60 Sherman tanks. They quickly overran the 1058th Grenadier Regiment, which broke up and ceased to exist as an organized combat force. The 709th Infantry Division was crippled. After this defeat von Schlieben gave up all thought of offensive action, and concentrated on blocking the American drive on Cherbourg,[18] which he knew would begin soon.

The most important battles of June 7 occurred north of Caen, on the right flank of the German battle line. This old university city was the most vital position in Normandy. Fifty miles from the Seine and only 120 miles from Paris, Caen was a departmental capital and the hub of the highway and railroad network in the Cotentin area; more important, it dominated the surrounding region. North of the city lay terrain well-suited for the defense, but south of it the ground was much flatter. Here lay ideal tank country. If the Allies reached this area, they could not be stopped. For this reason Rommel sent most of his best units to this part of the front. Montgomery's failure to capture Caen on D-Day would have bitter repercussions for him and his men. They would have the thankless job of holding off Rommel and pinning down his panzer reserves, while the Americans extended Rommel's left flank and tried to stretch it to the breaking point.

Montgomery was never the type to give up easily. He tried to take Caen by frontal assault on June 7. The British 3rd and Canadian 3rd Infantry divisions surged forward against the survivors of the 21st Panzer Division. Each Allied division was accompanied by an armored brigade. The British 3rd was halted by the panzer soldiers, but the Canadians continued forward, ignoring the fact that their left flank was now exposed. Their leading brigade, the 27th Armoured, drove to the Carpiquet Airfield, only two miles north of Caen, completely unaware that SS Colonel Kurt "Panzer" Meyer's 25th SS Panzer Grenadier Regiment, the advance guard of the 12th SS Panzer Division, had arrived at the airfield shortly before. Meyer, the veteran of a dozen campaigns, including three years on the Russian Front, lay a skillful ambush for the inexperienced Canadians. His young SS men maintained complete fire discipline until the tanks were within 200 yards of their positions; then they opened up on the sides of the steel monsters, where the armor was much thinner than in the front. Twenty-eight Shermans were quickly knocked out, while machine-gun fire riddled the ranks of the advancing infantrymen, who had needlessly exposed themselves. The Canadians suffered heavy casualties and retreated in disorder. Allied naval gunfire, however, prevented Meyer from following up his success to the utmost.[19]

Behind the front lines, events of even greater significance were taking place. The British 49th Infantry, 51st Infantry and 7th Armoured divisions were disembarking onto the mainland, almost totally unhampered by the German Navy and Luftwaffe. In the American sector, the U.S. 1st Army had a strength of five divisions by nightfall of June 7. The Allies' foothold in Europe was growing stronger by the hour. By June 12 they had 15 divisions ashore, and five more landed from June 13 to 19, along with several separate armored brigades and battalions.[20] The U.S. XIX and VIII Corps and British VIII Corps were all activated by June 16.[21] Table 4 shows the arrival of the Allied divisions in the first ten days of the campaign. The Allies had won the Battle of the Normandy Beachhead. The great buildup had begun, and the Battle of the Hedgerows was about to begin.

The fall of Bayeux placed the British in a position to wheel southward on Caen. However, by June 8 Rommel's reinforcements had at last reached

Table 4

The Allied Buildup, June 6–15, 1944

Division	Date of Arrival*
U.S. 82nd Airborne	June 6
U.S. 101st Airborne	June 6
British 6th Airborne	June 6
U.S. 4th Infantry	June 6
U.S. 1st Infantry	June 6
U.S. 29th Infantry	June 6
British 50th Infantry	June 6
Canadian 3rd Infantry	June 6
British 3rd Infantry	June 6
U.S. 2nd Infantry	June 8
British 7th Armoured	June 9
British 51st Infantry	June 9
U.S. 2nd Armored	June 13
British 49th Infantry	June 13
U.S. 30th Infantry	June 14
U.S. 90th Infantry	June 15
British 11th Armoured	June 15

Source: Montgomery: 51–60

---

*Refers to the date the division completed disembarkation; several of these divisions began arriving days earlier.

the area in significant numbers. Rommel's right flank was now held by the I SS Panzer Corps under Sepp Dietrich, and included the 12th SS and Panzer Lehr divisions, as well as the 21st Panzer and 716th Infantry divisions, although the latter was a broken unit. It had little more than an infantry battalion left, and only a dozen artillery pieces. The Allied landings had ground it to bits.[22] Marcks's LXXXIV Corps retained control of the left flank, with the remnants of the 352nd and 709th Infantry divisions, the disorganized 91st Air Landing Division and the newly arrived 6th Parachute Regiment, all operating primarily against the Americans.

Rommel, who personally liked Sepp Dietrich, apparently did not think much of the idea of entrusting him with responsibility for directing the great counterattack, especially since his staff was in such chaos. Dietrich, a butcher's son and World War I sergeant major, was a longtime Nazi. His personal friendship with Adolf Hitler was his chief qualification for high command. Von Rundstedt later referred to him as "decent, but stupid." Rommel probably shared this opinion, for he used his remaining influence in the High Command to get General von Schweppenburg appointed commander of the entire sector east of Dives as far as Tilly, thus placing all three panzer divisions under his personal supervision. Although Rommel and von Schweppenburg had had serious disagreements on strategic questions, Rommel recognized his tactical abilities, and so chose him to attempt to throw the Allies into the sea.

Von Schweppenburg had excellent human material with which to work. The 12th SS Panzer, nicknamed the "Baby Division" by the propagandists, consisted entirely of highly trained volunteers, most of them teenagers recruited from the Hitler Youth. It had three regiments: the 12th SS Panzer (two battalions) and the 25th and 26th SS Panzer Grenadier regiments. Panzer Lehr was much larger and, according to one source, was the only panzer division in the German Army at 100 percent strength. Although it was short a number of wheeled vehicles, it had 183 tanks and 800 tracked vehicles in three regiments: the Panzer Lehr Regiment, and the 901st and 902nd Panzer Grenadier regiments. This unit was specially designed to oppose the invasion, and its ranks were dominated by young veterans of North Africa and the Russian Front. The average age of its enlisted men was only 21½ years. Colonel General Heinz Guderian, the Inspector-General of Panzer Troops, said to the division commander in April 1944: "With this division alone you will throw the Anglo-Americans back into the sea."[23] However, like most of his contemporaries, Guderian was an

"Eastern General," and did not reckon with Allied air power when he made his estimate.

The units were ready on June 8, but von Schweppenburg was not. It takes time to move a major headquarters and set up communications, and without the headquarters of Panzer Group West the attack would surely fail, so the counteroffensive was postponed until June 9. Meanwhile, thousands of additional American, British, and Canadian soldiers poured onto the European mainland.

It was necessary to commit the bulk of the 12th SS and Panzer Lehr divisions in a defensive role on June 8, just to hold the line. Most of the 12th SS engaged the Canadians and immediately began launching local counter-attacks. They retook the villages of Bretteville and Putot-en-Bessin, although Putot changed hands again the next day. Panzer Lehr was also heavily engaged. By nightfall the lines were solidifying.[24]

Rommel himself turned up at Bayerlein's headquarters at the village of Le Mesnil-Patry on the evening of June 8. He angrily informed his former chief of staff that the British 50th Division had taken Bayeux. "The British 50th Division, Bayerlein!" he exclaimed. "Our very special friends from Africa!" He ordered Bayerlein to deploy Panzer Lehr in two combat groups from the Norrey-Brouay area to Tilly, so that he would be in a position to attack Bayeux on the morning of June 9. "The town will be taken!" the Desert Fox emphasized.[25]

However, before leaving, Rommel grew realistic again. He said to his old friend, "We shall suffer the same fate as in Africa, Bayerlein. Instead of the Mediterranean we shall have the Rhine—and we shan't get anything across!"[26]

On the German left flank, the Americans were trying to consolidate their hard-won gains and link up their beachheads. The U.S. V Corps at Omaha Beach and the U.S. VII Corps at Utah were prevented from joining hands by elements of the 352nd Division at Isigny (near the coast) and the 6th Parachute Regiment at Carentan. On the afternoon of June 8 Eisenhower ordered Bradley to take these positions immediately. Bradley sent the U.S. 29th Division against Isigny and the 101st Airborne Division against Carentan, while the U.S. 1st Infantry Division attacked eastward from Omaha Beach, with the objective of linking up the American and British sectors.[27]

The 29th Division met little organized resistance in its drive on Isigny. Major General Krauss's 352nd Division had already been shattered by two days of battle against five American divisions, the U.S. Navy, and huge numbers of aircraft. The rapid thrust of the U.S. 29th brushed aside the remnants of the 914th Grenadier Regiment and captured all the remaining guns of the 352nd Artillery Regiment. Isigny fell that night, and the American beachheads were effectively joined,[28] although the junction lacked depth.

The U.S. 101st Airborne Division had a much harder time against Lieutenant Colonel von der Heydte's parachute regiment. Here the American paratroopers met men of the same skill and toughness as themselves, and a bitter fight ensued. Baron Friedrich August von der Heydte's regiment had already lost all its vehicles at Ste.-Mère-Église, and one of its battalions had been cut off and was still missing. (Later, it was discovered that the Americans had trapped it against the swamp near the village of Ste.-Mère-du-Mont and destroyed it. Of its 700 men, over 200 were killed and 25 escaped. The rest were captured.)[29] Despite being shorthanded, the battle-hardened survivors of the 6th Parachute still had a lot of fight left; they also had excellent defensive positions, for this was hedgerow country.

The hedgerows of the French *bocage* country are not the simple bushes the normal American associates with the term "hedge." These are earthen dikes, averaging about four feet in height but frequently higher, constructed to box in fields and orchards of a few acres. None are large, but all are potential earthworks. Bushes, tangled vegetation, and even trees grow all over the dikes. In 1944, they provided the Germans with excellent concealment and cover. No sooner was one hedgerow taken than another faced the Allies. Each field became a separate battleground. The hedgerow country was ideal for the static defense, and very difficult for either side to launch even local attacks. Under these conditions, the U.S. 101st Airborne was unable to take Carentan on June 8. Bradley realized that this town must fall before the U.S. beachhead was completely out of danger. Against this background, the Battle of Carentan began in earnest. It would continue for six days.

While von Schweppenburg organized his counterattack on the right flank and von der Heydte held the center, Rommel turned his attention to the left, where General von Schlieben had organized a makeshift defensive line along the Montebourg—Ste.-Mère-Église—Fontenay—Rovenoville roads. He held this line with miscellaneous battle groups from the 243rd and 352nd divisions, as well as his own 709th. Most of these units had been badly damaged in the fighting of June 6 and 7, but the Americans were too busy at Isigny and Carentan to press their advantage on June 8, thereby giving Schlieben time to build a thin line to screen Cherbourg. Erwin Rommel, who had taken this port from the French in the campaign of 1940, realized that Cherbourg had to be Eisenhower's first strategic objective of the campaign. Rommel decided to reinforce Schlieben as rapidly as possible without jeopardizing von Schweppenburg's counterattack, so he ordered the 77th Infantry Division (then in Brittany) and the 17th SS Panzer Grenadier Division (which OKW had just released to him) to the left flank. The 3rd Parachute Division was also sent to the front, as was the Headquarters, II Parachute Corps, then in Brittany. It would take these units days to reach the front, but when they did arrive Rommel placed the 17th SS Panzer Grenadier and 3rd Parachute divisions under General Eugen Meindl's II Parachute Corps on the left-center of the German line, with the mission of holding St. Lô. Von Schlieben's makeshift force continued to hold the far left.[30]

On June 8, German military intelligence scored three important, if lucky, victories. About noon a bundle of captured documents was turned over to intelligence officers at LXXXIV Corps. They had been retrieved from a shell-riddled landing craft on the Normandy coast, where the body of an American naval beachmaster was found among the dead. The interpreters went to work immediately, and soon the Germans had the entire operations plan of the U.S. V and VII corps, as well as that of the adjacent British XXX Corps, including their day by day tactical objectives on the Cotentin Peninsula! The documents also revealed what Rommel had already guessed: Cherbourg was the strategic objective of the American landings.[31]

Elsewhere on the front, SS men took a map from a knocked-out Canadian tank. On it, Nazi positions were accurately marked, even down to individual light machine-gun positions. This document indicated the efficiency of the intelligence network against which the Germans were operating. From another damaged tank an Allied radio code book was lifted, and it gave the code names for all the German positions in the British zone. Inexplicably, the British continued to use this book long after it had been compromised, and thus allowed the Germans to see at least a portion of the Allied tactical plans.[32]

Although these finds were of great value, they could not be taken advantage of to the maximum extent for, despite the mounting evidence, Hitler still insisted that the invasion would come at Pas de Calais. The

fortunate triumphs of the German intelligence officers were largely thrown
away by the High Command.

On June 9 General von Schweppenburg was at last ready to launch the
long-delayed German panzer counterattack—at least two days too late.
That morning he conferred with SS Colonel "Panzer" Meyer at the
Ardenne Abbey, outside Caen. Meyer apparently brought up the subject of
how Germany could win the war by repelling the invasion. Von Schweppenburg cut him short by saying: "My dear Meyer, the war can only be won
now by political means."[33] Nevertheless, he ordered the attack. The 21st
Panzer on the right flank would attack out of the Caen area, accompanied by
the 12th SS Panzer in the center. On the German left, Bayerlein's Panzer
Lehr Division would retake Bayeux. The overall objective was to force a
breakthrough to the coast along a wide front. Further planning would
depend on the development of this thrust.

Meanwhile, Montgomery, Dempsey, and Bradley met and made some
plans of their own. As the senior ground commander, Montgomery ranked
above both Dempsey and Bradley and he ordered a double envelopment of
Caen. The British 6th Airborne Division, the 51st Highlander Division,
and the 4th Armoured Brigade would provide the left hook east of the city.
Their objective was to capture the village of Cagny and pin down the
German reserves. The main blow would be to the west, where the XXX
Corps, led by the 7th Armoured Division, would take Villers-Bocage and
Evrecy. When the two spearheads reached their final objectives, the British
1st Airborne Division would be dropped between them, and complete the
encirclement of Caen.[34] It was a bold plan, though decidedly overly
ambitious.

The German and British plans were in diametric opposition and their
timing was virtually identical. The result was a head-on collision all along
the line.

On June 9 the 21st Panzer Division attacked into the British airborne
bridgehead on the Orne, just as the 51st Highlander Division prepared to
attack out of it. The 12th SS Panzer struck north along the Caen-Bayeux
road, just as the Canadian 3rd Division prepared to move south along the
same road. Panzer Lehr, advancing on Bayeux from the south, ran directly
into the British 7th Armoured Division, which was advancing out of
Bayeux in the opposite direction. The Germans were forced to commit
their reserves far too early in the battle. On the other side, the British had

their tanks well forward, and initially did not have enough infantry up front to give them adequate protection.[35] Panzer Lehr penetrated to within three miles of Bayeux, but a hasty Allied counterattack forced Bayerlein to a halt. That night Dietrich ordered him to withdraw his division to defend the Tilly area, which now became the focus of British attention.[36] Meanwhile, with Rommel's consent, General von Schweppenburg went over to the defensive. He was ordered to regroup, await the arrival of the II Parachute Corps, and prepare to launch another attack.[37]

Tactically, the fighting of June 9 was inconclusive. Strategically, it was a major Allied victory which was completed the next evening when Allied radio intelligence pinpointed von Schweppenburg's Panzer Group West Headquarters. A saturation bombing raid knocked it out, and nearly wiped it out. General von Schweppenburg was only wounded, but Major General von Dawans, his chief of staff, was killed, along with the Group's operations officer and other key personnel. Only a few of the staff escaped injury. The Desert Fox himself barely escaped; he had just finished conferring with von Schweppenburg and left his HQ only an hour before the bombs fell. This raid was a turning point in the Battle of Normandy. After this, all German planning concentrated on the defense, and all serious talk of large-scale offensive action was silenced. No German counterattack of the magnitude of June 9 was ever again launched in Normandy.[38]

Rommel, in his *Papers*, listed five reasons for the Allied success up to June 10. First and foremost was Allied air superiority. Rommel estimated that the Americans and Royal air forces flew up to 27,000 sorties a day, and even the slightest daytime movement of the smallest German formation invited immediate aerial reprisals by the Allies. Movement, then, was restricted to night. In the short June nights of France, this often meant about nine hours. The flow of men and ammunition to the front was thus severely limited, especially when the disastrous state of the road and rail networks are taken into account. Second, the Allied heavy naval fire covered much of the Cotentin Peninsula. The Royal and American navies had 640 heavy guns; several valuable German units, including all three available panzer divisions, had been injured by these monsters. Third, the equipment of the Allies whose industry was largely intact, was much superior to the worn German equipment. Much of Rommel's material was captured foreign stock, dating back to the early 1930s, and even the better portion of the German-manufactured equipment had been used extensively on the Eastern Front; as a result, breakdowns were common and repairs were difficult.

Fourth, the Allies had an almost unlimited supply of ammunition, while Rommel's few stockpiles were dwindling fast. Fifth, the Allied use and threatened use of glider and paratroop units forced Rommel to hold back several units in critical sectors, to secure his rear from these elite forces. Otherwise, he could have moved these men to the front.[39]

Rommel's list is incomplete, probably because he feared that his papers might fall into the hands of the Gestapo. Therefore, criticisms of Hitler and his close associates is usually veiled, indirect, or omitted altogether. Nevertheless, the orders of the High Command hamstrung the Field Marshal's operations almost as much as the Allied air forces did. For instance, on June 9 Hitler and OKW issued a warning that Belgium was due to be invaded the next day and withheld the powerful 1st SS Panzer Division (now rebuilt to 21,000 men after returning from Russia) from Army Group B.[40]

On June 10 the Desert Fox reported that, owing to Allied air superiority, the enemy forces on the beachhead were building up faster than the reserves behind the German front. Rommel himself was very much aware of the enemy's aerial intervention, for he drove forward to Sepp Dietrich's headquarters that day. He was forced to abandon his car and take cover 30 times because of the fighter-bombers; he never did manage to reach the I SS Panzer Corps. Radio contact was also next to impossible. As of June 8, 16 of Dietrich's 20 radio sets had been knocked out, all or almost all by fighter-bombers or aerial-directed artillery fire.[41] Not only were the pilots keeping Rommel's orders from being obeyed, they were preventing him from issuing orders altogether!

Enemy air power made it impossible to bring up the I SS Panzer Corps, the 7th Nebelwerfer Brigade, Panzer Lehr, the III Flak Corps, or the II Parachute Corps in time to launch an effective, prepared counterattack. Those elements that did arrive more or less intact had to be thrown into the line as soon as they were available. No forces remained with which to establish a mobile reserve.[42] Rommel's report of June 10 was a veiled admission of defeat. His dispatches would grow less and less subtle as the situation in Normandy grew more and more desperate. In the days ahead he demanded the evacuation of the entire Brittany Peninsula, stating that it was strategically impossible to hold, and was now almost useless as a U-boat base anyway. By mid-1944 most of the German submarines had been sunk, and their gallant crews were dead. Rommel also demanded the evacuation of the Channel Islands, which had 35,000 soldiers on them. He also insisted that southern France be abandoned. Here the LVI Panzer

Corps, with its 9th, 11th, and 2nd SS Panzer divisions, lay inactive. If sent to Normandy, these units might well have been able to form the mobile reserve Rommel needed so badly. However, neither Hitler, OKW, nor OB West would approve any of these demands.[43] Also, the mythical Allied army group of George Patton continued to pin down the 15th Army in the vicinity of Pas de Calais, at a time when Rommel's front cried out for infantry. Hitler was still sure the real invasion would come here. This pigheadedness would eventually have the most disastrous results when the Normandy front broke.

Almost a year later, in May 1945, the Channel Island garrison (i.e., the 319th Infantry Division) surrendered, without ever having fired a shot in anger. Southern France and Brittany were overrun, with little loss to the enemy. Just as in North Africa, lack of support for Rommel's ideas was resulting in the defeat of the German armed forces; only the scale had changed.

After von Schweppenburg left the Western Front in an ambulance, Sepp Dietrich assumed temporary command of Panzer Group West and postponed all counterattacks indefinitely. Rommel's good friend and naval advisor, Admiral Ruge, wrote of this decision: "The Third Front had become a fact, and the fate of the Third Reich sealed."[44] Both Rommel and von Rundstedt realized now that it was hopeless to try to hold a line so far west.[45] The prudent thing to do was to retreat into the interior of France, out of the range of the huge Allied naval guns and before Eisenhower could build up his armored pursuit forces. The need to retreat would be especially acute if Cherbourg fell, which appeared likely unless 7th Army received massive reinforcements immediately. On June 11 von Rundstedt vocalized this notion to Hitler, stating that the situation would require "fundamental decisions" if the Cotentin port was lost. Rommel said virtually the same thing to Keitel the same day.[46] Both field marshals were ignored.

Two days later Rommel made yet another plea for infantry divisions and regimental combat groups from Pas de Calais. Again his request was rejected.[47]

On June 10 the Allies continued their offensive in both the American and the British sectors without letup. Colonel von der Heydte still held the Carentan position, but was gradually pushed back to the Vire-Taute Canal, which effectively sealed off the town to the east.[48] That night, in a rare performance, the Luftwaffe sent a flight of Ju-52s to Normandy. They dropped desperately needed mortar and machine-gun ammunition to the paratroopers. The next day fresh American troops launched heavy attacks and pushed back all sectors of the 6th Parachute Regiment's overextended perimeter. By noon they had gained a foothold in the town, and von der Heydte's exhausted men were unable to throw them out.[49]

That afternoon von der Heydte made a reconnaissance in the hills southwest of the town, to select defensive positions in case a retreat became necessary. He ran into SS Major General Werner Ostendorff, the commander of the 17th SS Panzer Grenadier Division, and his operations officer. The SS men were also on a reconnaissance. Ostendorff informed von der Heydte that the 6th Parachute Regiment was attached to his division for an attack against the Americans, scheduled for the next day. Von der Heydte asked for reinforcements, but Ostendorff denied his request. He wanted the colonel to hold out at Carentan until he could mass his division for the attack. The two officers argued briefly. Ostendorff discussed his experiences on the Eastern Front, and concluded, ". . . surely those Yanks can't be tougher than the Russians."

"Not tougher," replied von der Heydte, "but considerably better equipped, with a veritable steamroller of tanks and guns."

Ostendorff was not impressed. "Herr Oberstleutnant," he snapped curtly, "no doubt your parachutists will manage until tomorrow."[50]

Von der Heydte had no choice but to return to Carentan. When he arrived he found that his command post had been overrun.[51] He decided to disobey orders and abandon the critical position that evening. The U.S. Army's official history stated that the withdrawal was a "blunder," but this conclusion has been the subject of dispute. There is no doubt, however, that the unauthorized retreat was a severe blow to the German Army in Normandy, and that a great many in the High Command were furious at von der Heydte. The regimental commander reportedly escaped court-martial only because of his previous record. Ostendorff tried to retake the town on June 12 and 13, but failed.[52]

The victory at Carentan gave the American beachhead the depth it needed so badly, and Bradley was now in a position to cut across the Cotentin Peninsula and isolate Cherbourg to the northwest. This was the next stage of the American part of the campaign. However, events elsewhere assumed predominance, at least momentarily. On the other flank,

Field Marshal Montgomery was about to resume his offensive, which had been temporarily checked by von Schweppenburg's counterattack.

It will be remembered that Montgomery planned a double envelopment of Caen. The "left hook" was to be delivered from the airborne bridgehead east of the Orne. The "right hook" was to be launched from the Bayeux area, and was much stronger.

The left hook was, in fact, never delivered. Battle Group Luck, supported by elements of the 346th Infantry Division, continued to fight east of the Orne, and its operations assumed all the aspects of a spoiling attack. The German combat teams tied up the British 6th Airborne and 51st Highlander divisions, along with the 4th Armoured Brigade, until June 16. As a result, Monty's left hook never got out of its assembly areas. However, the price was high for the Germans. Combat Group Luck lost all but eight of the panzers loaned to it by the 22nd Panzer Regiment. The battle grew so fierce that hand-to-hand fighting took place in several spots.[53]

Montgomery's right hook was initially more successful. It was, however, facing groups of veteran soldiers who were rapidly gaining experience at fighting in hedgerow country. The German infantry set up in good defensive positions behind the hedgerows and in sunken lanes. Their elements set up in echelon, with overlapping zones of fire. The panzers often operated individually, with the infantry, as defensive weapons. They made superb armored machine-gun nests, and frequently spearheaded local counterattacks against Allied footholds. On the other hand, they were frequently knocked out by Allied fighter-bombers.

On June 11 the British 7th Armoured Division attacked through the 50th Infantry Division and began an attempt to encircle Panzer Lehr. This mission was ambitious in the extreme, because Bayerlein's division was perhaps the best equipped in the Nazi Army, with its fast, reliable PzKw IV's and Panthers. On the other side, the old desert soldiers of the 7th Armoured had left their reliable Shermans in Italy, and were now equipped with Cromwells, a tank that was excellent in pursuit, but inferior to the PzKw IVs and Vs in a tank battle, particularly if the fight became a slugging contest.

The 7th Armoured Division started the battle by capturing the village of Verrières-Lingevres. It fell quickly, but Panzer Lehr counterattacked just as quickly and soon a major armored battle raged around the village. In the center of the German line the British 6th Armoured Regiment, supported by the Canadian infantry, launched a second attack against the remnants of the 12th SS Panzer Division at Le Mesnil-Patry. The British tankers ran right into a nest of 88mm antiaircraft guns and were slaughtered. Thirty-seven tanks were knocked out, and only three NCOs and a handful of men ever came back. Every officer in the regiment was either killed, seriously wounded, or captured. The Canadians were also repulsed in savage fighting, although they did fare better than the 6th Armoured. The battle for Le Mesnil-Patry continued until June 14, but the SS line held.[54]

Meanwhile, at Tilly, Fritz Bayerlein discovered that he was being out-flanked. While the bulk of the 7th Armoured Division pinned down his reduced force, a brigade-sized combat group from the Allied armored division penetrated as far as Villers-Bocage, and took the pivotal village during the afternoon of June 12. This place was located on high ground well in the rear of the German line, in the void between the American and British sectors, which were still only loosely joined. Panzer Lehr's deep left flank was in grave danger and Bayerlein had already committed his reserves. There was nothing he could do but call for help.

Fortunately for Panzer Lehr, help was not far off. On the morning of June 13 the Allied combat group, which consisted of the 22nd Armoured Brigade, the 5th Royal Artillery Regiment, and the 1st Infantry Brigade, continued its advance toward Hill 213 (near Villers-Bocage), which con-trolled the vital road to Caen. They were spotted by SS Lieutenant Witt-mann, the commander of the 2nd Company, SS Heavy Panzer Battalion, 501st SS Panzer Regiment. Wittmann was no ordinary lieutenant. He had already personally destroyed 119 tanks and armored vehicles on the Rus-sian Front, and wore the Knights Cross with Oak Leaves, a decoration normally reserved for generals who had distinguished themselves by direct-ing a number of major operations. It was almost never awarded to company-grade officers.[55] Wittmann did not wait for the rest of his com-pany to come up, but immediately attacked the British with his own Tiger tank. Shell after shell from the Cromwells struck the huge PzKw VI, but bounded off its thick armored hull. Within five minutes the SS lieutenant had knocked out 25 British armored vehicles, bringing his personal total to 144. Soon the rest of Wittmann's company joined in the fight, in which a total of 25 British tanks, 14 half-tracks, and 14 Bren carriers were destroyed. The spearhead of the flanking column was annihilated.[56] Map 4 shows this battle.

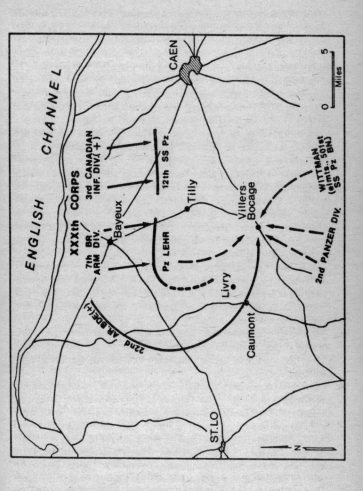

Map 4—The Battle of Villers-Bocage, June 13, 1944

The British combat group's troubles were just beginning. The weather had turned bad, and the R.A.F. was grounded, leaving the 22nd Armoured Brigade and its supporting units badly isolated. At just that moment the vanguard of Lieutenant General Baron Heinrich von Luettwitz's 2nd Panzer Division, en route to reinforce Panzer Lehr, arrived and joined in with Wittmann near Villers-Bocage instead. Also, Bayerlein had managed to scrape together a reserve and immediately dispatched it to the village, where the 22nd Armoured was soon trapped. Before it could make a getaway, the British brigade was severely mauled. Its brigadier was killed, along with 15 other officers and 176 men. Dozens of others were wounded and/or captured. The 1st Infantry Brigade left four officers and 60 men on the battlefield as well. The flanking column—or what was left of it—limped back to British lines. Montgomery's right hook had been blocked.[57]

Sir Bernard Law Montgomery was nothing if not persistent. Faced with four panzer divisions (including Luettwitz's previously undetected 2nd Panzer), he realized that he did not have the strength to carry out an offensive everywhere at the same time. Consequently, he decided to go over to the defensive in front of Caen, and launched an all-out frontal attack on the battered Panzer Lehr and Hitler Jugend divisions.

On June 15 Montgomery's second major thrust began with a massive aerial and artillery bombardment. Then the 50th Infantry Division, reinforced by new armored units, attacked the Panzer Lehr. The village of Lingevres fell, but the grenadiers held Tilly, thanks primarily to their excellent use of the Panzerfaust.[58]

At the same time that the 50th struck, the newly arrived British 49th Infantry Division attacked Witt's 12th SS Panzer Division at Putot-Brouary, on the Panzer Lehr's right flank. Once again the teenage SS men held fast.[59]

The battle continued on June 16. The British took Hottot and cut the Tilly-Balleroy road, but Bayerlein launched an immediate counterattack and the 902nd Panzer Grenadier Regiment, supported by 15 Panthers, retook the village in furious fighting. The British were not through, however. Their radio interceptors pinpointed the location of the Headquarters, 12th SS Panzer Division, 12 miles southwest of Caen, and informed the Navy, which blew it to pieces. SS Lieutenant General Witt jumped into a slit trench. A moment later a 16½-inch shell from a British battleship landed right beside it, killing him instantly.[60] Thirty-five-year-old SS Colonel (soon

Major General) Kurt "Panzer" Meyer replaced him as division commander.

Despite his heavy casualties, Montgomery attacked Tilly a third time on June 18. The bulk of the British VIII Corps took part in the battle for the ruins of the village. The R.A.F., the Royal Navy, and several fighter-bomber squadrons plastered the area, but to no avail: they were repulsed again. However, Panzer Lehr and the 12th SS Panzer divisions were being bled white. It was only a matter of time before they would be annihilated.[61]

The German ground forces called in vain for support from the Luftwaffe. It was simply not forthcoming. The German Air Force had been driven from the skies, never to return. The Chief of the Luftwaffe General Staff reported:

> The air officer commanding 3rd Air Fleet reports: Ground installations being systematically smashed, especially all fighter fields.

> The chief of operations of the 3rd Air Fleet reports . . . Ratio of air strength: generally 1 to 20, during major operations 1 to 40.

> The 2nd Fighter Corps reports: Own fighter operations now only conditionally possible. Effective reconnaissance and fighter operations entirely ruled out in the invasion area. Thirty Anglo-American airfields already constructed and operational in the bridgehead.[62]

While Erwin Rommel's men continued to hold on to their Cotentin line by their fingernails, the first V-1 weapon was fired on June 16. Traveling at 400 miles per hour, it crossed the English Channel and landed in the London area. Utter confusion resulted. "The Rocket Age had begun," Paul Carell wrote.[63]

Hitler intended to break England's spirit by employing these new weapons against her population. German scientists would win the war for the Reich, he said. The men of the Western Front would simply have to hold on until that day. Rommel protested that they could not, and demanded the High Command send representatives to Normandy to see for themselves what the true situation was. On June 14 he wrote, "Was up front again [today], the situation's not getting any better. We must be prepared for the worst. The troops—SS and army alike—are fighting with extreme courage but the balance of strength is remorselessly tilting against us every day." The Desert Fox was very depressed, reminiscent of those dreadful days in the desert after El Alamein, when it seemed as if Panzer Army Afrika would not make good its escape to Tunisia.[64] Perhaps in an attempt to rally the spirit of his marshals, Hitler ordered Rommel and von Rundstedt to meet him on the morning of June 16 at Margival, a Fuehrer HQ constructed in 1940. It was from here that Hitler had planned to direct the invasion of Great Britain. Those days seemed a long time ago indeed.

Rommel was off visiting the battlefield when the order arrived at his headquarters. He returned to La Roche-Guyon at 3:00 A.M. on the 16th, after a 21-hour trip to the front lines. Now he had to endure a 140-mile ride over damaged roads to Hitler's bunker. There was no time to make any preparations at all for the conference.[65]

Early the next morning Hitler and Jodl arrived at Margival. Hitler looked pale, sleepless, and ill. He played nervously with his glasses and some colored pencils, while sitting hunched on a stool, as the marshals stood in front of him. All his former hypnotic powers were gone. Bitterly he denounced Rommel and von Rundstedt for the success of the Allied invasion to date. Then it was the soldiers' turn to speak.

After a few introductory remarks, von Rundstedt turned the conference over to Rommel. With what General Speidel later called "merciless frankness," Erwin Rommel pointed out the hopelessness of the German position. Although he praised the fierce resistance of the German soldiers, he called the Cherbourg fortress "useless" and proceeded to denounce Hitler's whole concept of fortress-defense in the same, uncompromising terminology.[66]

Then the Desert Fox predicted what the Allies would do next: breakthrough from the Caen-Bayeux area and the Cotentin Peninsula, at first to the south, then in the direction of Paris. A secondary operation would attack past Avranches, to cut off the Brittany Peninsula. Germany had no way to prevent this in the long run. Eisenhower's 21st Army Group now had 22 to 25 mobile and armored divisions on shore, with two to three arriving each week. Rommel's dangerously understrength forces were being bled white, and could not hold on indefinitely.[67]

The tough Swabian categorically stated that there would be no secondary landing north of the Seine, and pointedly demanded freedom of maneuver. He proposed to withdraw from Caen to positions behind the Orne, beyond the range of the heavy guns of the Allied navies.[68] While the infantry

Rommel's official photograph, taken in December 1942, a year before he assumed command of Army Group B *(U.S. National Archives)*

Field Marshal Rommel inspects mobile troops behind the Atlantic Wall. His ideas on the employment of these troops caused great friction with Hitler and the High Command in 1944. *(Bundesarchiv)*

Rommel inspects the Atlantic Wall. (Bundesarchiv)

Rommel (right) and his chief of staff, General Speidel, share a map while an aide looks on. Speidel played an important role in the July 20 conspiracy to assassinate Adolf Hitler and encouraged Rommel to act against the dictator. (Bundesarchiv)

Adolf Hitler greets Rommel in one of their more cordial moments. Hitler only reluctantly gave Rommel command of the forces that met the Allies in Normandy. *(U.S. National Archives)*

Rommel (right) discusses strategy with Hitler and Field Marshal Wilhelm Keitel (center). Rommel and Hitler seem none too pleased with one another—a typical situation in 1944. *(U.S. National Archives)*

Field Marshal Rommel as he appeared on an inspection of the West Wall in early 1944. The Desert Fox was none too impressed with Hitler's great propaganda hoax. *(U.S. National Archives)*

SS Colonel General Otto "Sepp" Dietrich, who commanded the I SS Panzer Corps in Normandy, 1944 *(U.S. National Archives)*

The invasion coast at Grandcamp-Les-Bains, France, showing German teller mines affixed to posts and planted several hundred feet from the beach. At high tide they were covered with water and would cause considerable damage to landing craft. (U.S. Army)

One of the German gun positions at Azeville, neutralized by American paratroopers on D-Day (U.S. Army)

D-Day: U.S. fighter-bombers fly cover for troop-carrying gliders that have landed behind German lines. The Allies' absolute control of the air crippled Rommel's efforts to hurl the Americans, British, and Canadians back into the sea. *(U.S. National Archives)*

Utah Beach during the build-up phase, showing the masses of men and equipment being landed from various types of vessels offshore. Rommel could not match the overwhelming matériel superiority of the Allies. This photo was taken near Colleville on June 9, 1944. *(U.S. Army)*

A sniper takes aim. Individual fire-fights were frequent and deadly in the Battle for the Hedge-rows. *(Bundesarchiv)*

A German lieutenant in Normandy gives orders to his subordinates. *(Bundesarchiv)*

(top) A gunner places a victory strip on the tube of his assault gun while his lieutenant—a winner of the Knight's Cross—looks on. This gun has accounted for 16 Allied armored vehicles, some of which were probably destroyed in Russia. (Bundesarchiv)

(bottom) The commander of a panzer engineer battalion presents a corporal a special award for destroying an Allied tank in Normandy, 1944. The corporal has already been awarded the Iron Cross and the Close Combat Badge. (U.S. Army)

A German forward outpost, Normandy front, 1944 *(Bundesarchiv)*

A German soldier waits to ambush Allied armor *(Bundesarchiv)*

German heavy artillery
(Bundesarchiv)

(below) Artillerymen load their Nebelwerfer rocket launcher for another bombardment. *(Bundesarchiv)*

A U.S. Army medic examines a wounded German infantryman who was hit in the face by a rifle grenade during the battle for St. Lô. *(U.S. Army)*

A German killed near St. Lô on July 11th *(U.S. Army)*

This dead German soldier fell in the streets of Cherbourg. He still clutches in his right hand a hand grenade he never got to use. *(U.S. Army)*

A German assault gun, knocked out on the outskirts of Ste.-Mere-Eglise. (U.S. Army)

This self-propelled gun was knocked out by Allied fighter-bombers in Normandy in July 1944. (U.S. Army)

(top) "Ost" or Eastern Troops, captured in Normandy, await shipment to POW camps. These troops are from Georgia in the Soviet Union. One-sixth of the battalions of the LXXXIV Corps were made up of these unreliable soldiers, many of whom were returned to the Soviet Union and executed at the end of the war. *(U.S. Army)*

(bottom) Lieutenant General Karl Wilhelm von Schlieben, the commander of the Fortress of Cherbourg, surrenders on June 26, 1944. The soldier on the far right is carrying the hat and coat of Rear Admiral Hennecke, the German Naval Commander of Normandy, who surrendered with von Schlieben. *(U.S. Army)*

Field Marshal von Kluge, who replaced von Rundstedt as Commander-in-Chief, OB West, in July 1944. He and Rommel clashed almost immediately and, although united in purpose, they never became friendly. Von Kluge succeeded Rommel as commander of Army Group B after the Desert Fox was wounded on July 17, 1944. Kluge committed suicide shortly before Rommel met his own death. *(U.S. National Archives)*

Field Marshal Gerd von Rundstedt with U.S. Lieutenant General Alexander M. Patch, the commander of the 7th U.S. Army. Von Rundstedt had been restored to command of OB West in September 1944, only to be relieved again in March 1945. *(U.S. Army)*

Field Marshal Gerd von Rundstedt, May 2, 1945. He was captured at the hospital at Bad Tolz while undergoing treatment for arthritis. (U.S. Army)

retreated, the panzer divisions would cover them, and strike the Allied pursuit columns on the flanks. He conceded that the plan had only a one-to-four chance of succeeding, but attempting to hold the present line would eventually lead to disaster. Field Marshal von Rundstedt supported his subordinate's demands.[69]

Hitler did not want to listen to the unpleasant truth. "We have only to keep our heads . . . ," he said. "Hold the enemy in the East, defeat him in the West. If we ward off the invasion Britain will sue for peace under the effect of the V-weapons."[70]

Rommel and von Rundstedt requested that the V-1s be used against the Allied beachheads, but General Erich Heinemann, the General-in-Charge of V-weapons, pointed out that this was not feasible because the margin of error in the rockets' guidance systems was too great. The weapons usually landed within nine to twelve miles of where they were aimed, but they could not be accurately fired at tactical targets. The marshals then suggested that the weapons be turned on the port cities of southern England, but Hitler vetoed this idea too. He wanted to destroy London to make the British sue for peace.[71]

Somehow the commanders got the conference back on track. Rommel gave an account of the destructive powers of Allied weapons, but Hitler refused to believe his former favorite. Rommel then bluntly pointed out that no person of authority in Hitler's entourage had yet visited the front. Decisions were being made in the dark, he said, without firsthand knowledge. "You demand our confidence, but you do not trust us yourself," Rommel snapped at Hitler. The Nazi dictator flushed at this reprimand, but said nothing.[72]

An Allied air raid forced the conference to adjourn to an air-raid shelter. While there, Rommel continued to press his points to Hitler. He turned his attention to the political situation, and predicted the collapse of the German fronts both in France and in Russia, unless Hitler brought the war to and end.[73] He urgently implored the Fuehrer to sue for peace. "Don't you worry about the future course of the war," Hitler retorted, "but rather about your own invasion front."[74]

The Margival conference lasted from 9:00 A.M. to 4:00 P.M., with an hour break for lunch. During this period Hitler gobbled down a plate of vegetables, several pills, and small glasses of various medicines. The discussions ended without a single positive result.[75] The next morning an off-course V-1 rocket exploded near the bunker, and a shaken Hitler departed immediately. This reaction was a far cry from that of the Fuehrer whom Major General Rommel had guarded in 1939, when it seemed he enjoyed being under fire. Behind him, Hitler left an order. Victory, it said, was to be gained by "holding fast, tenaciously to every square yard of soil."[76]

4

Cherbourg

As we have seen, Lieutenant General Wilhelm von Schlieben was defeated in his attempt to retake Ste.-Mère-Église and retreated to a line overlooking the western edge of the American beachhead. Here he assembled what troops he could find, and what units Rommel could spare, while Bradley and Eisenhower were preoccupied with the Battle of Carentan. Between June 9 and 12 he established a line manned by miscellaneous units from the 709th, 243rd, and 91st divisions, as well as the 7th Army Sturm Battalion.[1] He organized them into three combat groups of approximately regimental size. These groups were Combat Groups Hoffmann and Mueller, of the 243rd Infantry Division and the 919th Grenadier Regiment of the 352nd Infantry Division.[2] Von Schlieben's main strength, however, was artillery. Several field artillery units had survived D-Day at least partially intact, and von Schlieben gathered all he could: a battalion from the 243rd Artillery Regiment, the 456th and 457th Motorized Artillery battalions, a battery of six French 155mm guns from the 1261st Artillery Regiment, five batteries from Flak Group Koenig, and part of the 100th Mortar Regiment. Major Friedrich Wilhelm Kueppers assumed command of the artillery forces.[3]

Utah Beach, on the east coast of the Cotentin, faced southwest, toward the interior of the peninsula. Twelve miles to the northwest was Cherbourg, the strategic objective of the American landings. As soon as they established some depth to their bridgehead, Rommel knew that the Americans would attack von Schlieben and go after this prize. However, he could spare little in the way of reinforcements from 7th Army, because he simply had to contain Montgomery in front of Caen and Bradley in front of St. Lô, or the Allies would break out of hedgerow country and reach the more favorable terrain to the south. This would allow their offensive to pick up steam, and the end of the Third Reich would be in sight. Rommel succeeded in halting both these forces by committing all of his mobile reserves as soon as they arrived. Unfortunately, this tactical plugging left von Schlieben pretty much on his own.

It was June 12 before Bradley captured Carentan and reduced the most significant strong points still holding out in the American rear. Although these battles tied up most of his divisions, General Bradley did make some preliminary moves to the west before then. From June 8 to 10 von Schlieben's makeshift corps fought against the 4th Infantry and 82nd Airborne divisions, which gradually pushed it back toward its main defensive positions along the Montebourg-Quineville line. By the time this German withdrawal was completed Carentan had fallen, as well as the coastal forts of Azeville, St.-Marcouf, and Crisbecq. These victories left Lieutenant General J. Lawton Collins's U.S. VII Corps free to attack the Cherbourg landfront. Von Schlieben, meanwhile, had at last received some additional reinforcements in the form of the 77th Infantry Division under Major General Stegmann. All other units in von Schlieben's command had been badly injured since D-Day, but the 77th was fresh from Brittany, and was still capable of offering prolonged resistance. When the Americans finally did advance on the "fortress" of Cherbourg, they faced a reasonably formidable combat force.[4]

On June 11 the U.S. VIIth Corps made its first major thrust toward Cherbourg with the 90th Infantry and 82nd Airborne divisions. The newly arrived 90th was stopped almost immediately, but the veteran paratroopers scored a potentially decisive breakthrough. They attacked the 100th Panzer Replacement Battalion, a unit made up mainly of foreigners in German service, which broke and ran in its first clash with the enemy. A combat group from the 265th Infantry Division arrived just in time to stabilize the situation, but the tactically important village of Pont l'Abbé was lost, so von Schlieben fell back a short distance and dug in for the next onslaught.[5]

Another major disaster overtook German arms on June 12, when General Erich Marcks, the tough and steady commander of the LXXXIV Corps (of which von Schlieben's command was a part), was caught by a fighter-bomber on the road west of St. Lô. He was critically wounded, and bled to death before help could arrive. General Wilhelm Fahrmbacher, the commander of the XXV Corps in Brittany, assumed temporary command of the LXXXIV Corps until a permanent replacement for Marcks could be named. The man chosen for this thankless job was General Dietrich von Choltitz, a veteran of the Russian Front, who arrived two days later.

Fahrmbacher immediately surveyed his new command and reported that it could not hold against a determined American attack. There were too few men, too much mixing and splitting of units, too many stopgap measures, and not enough ammunition.[6]

The defeat of von Schlieben's makeshift force was entirely predictable. The embattled veteran of the Eastern Front faced the U.S. 9th Infantry, 4th Infantry, and 82nd Airborne divisions, with the 79th and 90th Infantry divisions known to be in the VII Corps reserve.[7] Clearly von Schlieben was facing heavy odds, even if Anglo-American air superiority and naval support were not taken into account.

On June 15, after two days of skirmishing, the U.S. breakthrough came, with the 82nd Airborne spearheading the penetration.[8] German artillery slowed down the American advance by adopting a new tactic: it raked them with highly concentrated barrages of short duration. This method made it difficult for the ever-present fighter-bombers and spotter aircraft to pinpoint the location of German gun positions. At night especially, all Kueppers's guns would open up at once, but at different targets. As a result the attackers were suffering casualties, while German artillery units remained pretty much intact.[9] Such was not the case for the infantry units.

By June 16 the Nazi defenses were beginning to deteriorate. The 91st Air Landing Division was a shell. The other units, except for the 77th Infantry Division, were also in remnants. It would be impossible to halt the retreat east of the small Douve River, the last barrier between U.S. VII Corps and the western coast. General Collins wasted no time in exploiting his victory and pressed on with all possible forces toward St. Sauveur and the sea. His objective was obvious to anyone who could read a map: Collins wanted to cut the Cotentin and the LXXXIV Corps in half.

Field Marshal Rommel recognized the danger as early as June 14, even before the Americans launched their major offensive, but there was little he could do about it. As of June 12 he had only 12 divisions (perhaps 120,000 men) to face 326,000 Americans and British.[10] The odds would get even worse in the days ahead, and the Desert Fox knew he could not hold everywhere, so he ordered the 77th Infantry Division to break out of the trap before it was sprung. The 77th was almost the only cohesive force remaining north of Collins's probable route of advance, indicating that Rommel realized that Cherbourg was doomed and that he wanted to salvage all he could before the ultimate collapse of the northern half of the LXXXIV Corps. The other divisions in the enemy's path—the 91st, 243rd,

709th, and part of the 265th—were now of regimental size or less, burnt out, shattered beyond hope, and probably too disorganized to make good their escape in any event. On June 16, however, Hitler countermanded Rommel's order to Major General Stegmann. The 77th Infantry Division would defend Cherbourg to the bitter end.[11]

A few hours later the climax of the unequal battle was reached. The U.S. VII Corps flanked Montebourg to the south. Stegmann's 77th Infantry was unable to check the 82nd Airborne and 4th Infantry divisions, which reached the west coast of the Cotentin on June 17. Von Schlieben's men (now under the makeshift headquarters, Group von Schlieben) were virtually encircled.

The condition of Group von Schlieben continued to worsen on June 16 and 17, a deterioration that was no doubt accelerated by the death of one of von Schlieben's best subordinates. On June 16 Lieutenant General Heinz Hellmich of the 243rd Infantry Division was killed by a 20mm shell from an American fighter-bomber.[12]

To defend the southern edge of the corridor now extending across the Cotentin from German counterattacks, Bradley committed another U.S. corps: the VIII, under Major General Troy H. Middleton. Middleton was given the 82nd and 101st Airborne divisions, and ordered to cover Collins's rear as he advanced northward on Cherbourg.[13] Like Rommel, Major General Stegmann realized that the Americans were turning north to wipe out the Cherbourg pocket. Unlike Rommel, he decided that the 77th Division had to be saved, even if it meant flagrant disobedience of the Fuehrer's direct orders. On the evening of June 17 he turned south and struck out across the American corridor. At that moment the Allied front across the peninsula was far from solid; this situation, however, could not be expected to exist for long. Stegmann decided to get his men out of the trap while he still had the chance.

Although he saved much of his command, General Stegmann could not save himself. Near the village of Bricquebec fighter-bombers destroyed his horse-drawn columns. As he tried to reorganize what was left, the aircraft attacked again and his body was ripped apart by 20mm shells. He died instantly.[14]

Colonel Bacherer, the commander of the 1049th Infantry Regiment, assumed divisional command and continued with Stegmann's plan. Late on June 17 he surprised an American infantry battalion and took 250 prisoners. With his remaining 1,500 men he broke through the corridor and reached the southern front of LXXXIV Corps near La Haye-du-Puits the next day.[15]

Meanwhile, the jaws closed inexorably on Cherbourg. Hitler ordered: "The present positions are to be held at all costs." This command was meaningless, for the Americans were already in von Schlieben's rear. The escape of the 77th stripped his right flank of men. If the Americans discovered this (as they surely would) they could swing north along the western coast of the peninsula and bag the entire force before it even reached Cherbourg. Rommel therefore changed Hitler's order to read: "The fortress of Cherbourg is to be held at all costs. . . ."[16]

By mid-1944 Hitler's insanity was far advanced and he lived in a dream world. His grasp of reality was steadily slipping as the military situation got more and more out of control. He even went so far as to order Rommel to counterattack and relieve von Schlieben. "Fancy ordering me to attack Cherbourg!" Rommel exclaimed to Admiral Ruge later, as they went on one of their walks near the Château La Roche-Guyon. "I was glad enough to have managed to piece together even a semblance of a defensive front."[17]

On June 19 the Allied advance on Cherbourg resumed. The Germans resisted at Montebourg on the eastern flank against the U.S. 4th, 9th, and 79th Infantry divisions, until the artillerymen fired all the ammunition they could not carry with them in their limited transport; then the surviving infantrymen retreated as rapidly as they could into the fortress. Most of them reached the city by the end of the next day.[18]

The siege of Cherbourg began on June 21. General von Schlieben realized that he could not hold out indefinitely and that there was little chance for relief. His objective, then, was time. Time to allow the sailors and engineers to destroy the harbor; time to enable Rommel to establish a solid defensive line to the south; always time!

He did not have much left with which to fight. The units involved were already burned out, and most of them were below 50 percent of their original strength. However, a major storm did give the trapped garrison some respite, even though it also underlined to the enemy the necessity of taking Cherbourg as soon as possible.

The weather began to change on June 20. A gale was brewing. It was what Montgomery later called "the most famous gale since the Armada." For three days breakers rolled across the beaches. They held up landings for

several days, and endangered the success of the invasion.[19] British Squadron
Leader Hill remembered:

> On the beach just west of where I was at Juno, there was utter chaos; literally
> hundreds of small craft were washed ashore by the gale at high tide and lay on
> the road which traversed the beach, rather like a cargo of timber logs.[20]

The smaller Allied landing vessels, such as LSTs and LCMs (Landing
Ship, Tank; and Landing Craft, Mechanized; respectively), were particularly hard hit. Off Omaha Beach alone 90 ferrying vessels were lost, and the
British lost another 250 such vessels. Eight hundred small vessels were
grounded on the beaches and left stranded when the water receded.[21] Many
of these had to be written off.

The storm, labeled by the British official historian as the worst June
storm to hit the Channel in 40 years, wrecked the two artificial harbors
which the Allied High Command depended on. The British harbor was
eventually repaired, but the American harbor off Omaha Beach was totally
destroyed. Omar Bradley was left with only three days' supply of ammunition, which meant he had to delay his planned attacks in the St. Lô region.
Likewise, Montgomery's June 22 attack on Caen had to be postponed.[22]

To add to the Allies' supply problems, the Luftwaffe began night drops
of a new type of mine into the waters off the beachhead. It was a pressure or
"oyster" mine, which was activated by the pressure change caused by a
ship's hull moving through the water, and was unsweepable by any method
known in 1944.[23]

German submarines also became active, although there were few of
them left in the Navy of the Third Reich. Forty-three of them left bases in
Norway, Germany, and the Bay of Biscay region, with orders to attack the
Allied ships off the Normandy coast. A dozen of these had to return
prematurely because of mechanical defects or damages inflicted by depth
charges. Ten were sunk before they could reach the area of operations and
eight more were destroyed while there. Only 13 of those engaging the
Royal and American navies ever returned. In this "last hurrah" of the Nazi
Navy, U-boats destroyed seven warships, two LSTs, one LCI (Landing
Craft, Infantry) and 13 transport ships totalling 50,000 tons, while six other
transports (totalling 49,000 tons) were damaged. The German submari-
ners had suffered a major defeat in this, their last major battle of World War
II. There were simply not enough of them to disrupt the Allied invasion.[24]

The oyster mines did almost as much damage to the Allies' shipping as did the German Navy. In the week of June 22–29 alone they sank four warships, as well as four other vessels, while seven other warships were damaged. One oyster mine blew up the *Derry Cunihy*, with the British 43rd Reconnaissance Battalion on board. Of its 500 men, 150 were killed and 180 wounded, and all its equipment was lost. The 43rd was eliminated as a combat force even before it reached the mainland.[25]

In Cherbourg, however, nothing could save the doomed garrison. On June 22, even before the storm had completely dissipated, approximately 1,000 aircraft pulverized the defensive positions of Group von Schlieben. The cornered soldiers resisted stubbornly that day and the Americans gained little ground, but the next day resistance began to weaken. The U.S. VII Corps established four wedges in the fortified line. Hitler ordered von Schlieben ". . . to defend the last bunker and leave the enemy not a harbor but a field of ruins. . . ."[26]

Wilhelm von Schlieben had few resources left with which to carry out this order. He reported on the morning of June 24 that he had no more reserves and that the fall of the fortress was inevitable. Nevertheless he ordered his men to resist until the last cartridge.[27]

The next day the Americans took Fort du Roule and entered the suburbs of Tourlaville and Octeville, thus putting the headquarters of Group von Schlieben in the immediate front of the battle. The lieutenant general signaled Rommel:

Enemy superiority in material and enemy domination of the air overwhelming. Most of our own batteries out of ammunition or smashed. Troops badly exhausted, confined to narrowest space, their backs against the sea. Harbor and all important installations effectively destroyed. Loss of town unavoidable in nearest future, as enemy has already penetrated outskirts. Have 2,000 wounded without possibility of moving them. Is there any point, in view of the overall situation, in having our remaining forces entirely wiped out, as seems inevitable? . . . Urgently request instructions.[28]

Rommel replied: "In accordance with the Fuehrer's orders, you are to continue fighting to the last round."

"Is that all?" von Schlieben asked his radio operator.

"That is all, Herr General," the operator replied.[29]

Erwin Rommel, it seems, had temporarily been cowed by the pressure from Hitler and the High Command. He spent the entire day moping about La Roche-Guyon in a state of abject depression.[30] Von Schlieben had no way of knowing that, even as Cherbourg went through its death agonies, the commander of Army Group B was involved in a plot to bring about the end of the Nazi dictatorship.

At 7:00 P.M. on June 25 naval demolition teams under Captain Witt blew up the remains of the harbor with 35 tons of dynamite. Ten minutes later von Schlieben burned his secret papers. The Americans were within 100 yards of his command bunker.[31]

The defenders held the bunker until 1:30 P.M. the next day. Then von Schlieben turned to Vice Admiral Walther Hennecke, the Naval Commander, Normandy, and said, "If my superiors thought fit to make me a general, then they've got to accept the fact that I will act in accordance with the situation and my conscience." This was the second time in his career von Schlieben had defied orders. As the commander of the 18th Panzer Division in Russia he had led his men out of encirclement against orders.[32] Now he gave the command to surrender.

Von Schlieben's order involved only his own headquarters. The leaders of the various sectors were left on their own, to surrender or keep fighting as they saw fit. The city commander, Major General Robert Sattler, capitulated the next morning, along with 400 of his men. Harbor Commander Witt, Major Kueppers, and others continued to resist.[33] It was a hopeless struggle, however, and the agony was soon over. The last pockets of resistance (on the northwest corner of the peninsula) were overcome on July 1—three weeks behind Eisenhower's schedule.[34]

The fall of Cherbourg released thousands of men in mobile forces, who would soon be sent against the left flank of Rommel's Normandy front. However, the prize the U.S. VII Corps had fought so hard for turned out to be of much less value than expected. The American engineer officer charged with the task of rehabilitating the port reported: "The demolition of the port of Cherbourg is a masterful job, beyond a doubt the most complete, intensive, and best-planned demolition in history."[35] The U.S. Army's official history recorded that "the whole port was as nearly a wreck as demolitions could make it." Three weeks would elapse before the Americans could get the slightest use out of the fortress-harbor.[36] Hitler was so pleased that he awarded Admiral Hennecke the Knights Cross, even though he was in captivity.

The collapse of resistance in the northern Cotentin ended a major phase of the Normandy campaign. The Allies had achieved their first strategic objective. They no longer had to worry about the fortress of Cherbourg holding out in their rear, and they could now turn their full attention to the south, where Erwin Rommel had established a thin line in hedgerow country. Against the Americans in the western half of the Cotentin Peninsula, he now had four fewer divisions and 39,000 fewer men with which to defend "Fortress Europe."[37] As of June 18 he faced approximately 600,000 enemy soldiers, and by July 1 the total number of Allied troops who had landed in Europe stood at 929,000, or about three times what Rommel could muster. In addition, the Allies were increasing their strength at a rate of two to three divisions per week.[38] If they could force the Desert Fox out of hedgerow country, the German armies in the West would be facing annihilation. The floodgates were creaking.

5

The Crumbling Fortress

As the U.S. VII Corps advanced on Cherbourg, Erwin Rommel desperately hung on to the hedgerow country against the sledgehammerlike blows of the British 2nd and American 1st armies. He held out pretty much with his own resources, for little help was sent by Berlin. From D-Day to the third week in July, Rommel lost 2,722 officers and 110,357 men, of which only 10,078 were replaced. In the same period the Allies lost 117,000 men. These casualties were more than fully replaced.[1]

As resistance in Cherbourg deteriorated from furious to weak, more German divisions sat idle between the Seine and the Scheldt than were fighting in Normandy. The reason for this situation was that, even at this late date, Adolf Hitler refused to believe the invasion had come! As incredible as it may seem, the Fuehrer and OKW still believed the Normandy landings were a diversion, and that the main blow would come at the Pas de Calais. A force equivalent in strength to an army group, with 24 infantry divisions, five Luftwaffe field divisions, and six panzer divisions, sat motionless.[2] Meanwhile, in the American sector alone, Rommel faced four full corps of 14 divisions, against which he could field only three intact divisions, three decimated divisions of approximately regimental strength, and a few miscellaneous formations.[3] On July 3 OKW estimated that the Allies had landed 225,000 to 250,000 men with 43,000 vehicles. Actually, they had landed 929,000 men, 177,000 vehicles, and 586,000 tons of matériels.[4] Rommel was outnumbered roughly 3 to 1.[5]

On June 20, the High Command ordered von Rundstedt and Rommel to launch a massive armored counterattack and hurl the Allies into the sea. This order was ridiculous in the extreme. It was far too late for that, and probably had been since June 7. Three of the panzer divisions earmarked for the participation in this attack (the 1st SS, the 9th SS, and the 10th SS) had not yet arrived, and would be delayed even longer by the U.S. and Royal air forces, as was the case with other units en route to the front. A week later, for example, a battle group from the 265th Infantry Division was assigned to 7th Army, to replace a battle group from the same division which was destroyed at Cherbourg. It took the new unit five days to cover the 180 miles to the front, but it took seven days to transport its heavy equipment 100 miles by railroad; then it had to proceed by highway.[6] As a result of such delays, two of the panzer divisions in the line—the Panzer Lehr and 12th SS—could not be taken out, because the two infantry divisions sent from southern France to replace them in the front line (the 276th and 277th Infantry) were also seriously delayed by enemy aircraft. Neither the Panzer Lehr nor Hitler Jugend could properly be called a division in any case, inasmuch as half their men or more had become casualties since June 6. Only the 2nd SS Panzer Division "Das Reich" was in a position to launch the ordered attack, and a single division would be easily repulsed. Besides all this, the Allied aerial domination had reduced Rommel's resupply effort to a trickle. The Field Marshal had approximately 637 guns, but they only had a few shells each, not even enough to carry out all of their defensive fire missions. Counterattack was, of course, out of the question.[7] As von Rundstedt's chief of staff, Lieutenant General Guenther Blumentritt, said: "As he [Hitler] would not modify his orders, the troops had to continue clinging on to their cracking line. There was no plan any longer. We were merely trying, without hope, to comply with Hitler's order that the line Caen-Avranches must be held at all costs."[8]

Montgomery had brought a new corps ashore by June 18: the British VIII. He planned to close on Caen with another pincer attack, this time nearer to the city. The fresh VIII Corps would provide the main punch. It was scheduled to begin on June 22, but was delayed three days by the gale.[9]

Meanwhile, Battle Group Luck launched its last counterattack. The group had lost several commanders over the past three weeks, and was now led by Captain von Gottberg, the former battalion commander in the 22nd Panzer Regiment, 21st Panzer Division. His objective was the village of St. Honorine, three miles northeast of Caen, which had just been taken by the British 51st Infantry Division. Gottberg tried to take it back, but was stopped by British artillery and naval gunfire. The battle group's tank contingent was reduced to seven panzers.[10] Like so many units before it, the group was now burnt out. Nevertheless, its survivors remained in the line.

On June 22 Montgomery attacked again. Even though this assault was not his major offensive, it was serious enough. His objective was the vital Hill 112, which dominated the city of Caen. The British attack was spearheaded by the newly arrived 11th Armoured Division, which faced the nearly exhausted survivors of the 12th SS Panzer Division. The Hitler Youth Division still continued to resist with fanatical courage, and the struggle for the hill became one of the most bitter small battles of World War II. Even the divisional commander, SS Major General Kurt Meyer, manned a Panzerfaust (antitank weapon). A counterattack by a small force of Tiger tanks ended the battle. The teenage SS men continued to hold the vital position.[11]

Shortly after the repulse of the 11th Armoured Division, Montgomery launched a night attack further east, and broke through the positions of the 192nd Panzer Grenadier Regiment of the 21st Panzer Division. However, Major General Feuchtinger immediately counterattacked with his reserve, and again closed the road to Caen.[12]

For the next two days heavy skirmishing continued all along the Caen front, particularly between the 11th Armoured and 12th SS Panzer divisions.[13] On June 25 Montgomery's long-delayed offensive, code-named "Epsom," began. The plan was relatively simple: the XXX Corps would start by attacking east of Tilly, to pull in the German reserves. The next day the British VIII Corps, with one armored and two infantry divisions, would pass through the Canadian 3rd Division and attack east of Caen, from the Orne bridgehead. Its objective was the area around St. Mauvieu, southeast of the city. If it was reached, Montgomery would be out of *bocage* (hedgerow) country.[14] Meanwhile, the British I Corps would engage in a flanking attack even further to the east, while the Canadians again tried to take the airfield at Carpiquet.[15] Map 5, page 124, shows the "Epsom" offensive.

The XXX Corps attack was spearheaded by the 49th Division with the 8th Armoured Brigade attached. It struck toward the critical Fontenay and Rauray ridges, where it was met by the remnants of Bayerlein's Panzer Lehr Division.[16] The battle here grew fierce. McKee wrote: "Germans and British became inextricably intermingled in the fog and bitter hand-to-hand fighting developed where no quarter was given on either side."[17] The British 49th Division suffered heavy casualties against the Panzer Lehr, and only managed to secure a small foothold on the western end of Fontenay Ridge.[18]

The VIII Corps struck the next day, as planned. This force alone included 60,000 men, 600 tanks, and 300 guns. They were further supported by 400

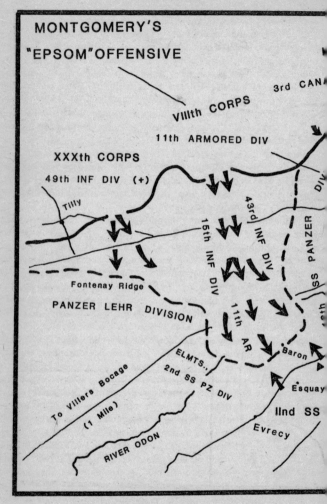

Map 5—Montgomery's "Epsom" Offensive

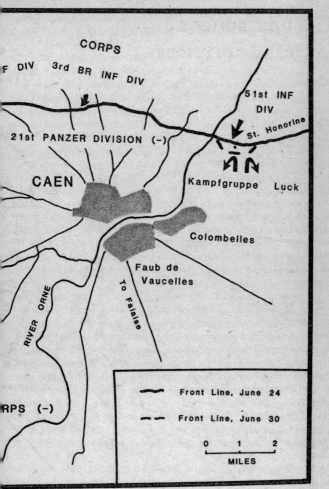

CORPS

F DIV   3rd BR INF DIV

51st INF DIV

St. Honorine

21st PANZER DIVISION (−)

CAEN

Kampfgruppe   Luck

Colombelles

Faub de Vaucelles

To Falaise

RIVER ORNE

RPS (−)

―――― Front Line, June 24

― ― ― Front Line, June 30

0   1   2
MILES

guns from the XXX and I corps on their right and left flanks, respectively. Three cruisers from the Royal Navy and 250 R.A.F. bombers also pounded German positions.[19]

The greatly reduced 12th SS Panzer Division opposed the advance of the VIII Corps, which included the 15th Scottish Infantry, 11th Armoured, and 43rd Wessex Infantry divisions, along with the 31st Army Tank and 4th Armoured brigades. In addition, the Canadian 3rd Infantry Division of the British I Corps supported the main drive by launching yet another attack on Carpiquet Airfield.[20] The Germans were outnumbered at least six to one. To make matters worse, Sepp Dietrich, whose I SS Panzer Corps controlled both the Panzer Lehr and the "Hitler Jugend" divisions, committed his last reserves prematurely. Kurt "Panzer" Meyer of the 12th SS objected, but to no avail. As a result, the 26th SS Panzer Grenadier Regiment was left unsupported at 7:00 A.M. on June 26, when the bulk of the British VIII Corps fell on its positions. The regiment was overrun, as was much of the 12th SS Panzer Engineer Battalion. The British, however, allowed the German artillery to separate their infantry from their armor, and the attack bogged down. SS Major Siegfried Mueller, the commander of the SS engineers, turned his headquarters into a strong point, and held out well into the night before slipping away to the west with the survivors of his command.[21]

The stubborn resistance of the SS men gave the 7th Army time to take countermeasures. Colonel General Dollmann rushed most of the Army's reserves to the threatened sector. These included three battalions from the 2nd SS Panzer Division, the entire 7th Mortar Brigade, and a small battle group from the 21st Panzer Division. Rommel also took a hand in the battle. He ordered the II SS Panzer Corps (9th and 10th SS Panzer divisions), which was just arriving from Russia, to head for the Caen sector. This unit, however, was still en route from Paris and was under heavy aerial attack. Its arrival would be delayed until June 29. Rommel also sent in that part of the 2nd SS Panzer Division that was in Army Group reserve. The Desert Fox considered the situation so serious that he halted all supply movement on the roads and gave the armor emergency priority of movement.[22]

Late on the afternoon of the 26th "Panzer" Meyer led a desperate counterattack on the right flank of the British spearhead. He struck with everything he could lay his hands on. The SS were met by the 15th Scottish and 11th Armoured divisions and were beaten back. They had, however, achieved their objective: the British advance was halted, at least temporarily.[23]

On June 27 the Allies got their attack going again, but at a much slower pace. The British 11th Armoured and 15th Scottish divisions suffered heavy losses against well-placed German artillery fire, not to mention antitank gunners hidden in the hedgerows. The Scottish Division finally managed to break the thin SS line and establish a bridgehead over the Odon River near Baron.[24] The fighting reached General Meyer's headquarters at Verson before the evening had ended. Slowly the British and Scots continued to inch toward Hill 112.[25]

On the morning of June 28, the men of the British VIII Corps faced what they thought was a screen of German snipers and machine gunners. They were wrong: this was the main body of the German line, all that was left of the once-proud 12th SS Panzer Division "Hitler Jugend." Once again the British attacked and slowly pushed "Panzer" Meyer back, before he was reinforced by a company from the 22nd Panzer Regiment of the 21st Panzer Division. He threw them into battle immediately, along with a few SS grenadiers and a Panther or two. Again there was heavy fighting, and again the Allied attack was halted by the last German reserves.[26]

On the night of June 28/29 the vanguard of the II SS Panzer Corps began to arrive. It was led by SS General Paul Hausser, who had retired from the Army as a lieutenant general before joining the SS. His 9th SS and 10th SS Panzer divisions, nicknamed "Hohenstauffen" and "Frundsberg" respectively, were made up entirely of veterans, toughened by months of combat on the Eastern Front. In April they had broken the Russian spring offensive before being sent into reserve at Tarnopol. On June 13 they entrained at Tarnopol and moved directly to Normandy. Most of their combat units were up by June 29. Hausser immediately grouped his men for a counterattack; however, Montgomery caught this "Eastern General" in his assembly areas and subjected the II SS Panzer Corps to a massive aerial, naval, and artillery bombardment. By the time Hausser could regain his balance, Hill 112 had fallen.[27]

June 29 was another day of desperate fighting. Hill 112 had to be retaken, or Caen was doomed. Meyer slugged at the vital position with all his remaining artillery.[28] Meanwhile, General von Schweppenburg prepared for an immediate counterattack with all the forces he could throw together. Von Schweppenburg's Panzer Group West Headquarters, which was upgraded and redesignated 5th Panzer Army a few days later, had been reactivated the day before and took over the right flank of Rommel's Normandy Front. His forces included the XXXXVII Panzer, I SS Panzer, II SS Panzer, and LXXXVI Infantry corps, the last of which was en route from the 1st Army in southern France. Dollmann's 7th Army was transferred to the western (St. Lô) sector, where it commanded the LXXXIV and II Parachute corps.[29] These dispositions indicate that Erwin Rommel felt von Schweppenburg was his best tactical commander, for he entrusted him with his most critical and dangerous sector.

Unfortunately for General von Schweppenburg, he took over a battle already in progress with practically all his reserves committed. Rommel was unable to help, because local American attacks had forced him to commit his last reserve (a battle group from the 2nd SS Panzer Division) to prevent the collapse of his left flank.[30] To make matters worse, Fuehrer Headquarters ordered von Schweppenburg to throw the newcomers from the II SS Panzer Corps into the battle before they were ready. "By this order the Panzer Group is already sold out!" von Schweppenburg snapped, bitterly.[31] The results were predictable: the attack began in the afternoon and had been defeated by nightfall. Hill 112 remained in British hands.[32]

Meanwhile, Rommel lost yet another senior commander. Colonel General Friedrich Dollmann, chief of the 7th Army since 1940, died of a heart attack on June 29. Hitler had wanted to sack him for some time, but Rommel had insisted that he be allowed to remain at his post. The Desert Fox, who had had no idea that Dollmann's health was so bad, had appreciated the fact that Dollmann was loyal, even if he was not the best tactical commander in the world. Hitler finally overrode Rommel and issued the order relieving Dollmann of his command; however, the 7th Army leader dropped dead just before the order reached his headquarters.

Hausser replaced Dollmann as commander of the 7th Army, a change that did not entirely please Erwin Rommel. The SS man had been a General Staff officer and was able, courageous, and energetic, but definitely a Nazi.[33] SS Lieutenant General (soon General) Willi Bittick, the leader of the Hohenstauffen Division, succeeded to the command of the II Panzer Corps. Bittick was a fine leader in his own right. He had been a Luftwaffe officer, but joined the Waffen-SS in order to gain faster promotions. Already he had commanded the 2nd SS Panzer Division in Russia and the 8th SS Cavalry Division in the Balkans, but his most famous victory lay ahead of him: Bittick would all but annihilate the British 1st Parachute Division at Arnhem the following September. SS Colonel Mueller, the commander of the 20th SS Panzer Grenadier Regiment, became acting commander of the 9th SS Panzer Division when Bittick moved up.[34]

On June 30, his first day as a corps commander, Bittick won a major victory by recapturing Hill 112 from the British 29th Armoured Brigade. His trump card was the 7th Mortar Brigade (a unit supplied by 7th Army Headquarters), which trained 300 tubes on the heights. Before the Battle of Normandy was over, this unit fired some 8,000 tons of mortar-shells at the Allies. While the II SS took Hill 112, Panzer Lehr Division beat back attacks from Montgomery's 49th and 50th Infantry and 2nd Armoured divisions a few miles to the west.[35] The German line had been bent and pushed back, but it had not broken.

A dangerous gap had existed on the left (western) flank of the Panzer Lehr Division for several days. Field Marshal Rommel was aware of this fact, but was too occupied with the battle for Hill 112 to do anything about it. Fortunately for him, the British 2nd Army failed to detect it. On June 30 a battle group from the 2nd SS Panzer Division was finally available to fill the hole. The relatively fresh 2nd SS and the nearly exhausted Panzer Lehr were now placed under the command of Baron von Funk's veteran XXXXVII Panzer Corps Headquarters, which soon exerted a real control over the battlefield. The Allies had missed another golden opportunity to score the decisive breakthrough.[36]

The reason for the British failure at Hill 112 was that, despite their overwhelming air superiority which crippled German movement, they were still too slow. They had suffered heavy casualties on the road to the hill, but failed to bring up reinforcements for the 29th Armoured Brigade when it finally took the key position. The Germans under Rommel, on the other hand, threw everything into the breach so soon as it became available. It had been just barely enough to prevent the decisive breakthrough.[37]

General Speidel, the chief of staff of Army Group B, called the Battle of Hill 112 "tactical patchwork," and "unsound in every respect."[38] He was right, of course, but there was little else his chief could do. Rommel's emergency measures had prevented a catastrophe once more—but only by a hair.

While the all-important Battle of Hill 112 was reaching its climax, Erwin Rommel was hundreds of miles away, waiting. He and his immediate superior, Field Marshal von Rundstedt, sat at Hitler's Bavarian residence from late morning until early evening, a total of roughly six hours. Von

Rundstedt was heard to mutter something about how this would be a good way to kill an old man. Rommel also let his feelings show. "Herr von Rundstedt," he said, "you and I both believe that the war must be stopped now. I intend to make no bones about it when we see the Fuehrer."[39] He also spoke with Goebbels and Himmler, both of whom agreed to support his position in the Fuehrer conference.[40] Rommel was optimistic when Hitler at last decided to see them. The conference took place in front of a large audience, which included the unemployed Field Marshal Gunther von Kluge, who had just recovered from injuries suffered on the Eastern Front some months before. Rommel and von Rundstedt twice requested a private audience with Hitler and were twice rejected. Rommel finally cleared his throat and said: "Mein Fuehrer, I am here as commander of Army Group B. I think it is high time that I—on behalf of the German people to whom I am also answerable—tell you the situation in the West. I should like to begin with our political situation. The entire world is arrayed now against Germany, and this balance of strength. . . ."

"Field Marshal!" Hitler cut in, beating his hand on the table. "Please stick to the military situation!"

"Mein Fuehrer," Rommel replied, "history demands of me that I should deal first with our *overall* situation."

"You will deal with your military situation, and nothing else," Hitler ordered, emphatically.[41]

After this exchange, Rommel tried to give him a realistic report, but Hitler did not want to listen. The Nazi dictator reprimanded Rommel for failing to launch a relief attack on Cherbourg as he had commanded.[42] He also bluntly informed von Rundstedt that Army Group B would not be allowed to withdraw behind the Seine and southern France would not be evacuated, as the Prussian marshal had suggested.[43] Rommel would not be given any of the 15th Army's divisions, Hitler continued, for they would all be needed when the real invasion came. The Desert Fox was to concern himself with holding his present line, to prevent the enemy from reaching open country and driving on Paris.[44] Then, in a discussion General Blumentritt described later as "fantastic,"[45] Hitler lapsed into a monologue about his miracle weapons, such as the jet airplane and the V-1 and V-2 rockets, which would bring the Allies to their knees. Finally, weary of this tirade, Rommel asked Hitler point-blank how he imagined the war could still be won,[46] and he called on the others in the room to express their views. Goebbels and Himmler maintained a guilty silence. Even without the promised support, the Field Marshal faced Hitler with a courage the dictator was not accustomed to from his generals. "Mein Fuehrer," he said, "I must speak bluntly: I can't leave here without speaking on the subject of Germany."

"Field Marshal," Hitler replied, "be so good as to leave the room. I think it would be better that way."[47] Rommel turned on his heel and left Hitler's presence, never to see him again.

After the conference, Rommel said to Field Marshal Keitel: "A total victory, to which Hitler is still referring even today, is absurd in our rapidly worsening situation, and a total defeat can be expected. . . ."[48]

Even Keitel, Hitler's notorious yes-man and longtime enemy of the Desert Fox, agreed. "I too am aware that there is nothing more to be done," he said. He promised to present the situation to Hitler along the lines Rommel described. However, it is highly doubtful that he ever attempted to do so.[49]

Despite all that had happened, Hitler still refused to believe that the major Allied invasion had come. He repeated his orders to Rommel and von Rundstedt to hold every inch of ground at all costs. Any thought of mobile warfare was to be forgotten. When Rommel returned to la Roche Guyon he was given an estimate of the situation, written by General von Schweppenburg and 7th Army's new chief, SS General Hausser. They both called for the evacuation of the Caen pocket and a retreat to the shorter Orne River-Bully-Avenay-Villers-Bocage-Caumont line. This retreat would at last place the German forces out of range of Allied naval guns and allow Rommel to create an armored reserve; however, it would also put the Allies on terrain favorable for armored operations. Obviously these proposals were in complete opposition to the orders Hitler had just issued. Rommel approved the plan anyway, and hastily forwarded it to von Rundstedt at OB West Headquarters in Paris. The reason for the sense of urgency was that both field marshals expected to be relieved of their commands as a result of the Berchtesgaden conference. The documents arrived in Paris a few minutes after midnight on July 1. Von Rundstedt quickly endorsed them, and requested a free hand in the evacuation of Caen. Jodl recommended the rejection of these ideas, and brought the matter before Hitler. The Nazi chieftain turned down the proposals as expected, and again ordered OB West to hold every position presently occupied, and to halt every Allied breakthrough by local counterattacks.[50]

Hitler's reaction to the insubordination of his top generals was quick in coming. General von Schweppenburg was dismissed from active service on July 2. Hitler blamed von Schweppenburg for the defeat of the counterattack of June 29 and considered him a defeatist. Rommel protested his removal but was brushed off by Keitel.[51] Fifth Panzer Army was turned over to General Heinrich Eberbach, who had commanded the 4th Panzer Division on the Eastern Front. Eberbach's chief of staff was Major General Alfred Gause, the former chief of staff of Panzer Army Afrika. At the same time as von Schweppenburg's dismissal, Colonel Heinrich Borgmann, one of Hitler's army adjutants, entered von Rundstedt's command post. He politely presented the aging field marshal with the Oak Leaves to the Knights Cross and a handwritten letter from Hitler.[52] It was a polite note ordering von Rundstedt into retirement on the grounds of age and health. "I shall be next," Rommel remarked when he heard the news.[53] Of the top German commanders on the Western Front six weeks before, only he remained.

As he left for Germany, General von Schweppenburg wrote a letter to Erwin Rommel. It is worth reprinting here in full, because it shows the measure of the man and his changed opinion of Rommel, to whom he had resolved not to speak only a few weeks before:

6 July 1944

Dear Field Marshal:

On relinquishing my command, may I be permitted to add a few words to my official leave-taking. The recent battles in a theater of war more exacting than any I had hitherto experienced have, in addition to providing me with my posting to Army Group B and uniting me in purpose with yourself, wrought an inner change in me. Your soldierly qualities and experience have transformed the temper of my obedience into something different and finer than the effort of will it had hitherto been.

I feel I may ask you, Herr Field Marshal, to accept my thanks for the confidence which you placed in me and my troops in those brief hard days of battle which we went through together. Since I regard my military career to be at an end, I think that I can say this without fear of misinterpretation.

I am, Herr Field Marshal,
Yours obediently,
FREIHERR VON SCHWEPPENBURG[54]

Although Rommel was by seniority next in line for the post, Hitler named Field Marshal Guenther von Kluge as replacement for von Rundstedt as Commander-in-Chief of OB West. The 61-year-old von Kluge, called "Clever Hans" in top army circles, was in no way prepared for what he would be facing in Normandy. He had served in World War I as an artillery officer and rose to command the VI Corps in prewar Germany, but had lost this command when the Nazis purged Army Commander-in-Chief General Werner von Fritsch and his allies in 1938. Von Kluge was recalled to active duty in January 1939, when he commanded the 6th Army Group in Hanover. He later led the 4th Army in Poland and the French campaign of 1940, where Rommel had been one of his divisional commanders. Since then his services had been entirely in the East, where he led the 4th Army on the drive toward Moscow. In December of that year Hitler relieved Field Marshal Fedor von Bock of the command of Army Group Center, and named von Kluge to succeed him. Von Kluge soldiered here, without particular distinction, until he was injured in an automobile accident on a snow-covered Russian road in early 1944. Now he faced his greatest challenge. Von Kluge was a non-Nazi, as opposed to being an anti-Nazi, and he had no idea of what he was up against in the West.[55] It was his type of officer about whom Rommel had spoken to Bayerlein at la Roche Guyon two months before, when he told his old companion: "Our friends from the East cannot imagine what they're in for here. It's not a matter of fanatical hordes to be driven forward in masses against our line, with no regard for casualties and little recourse to tactical craft; here we are facing an enemy who applies all his native intelligence to the use of his many technical resources, who spares no expenditure of material and whose every operation goes its course as though it had been the subject of repeated rehearsal. Dash and doggedness alone no longer make a soldier, Bayerlein; he must have sufficient intelligence to enable him to get the most out of his fighting machine. And that's something these people can do, [as] we found out in Africa."[56]

Von Kluge had already been influenced against Rommel at Fuehrer Headquarters, where Hitler, Keitel, and Jodl spoke of him as being disobedient and a defeatist. Von Kluge spent several days at Berchtesgaden, where he let himself be convinced that the disasters on the Western Front were attributable solely to poor generalship. Consequently he was overly optimistic when he arrived at Rommel's headquarters on July 5. At first the conference was chilly as von Kluge listed Rommel's sins: he was too pessimistic, and too easily influenced by the "allegedly overpowering effect of the enemy's weapons," both in France and in North Africa. Rommel was too obstinate, and did not carry out the Fuehrer's orders as wholeheartedly as he should. "Field Marshal Rommel," he said, "even you must obey unconditionally from now on. This is good advice that I am giving you."[57]

Rommel grew angry and then furious. He had never been the type to take unwarranted criticism lying down. The insult was doubly humiliating because Dr. Speidel and Colonel von Tempelhoff were present. The Swabian heatedly demanded that von Kluge draw his conclusions only after he had visited the front. He denounced Hitler's criticisms of him as unjustified, and then proceeded to censure the High Command itself in no uncertain terms. The argument grew so violent that von Kluge ordered everybody to leave the room except Rommel and himself.[58]

Von Kluge arrogantly demanded to see the negative reports Rommel claimed to be getting from his subordinate commanders concerning the situation at the front. He was obviously insinuating that Rommel did not have them because they did not exist.

"You seem to be forgetting that you are talking to a field marshal!" Rommel retorted, challengingly.

"I'm perfectly well aware of it," von Kluge came back. "But you have taken very independent positions up to now, and you always got your own way in defiance of your immediate superiors by going over their heads to the Fuehrer."

"My job is quite clearly defined," Rommel replied. "I have to defend the coast and I demand that the Commander-in-Chief West [i.e., von Kluge himself] place all the necessary forces at my disposal to that end." He added that von Kluge would have enough trouble merely with his own job, without meddling into Rommel's. "Just look at the bungling of your [own] quartermaster!" the Desert Fox snapped, referring to the mess the rear areas of France were in.

What did Rommel know about high command? Von Kluge wanted to know. "Up to now you haven't ever really commanded any unit bigger than a division!"

"And you still have to meet the British in battle!" Rommel yelled back.[59]

The Desert Fox insisted that von Kluge withdraw his accusations and apologize in writing. The new C-in-C of OB West refused to do this, and the two were at loggerheads. After this meeting, there was an intense resentment between them; it did not completely dissipate even after von Kluge had come around to Rommel's viewpoint.[60]

Von Kluge told his staff that he felt sure he had scored more points than Rommel in their shouting contest, and that the Desert Fox would not try to go over his head and deal directly with Hitler, as he had done under Field Marshal Kesselring in North Africa and under von Rundstedt in the West. Even as he spoke, Rommel was sending another ten-page letter directly to the Fuehrer, listing his previous demands and requesting that the appropriate conclusions be drawn.[61]

Rommel was never one to let an unfinished argument lie. That very afternoon he wrote the following letter to von Kluge:

HQ, 5 July 1944

To: C-in-C West

Herr Generalfeldmarschall von Kluge

I send you enclosed my comments on military events in Normandy to date.

The rebuke which you leveled at me at the beginning of your visit, in the presence of my Chief of Staff and Ia, to the effect that I, too, "will now have to get accustomed to obeying orders," has deeply wounded me. I request you to notify me what grounds you have for making such an accusation.

(Signed) ROMMEL
Generalfeldmarschall[62]

Rommel's attached document, which had already been forwarded to Hitler, was a severe indictment of the way the Nazi High Command had conducted the war in Normandy to that date. It started out with the statement that the Normandy garrison was too weak to begin with, its equipment outdated, ammunition stocks too small, construction of fortifications too much in arrears, and "the supply situation . . . utterly inadequate."[63]

The report went on to give a laundry list of the reinforcements and countermeasures he had requested, and how he had been turned down almost every time. Rommel spared no one, including the Quartermaster General Wagner, Jodl, the Navy, and the Luftwaffe. He was, however, at least diplomatic enough to make his criticism of Hitler himself implied or indirect, rather than blatant and personal.[64]

Meanwhile, von Kluge was coming round to Rommel's view of the military situation. Of his new commander, the Chief of Staff of OB West wrote: "Field Marshal von Kluge was a robust, aggressive type of soldier. At the start he was very cheerful and confident—like all newly appointed commanders.... Within a few days he became very sober and quiet. Hitler did not like the changing tone of his reports."[65]

It took von Kluge only one inspection of the front to make him realize that he was wrong on the Rommel question. He reversed himself completely, and even acknowledged the justification of a memorandum which Rommel had written to Hitler at the end of June, in which Rommel had commented: "The enemy's command of the air restricts all movement in terms of both space and time, and renders calculation of time impossible."[66]

The supply situation, already at the crisis stage, reached astronomical proportions by July 2. Colonel Lattmann, the Army Group's artillery expert, reported that he needed a minimum of 3,500 tons of supplies per day, but he was not even getting 350 tons. Von Rundstedt's old supply officer had already been sacked, but the new one could do no better,[67] in view of the total Allied control of the air.

The Allies did not give Army Group B any respite while the Germans tried to work out their supply problems, command structure, and personality and policy conflicts. Montgomery continued his strategy of continuous alternation of the center of gravity between the British on his left flank and the Americans on his right. This method forced the Germans to rush their armored forces from one crisis point to another. They grew steadily weaker without seriously challenging the Allied foothold in Europe, because there were simply not enough reserves to permanently deal with both the Caen and the St. Lô sectors at the same time. Rommel asked of OKW in early July: "How can they expect me to hold out with a quarter of a division when three American divisions are attacking?"[68]

Throughout his last campaign, Rommel naturally chose to concentrate most of his armor against the British in the eastern (Caen) sector, rather than against the Americans on his left flank. The reasons were fundamental: if the Americans broke through, the Battle of Normandy would be lost, but Army Group B would still be in a position to retreat across the Seine. If the British broke through, they would be between the Germans and the Seine, in a position to cut the Army Group off from its bases, Paris and the Reich. At best the 7th and 5th Panzer armies would be routed and most of their heavy equipment would be lost. They would then be unable to prevent the Allies from overrunning France and thrusting into Germany itself, possibly into the Ruhr industrial area. The Third Reich would have lost whatever feeble chances it had left of staving off defeat. For these reasons, Rommel's left wing was always weaker than his right, although many of the Americans slugging their way through the hedgerows would have questioned this fact in 1944.

The key position in the American sector was St. Lô. It was a road center rivaling Caen, and its capture would give Bradley the additional lateral communications he needed, as well as road routes to the south, out of hedgerow country. Methodically he plotted his next offensive.[69] Map 6, page 138, shows the Normandy Front on July 2, 1944, the day before the U.S. offensive began.

The American offensive was launched in corps attacks by echelon. The VIII Corps on the American right (coastal) flank attacked the far left flank of the LXXXIV Corps on July 3. The next day, July 4, the VII Corps in the right-center of the American line jumped off. Three days later the newly committed XIX Corps went over to the offensive against the right flank of von Cholwitz's LXXXIV Corps and the left flank of Meindl's relatively weak II Parachute Corps. The fourth and final U.S. thrust would be launched by their V Corps. It would also attack on July 7, on the far left of the American line, against the right flank of Meindl's Corps.[70]

On the western coast of the Cotentin, the U.S. VIII Corps massed thousands of men, including the 8th Infantry, 79th Infantry, 82nd Airborne, and 90th Infantry divisions. Against this huge force, von Cholwitz could commit only the understrength 353rd and the greatly understrength 243rd and 77th Infantry divisions.[71]

The Americans were confident of victory and General Middleton's VIII Corps was expected to advance 20 miles against light German resistance. One U.S. Army Intelligence estimate, dated June 28, stated that "the German division unit as such . . . has apparently ceased to exist."[72] However, as the American official history pointed out, this may have been true in the last week of June, but it was certainly not the case in the first week of July.[73]

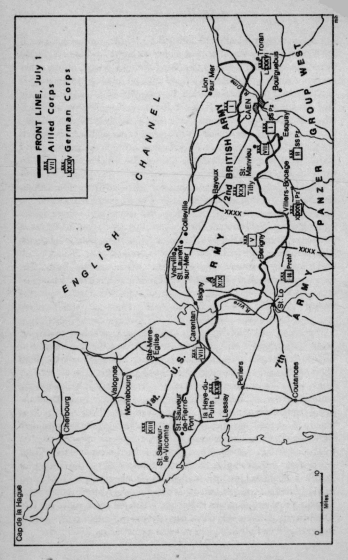

Map 6—The Situation in Normandy, July 2, 1944

The Germans were badly outnumbered. Each American division, except the 82nd Airborne, was at or near its full authorized strength of 14,000 men. Colonel Eugen Koenig's 91st Air Landing Division, on the other hand, was fairly typical of the German units on July 3. It had only 3,500 effectives, and this figure included the remnants of the 243rd Infantry Division and a battle group from the 265th Infantry Division, as well as other miscellaneous formations.[74] Colonel Rudolf Bacherer's 77th Infantry Division, which had been mauled in its breakout two weeks before, was well under half its original strength.[75] The German command in this sector had also suffered heavy losses. Both the 77th and the 91st divisions had seen their commanders killed in recent actions, and their Army commander was also dead, while LXXXIV Corps now had its third leader since D-Day. Despite its staggering losses, the LXXXIV again rose to the occasion. Its men, well dug-in in the hedgerows, gave ground slowly and only after bitter fighting. The U.S. 82nd Airborne managed to advance only four miles in three days. Although it did take the tactically important Poterie Ridge, the 82nd's casualties were tremendous. The strongest company left in its 325th Glider Infantry Regiment, for example, now numbered only 57 men. One company could field only 12—the normal size of an augmented squad! The division had lost over half its men since D-Day. Now it was withdrawn from the line and returned to England, to rebuild and get a well-deserved rest.[76]

There was no rest for Rommel's divisions, no matter how much they deserved or needed it. Major General Middleton sent the 90th Division of his VIII Corps against the important heights of Mont Castre, in the main effort of his corps. This attack was backed with the heaviest artillery support and was stubbornly opposed by two of Koenig's battalions, the remnants of the 77th Infantry Division and a battalion from the 353rd. On July 3, the first day of the attack, the Americans gained less than a mile, at the cost of over 600 casualties. The next day they advanced two more miles, with even higher casualties. Finally Middleton captured the high ground on July 6, only to face immediate counterattacks. Rain prevented the U.S. air power from intervening as SS General Hausser threw the fresh 15th Parachute Regiment, just up from Brittany, into the struggle. The fighting in and around Mont Castre lasted for three more days, before the advanced American combat group was wiped out. When the battle ended the U.S. 90th Infantry Division held only a part of the reverse slope of the heights. In five days it had advanced four miles, at a cost of over 2,000 men.[77]

On the extreme left flank of Rommel's line, the U.S. 79th Division attacked along the Atlantic coast against the remnants of the 243rd Division. Its objective was the high ground in the vicinity of La Haye-du-Puits. In five days it suffered over 2,000 men killed, wounded, and captured. Hausser had to commit two battalions of the 2nd SS Panzer Division to prevent a breakthrough, but by July 8 the 79th had stalled, and the VIII Corps offensive had failed all along the line.[78]

Meanwhile, the U.S. VII Corps began its attack on July 4, America's Independence Day. The victors of Cherbourg found themselves in swampy terrain, with inadequate space to commit all their forces. It was hoped that they could quickly reach the Périers-St. Lô highway, for south of this the ground was drier and the corps could fan out, and commit the bulk of its infantry.[79]

Although American Lieutenant General Collins had the 4th, 9th, and 83rd Infantry divisions under his command, he could commit only the 83rd initially, because of the terrain. His attack was met by the survivors of von der Heydte's 6th Parachute Regiment and elements of the 17th SS Panzer Grenadier Division. The attack started badly. The commander of the American spearhead was killed before he could advance 200 yards. The 83rd Division lost 1,400 men on the first day. The slaughter was so bad that Colonel von der Heydte returned captured American medical personnel, so that they could aid in evacuating the wounded.[80]

The terrain—swampy, hedgerow country—could hardly have been less suitable for offensive action, and the rainy weather eliminated the Allies' air cover, but the U.S. forces attacked again on July 5. The VII Corps managed to gain a mile along the Carentan-Périers road, at the cost of another 750 casualties.[81]

Despite the narrowness of the front, General Collins threw his veteran 4th Infantry Division into the battle, but they also failed. The paratroopers and SS men were generally of a very different character, but they possessed a common toughness and fought with bitter determination. Although Hausser was forced to send part of SS Lieutenant General Heinz Lammerding's 2nd SS Panzer Division (which was now being split and scattered all over the battlefield) into the fight, the Americans were halted by July 7. They had advanced less than 2½ miles in four days.[82]

With the U.S. VIII and VII corps decisively engaged in heavy hedgerow fighting, the U.S. XIX Corps started its offensive on July 7. It was approximately 11 miles due north of St. Lô when it began its drive on the city.

Initially it had three infantry divisions: the 30th on the right, the 29th on the left, and the 35th in the center.[83]

To the surprise of the American High Command, Major General Colbert's XIX Corps made rapid headway. The reason for this was simple: the Allies' tactic of continually shifting the center of gravity was paying off. Rommel and Hausser had been forced to commit all of 7th Army's and Army Group B's reserves to halt the attacks of the U.S. VIII, U.S. VII, British XXX, British VIII, and British I corps all along the line from the Orne bridgehead to the west coast of the peninsula. These attacks by over half a million men had come within a four-day period. All that remained to defend St. Lô was Battle Group Heinz: a reduced regiment from the 17th SS Panzer Grenadier Division, augmented by three battalions from the 275th Infantry Division.[84] It faced three full-strength American divisions.

At 3:30 A.M. on July 7 eight field artillery battalions, including one of heavy 8-inch guns, blasted Colonel Heinz's positions. By 6:00 A.M. the Americans had a foothold across the small Vire River, a position which U.S. Army Intelligence expected to be strongly held. Only one machine gun fired on the American infantry as they crossed the stream. By nightfall the bridgehead across the Vire was definitely established. General Bradley decided that the time had come to commit his armor for the decisive thrust toward St. Lô, so he sent the 3rd Armored Division into the battle.[85]

Rommel's line was reeling. Not only was his St. Lô sector threatened with immediate collapse, but Caen was also in imminent danger of falling. On July 2 Rommel had taken the battered Panzer Lehr Division out of the line and replaced it with the newly arrived 16th Luftwaffe Field Division. The next day Montgomery struck with his veteran British 3rd Infantry Division at the exact point Panzer Lehr had vacated. Despite the support of the 12th SS Panzer Division—itself a mere skeleton—the green air force unit broke and ran. It was a complete rout. The Luftwaffe unit lost 75 percent of its men (mostly captured) and almost all of its artillery. The remainder of the unit was so demoralized that Rommel attached it to the 21st Panzer Division, probably in the hope that the latter could restore some fighting spirit to the survivors. The divisional commander, Major General Sievers, wandered about the battlefield on July 3, vainly trying to restore some cohesion to his disintegrated command.[86]

The Luftwaffe Field Division reflected one of the worst aspects of Nazi Germany's military system: the personal empire. The rout of the 16th Field Division is an excellent example of the results of such a system. These men were not cowards but highly trained and skilled air force personnel, perfectly competent when it came to repairing Messerschmitts, building airfields, or directing air traffic. As the Reich's air power declined, however, they became excess baggage. Instead of transferring them to the Army, where they could have been properly retrained for ground combat, Reichsmarschall Hermann Goering insisted on keeping them under his personal control, and persuaded Hitler to create the Luftwaffe Field Division for that purpose. They would serve as infantry, but under Luftwaffe leadership and command. As a result, both officers and men were insufficiently prepared for land battles, and the Allies smashed them in almost every encounter. Now, thanks to the collapse of the 16th Field, the British closed in on Caen. However, the fanatical 12th SS Panzer Division—no matter how greatly reduced—was still a force to be reckoned with.

No better example of the tenacity and blind courage of these young SS men can be found than their conduct at the Battle of Carpiquet. In peacetime this place was the airport for Caen; in 1944 it was the best constructed and defended strong point in the whole Caen defensive network. On July 4, it was attacked by the Canadian 8th Infantry Brigade, two battalions of the British 79th Armoured Division, and a battalion of the Canadian 7th Infantry Brigade. The Canadians were supported by 428 artillery pieces, plus the 16-inch guns of the battleship *Rodney* and the 15-inch guns of the mortar ship *Roberts*. The airfield was defended by only 150 Germans, almost all of them in their teens. This was all that was left of the once impressive 25th SS Panzer Grenadier Regiment.[87]

When the division commander, SS Major General Meyer, realized that an attack on Carpiquet was imminent, he rushed all his reserves to the threatened zone. This "divisional reserve" consisted of two or three worn tanks and one 88mm antiaircraft gun.[88] Clearly "Panzer" Meyer was also scraping the bottom of the barrel.

Remarkable as it may seem, the Allies came out of this battle second-best. The SS lost the village of Carpiquet, but held the more critical airfield position against all comers. Even Field Marshal Montgomery complimented them on their "stout fight."[89] The Canadians fell back with "relatively enormous losses."[90] Neither side took prisoners in the desperate struggle. The Canadians tried to storm the airfield again the next day, but were again turned back.[91] Erwin Rommel had picked the right unit to defend the all-important city on the Orne.

Meanwhile, the men of the U.S. XIX Corps had pushed their way across the Vire and were smashing Combat Group Heinz, the last force between them and St. Lo. To prevent Rommel from pulling men out of his front lines to save St. Lo, Omar Bradley ordered his 1st Army to attack all along the line. Troy Middleton committed the VIII Corps reserve—the fresh 8th Infantry Division—to the fighting, and on July 9 the village of la Haye-du-Puits finally fell. At last the weather broke and U.S. fighter-bombers blasted German positions near the western coast of the Cotentin. Mont Castre fell on the evening of July 10. By July 13 German resistance on Rommel's extreme left flank had definitely weakened, and the U.S. VIII Corps had reached the high ground overlooking the Ay and Seves rivers. It had advanced across seven miles of hedgerow country in 11 days, at a cost of over 10,000 killed, wounded, or missing.[92]

General Collins' U.S. VII Corps also kept up the pressure, but not as effectively as Middleton's men. From July 8 to 15 it attacked the 17th SS Division and the remnants of the 6th Parachute Regiment, now supported by panzers and artillery elements from the 2nd Panzer Division. The VIIth gained very little ground in spite of tremendous losses. Major General Raymond Barton's 4th Infantry Division alone lost 2,300 men from July 5 to 15, including three battalion and nine company commanders. The 83rd Division lost 5,000 men in a similar period, along with half of its attached tanks, and also failed to break the thin German line. "The Germans are staying in there just by the guts of their soldiers," General Barton commented. "We outnumber them 10 to 1 in infantry, 50 to 1 in artillery, and by an infinite number in the air."[93] Just as in North Africa, Erwin Rommel was getting the maximum possible effort from his men; just as in North Africa, it would not be enough.

At the same time, 200 miles away, the strong 15th German Army—more than half the combat forces in Army Group B—lay idle. Adolf Hitler even now clung to the notion that this was not the invasion. The Allies, he maintained, would come at the Pas de Calais. The 15th Army sat inactive while her sister 7th Army and the 5th Panzer Army bled to death in the hedgerows of Normandy.

Meanwhile, as we have seen, Omar Bradley committed the 3rd Armored Division into the Vire bridgehead north of St. Lô while successfully pinning down all of Rommel's other forces in the U.S. zone. The order sending in the U.S. 3rd Armored could have been the key decision of the campaign if it had been made 24 hours later. On July 7, however, the bridgehead was not yet large enough to accommodate such a large tank force. The 3rd Armored was one of the two oversized American tank divisions. It had three main components: Combat Commands A, B, and Reserve (CCA, CCB, and CCR, respectively). It included 232 tanks instead of the normal 168, and 16,000 men instead of the standard 12,000. In the congestion of the battle area, CCB strung out for 20 miles on the single, rain-drenched, dirt, approach road. This bulky column crossed the single engineer tank bridge on the night of July 7/8, maintaining radio silence as ordered. This silence was a serious error. By the time its crossing was completed CCB was badly disorganized, and from that point on, almost everything that could go wrong did. Communications failed, coordination between tanks and artillery and tanks and infantry was almost nonexistent, a hasty infantry divisional commander relieved the leader of CCB, thus further disrupting U.S. Command channels, the commander of the XIX Corps fell ill, and the congestion on the single road south of the Vire severely restricted resupply efforts.[94] The entire operation—which could easily have been a victorious march into St. Lô—degenerated into a dreadful mess.

Erwin Rommel was quick to take advantage of his opponent's disorganization. He correctly judged the situation on the Vire to be more critical (at the moment) than that on the Orne, so he threw Panzer Lehr—his one reserve panzer division which he had just taken out of the line—into the contest. Rommel shifted this formation laterally across the rear area of the battle zone (a tricky maneuver), toward the crumbling sector. He also sent into the battle that part of the 2nd SS Panzer Division not yet engaged. This particular SS combat group amounted to a battalion of infantry and a company of tanks. Its mission was to slow down the Americans until General Bayerlein's armor arrived for the counterattack.[95]

Rommel's desperate measures should not have worked, but they did. The Americans had penetrated the Vire River against minimal opposition on July 7. Rommel put his counterattack plans into operation the same day. The U.S. forces which had brushed aside Combat Group Heinz had a clear shot for St. Lô late on the 7th, but the hasty commitment of the 3rd Armored Division had paralyzed their advance. It was July 10—two-and-a-half days later—before the confusion caused by this premature commitment abated, and the resupplied American drive could start up again. By that time the opportunity was lost, for the vanguard of Panzer Lehr had arrived on the battlefield.[96]

Bayerlein's attack, delivered in poor weather, knocked the breath out of the renewed American thrust for St. Lô. Unhindered by the U.S. Air Force, Colonel Joachim Gutmann's 902nd Panzer Grenadier Regiment, supported by 20 tanks, struck the U.S. 30th Infantry Division. On Gutmann's left Colonel Scholze's 901st Panzer Grenadier Regiment, supported by a dozen Panther tanks, mauled a regiment from the U.S. 9th Infantry Division. By 6:30 A.M. Panzer Lehr had pushed the Americans back two miles. The attack began to weaken before noon, however. The panzer division, down to one-third of its June 5 strength, proved too weak to defeat the combined efforts of the 3rd Armored, 30th Infantry, and 9th Infantry divisions. Bayerlein lost over 500 men and 32 tanks in the attempt, but American casualties were also high. The U.S. breakthrough was sealed off and the stalemate reimposed—at least temporarily.[97]

Rommel's days must have seemed to run together as crisis followed crisis, almost without letup. Each day he was relatively weaker than the day before. Eisenhower now had a million men in Europe. Rommel had probably fewer than 250,000. The 15th Army still idly guarded its unthreatened sector, while Hitler and his lackeys vacillated in East Prussia. In Normandy, the front was on the verge of collapse. Bradley and Montgomery ruthlessly threw fresh reserves into the cauldron, and Rommel met them with the same jaded forces. He knew that the day was rapidly approaching when they would break, and he said so. As usual, the Nazi High Command viewed him as an alarmist and ignored his pleas. Yet, he continued to hold off the invaders with all the genius and force of will he could muster.

The American offensive was not really defeated on July 11: it was simply checked for the moment. Meanwhile, with Panzer Lehr out of the line, Montgomery had launched yet another massive offensive against Caen. It began on the evening of July 7, the same day the American XIX Corps began its attack north of St. Lô. First a massive artillery bombardment virtually leveled the city, and then 500 R.A.F. four-engine bombers dropped 2,560 tons of high explosives on the ruins. The bombings lasted from 9:50 to 10:30 P.M., and killed an estimated 5,000 French civilians. Monty's ground attack began six hours later. The British field marshal ignored the advice of General Bradley, who recommended that he attack immediately after the last bomb fell. "Rush it and you'll get it," were his exact words.[98] Instead, Montgomery—showing the excessive caution which was his only major weakness as a military commander and for which he has been severely criticized—allowed the men of the 21st Panzer and Hitler Jugend divisions six hours to recover. When he struck at dawn, they were ready and waiting for him.[99]

About all the massive aerial and artillery bombardments had accomplished was to tip off the Germans that the offensive was coming. At 4:20 A.M. on July 8 General Dempsey's British 2nd Army attacked with 115,000 men, spearheaded by the fresh 59th (Staffordshire) Infantry Division, supported by the 3rd Armoured Division, and two Canadian tank brigades.[100] By July 9 the 12th SS Panzer Division had been pushed back about two miles and there was fighting in the northern suburbs. Hitler's orders were uncompromising: "Caen must be defended to the last man." The SS men responded, and bitter house-to-house fighting took place. The 1st Battalion of the 26th SS Panzer Grenadier Regiment particularly distinguished itself. The 1st Flak Battery of the 12th SS Flak Battalion knocked out a large number of Sherman tanks before it was overwhelmed. Obeying Hitler's order to the letter, it was completely wiped out.[101]

Fighting of this nature was too much, even for a hardened veteran like "Panzer" Meyer. He requested permission to evacuate the city, but his corps commander, Sepp Dietrich, turned down the request on the grounds that Hitler had forbidden it. Meyer retreated anyway. Later he said, "We were meant to die in Caen, but one just couldn't watch those youngsters being sacrificed to a senseless order."[102] That night he fell back south of the Orne, to the industrial suburbs of Colombelles and Faubourg de Vaucelles. Most of Caen was now in British hands.[103] The next morning, July 9, the British 3rd Division entered the city from the east and linked up with the Canadian 3rd Division, advancing from the west. By the end of the next day, the last cut-off pockets of German resistance had been mopped up.[104] Montgomery had his prize, which was now a sea of rubble. It had taken him more than four weeks to advance eight miles. The British 2nd Army had suffered more casualties than the British General Staff had projected for the entire balance of the war, and yet the German line was still intact. Rommel reestablished a front along the east bank of the Orne, [105] and most of his men were still in the hedgerows. The British still had not reached tank country, but they were only a river crossing away and in a position to establish themselves on the flat ground southeast of Caen. From there they could threaten the communications centers of Falaise and Argentan, which were critical to Army Group B; they could also threaten the Seine basin, Paris, and/or

Rouen and Le Havre; they would also be in a position to drive a wedge between the 5th Panzer and 15th armies.[106] Rommel had no choice but to defend this flat ground with the bulk of his surviving armor, at the expense of his western flank.

To the west of the burning city the Battle of Hill 112 was renewed on July 10. Meanwhile, a few miles away, Erwin Rommel met with Eberbach's chief of staff, Major General Gause. He and Rommel had served together from July 1941 until March 1944, except for about half of 1942, when Gause was recovering from wounds suffered in the Battle of the Gazala Line.[107] Early in the spring of 1944 they had had a personal falling out, and Rommel had replaced him as Chief of Staff of Army Group B. The Desert Fox continued to respect his former subordinate, however, and had asked General Rudolf Schmundt, the Army's chief personnel officer, to give Gause command of the next available panzer division.[108] Their personal differences now seemed to be entirely forgotten. Gause told Rommel that 5th Panzer Army was critically short on shells, but this was nothing new—all of Rommel's units were short on supplies of every description. The Allied air forces had totally disrupted the army group's rear area; bridges were down, railroads cut, barges sunk, transport destroyed, facilities demolished, depots smashed, and cities in rubble. Germany still had supplies, but it simply could not get them through to Army Group B. Gause told Rommel: "Our troops' morale is high, but courage alone won't be enough against the enemy's sheer weight of metal. Even our First World War veterans say they've never known anything like it. The enemy make up for their own poor morale by shelling and bombing."[109]

Even without the city, the high ground of Hill 112 was of great significance, because it still controlled the terrain between the Odon and the Orne. South of the Orne the *bocage* ended; therefore, to keep his right flank in good defensive territory, Rommel needed to hold this vital terrain feature. SS General Hausser, the 7th Army commander, considered Hill 112 to be the key to Normandy. General Bittick, leader of the II SS Panzer Corps, apparently agreed, because he committed the 502nd SS Heavy Panzer Battalion to the struggle. This elite group included the best of the SS tankers, mostly drafted into the unit from the Eastern Front. They were equipped with the PzKw VI (Tiger) tank, the best in the German arsenal. It was fortunate for the Germans that Bittick placed them here, for on July 10 the British hurled the 43rd Wessex Division, the Canadian 3rd Division, the 46th (Highland) Brigade, the 4th Armoured Brigade, and the 31st

Army Tank Brigade into the struggle for the hill. By midnight the situation was critical, despite the skill of the defenders. Each side occupied half of the hill by that time.[110]

The next day the grenadiers of the 9th and 10th SS Panzer divisions (II SS Panzer Corps) launched a counterattack. They gained some ground, but not much. Both sides suffered heavy losses in hard fighting.

In the next week the battle tottered back and forth in a real slugfest. On July 12 the British took the hill, but the SS took it back the next day. By July 15 the Tiger battalion was isolated on the crest, but they held on, despite the cost. The next day they were rescued by the 9th SS Panzer Division.[111] Meanwhile, the British I Corps, led by the 51st Infantry Division, attempted to take Colombelles (across the river from Caen) but was thrown back. At last, the Allies gave up the contest and regrouped. Montgomery reorganized, committing the Canadian II Corps (2nd and 3rd Infantry divisions) and the British XII Corps to the line.[112] The Germans also took advantage of this short lull by digging in. The SS panzer troops entrenched themselves on Hill 112 so well that they held it until the end of July.[113]

In Washington and London, top-level staffs and politicians spoke of the crisis in Normandy. Even General Eisenhower was worried. It seemed that Hitler's "hold at all costs" strategy was working. Montgomery's invasion force was pinned down by Field Marshal Rommel. It occupied a narrow bridgehead 10 to 20 miles deep—hardly a fifth of what Eisenhower and his Supreme Headquarters planned for it to hold by that date. It was feared that the Germans might bring up their reserves and hold the Allies in the Cotentin until the onset of winter. This would be a disaster of unforeseeable magnitude. Winter weather would deny the Allies the use of their most important weapon: air power. Also, it was by no means certain that they could continue to supply their huge 21st Army Group throughout the winter. Cherbourg was still virtually useless and the winter storms would doubtless wreck the surviving artificial harbor. With no other port facilities, the supply situation could conceivably grow very bleak indeed. Rommel might even succeed in pushing the Allies back into the sea.[114]

At last Hitler and his advisors were weakening in their insistence that the Normandy landings were not the real invasion. In the first and second weeks in July they released four infantry divisions from the 15th Army at Pas de Calais. Three of these were earmarked for the Caen sector, where elements of the 5th Panzer Army could expect some relief at last. It might even be possible for Rommel to establish a significant mobile reserve.[115] Montgomery was certainly concerned about this possibility. He wrote later:

> There were two very disquieting developments in the enemy situation during the first week in July. The identification of the 2nd SS Panzer Division in the American sector . . . showed the enemy's determination to strengthen his resistance in the west in spite of 2nd [British] Army's endeavours to prevent it. Moreover, we had identified fresh infantry divisions on the eastern sectors, which were relieving Panzer formations in the line; during the week 1st SS, 2nd SS, Lehr and 21st Panzer divisions were known to have been withdrawn wholly or partially into reserve.[116]

The situation was not quite as dark as this passage might suggest, for all these German units were wholly or largely burnt out. Still, it was a dangerous trend: the Desert Fox was trying not only to stall the invasion but to seal it off in depth. Despite all obstacles, he was beginning to meet with some success.

Rommel was not going to form a strong mobile reserve if the Americans could prevent it. Doggedly, they launched another series of attacks near St. Lô, using their XIX and V corps. Major General Gerow's V included the 1st Infantry, 2nd Infantry, and 2nd Armored divisions. Colbert's XIX Corps still had the 29th, 30th, and 35th Infantry divisions. Again they faced the II Parachute Corps of General Eugen Meindl. He had an assortment of battered and understrength units, which were formed up in two very mixed divisions. On the left flank, a battle group from each of the 266th, 352nd, and 353rd Infantry divisions was placed under the operational control of the 352nd Infantry Division Headquarters. On the right flank stood the reduced 3rd Parachute Division. The 12th Assault Gun Brigade was in support. Panzer Lehr, which was exhausted, was transferred to the LXXXIV Corps, and occupied a sector of the front line further west. Meindl had almost no tanks and very few reserves.[117]

The Americans began to close in on St. Lô on July 11, when the V Corps attacked Hill 192, which overlooked the St. Lô-Bayeux road east of the city. The hill was defended by a single parachute battalion. It was attacked by the entire U.S. 2nd Infantry Division. The 2nd's divisional artillery alone fired 20,000 rounds that day. In all, 45 tons of high explosive shells were hurled at the position. The battle began at 6:00 A.M., and the hill fell at noon. Only 15 paratroopers surrendered.[118]

Hausser ordered Meindl to retake the hill at all costs. That paratroop general, however, was more concerned with holding his disintegrating front together than with trying to obey an order that no longer made sense. He had almost nothing in reserve, and certainly not enough to eject the entire U.S. 2nd Infantry Division. He was very much relieved when the Americans did not press their success by continuing to attack southward. Had they done so, they might have achieved their decisive breakthrough then and there.[119]

Bradley was more concerned with St. Lô at this moment than with a long-range breakthrough. Indeed, the capture of this ruined departmental capital preoccupied the minds of the American political and military leaders at this time. They badly needed a victory, for propaganda reasons if nothing else. They also needed the road network of which St. Lô was the major junction; in addition, the high ground near the city dominated a considerable stretch of hedgerow country. However, St. Lô was not as important as Caen in the strategic sense, because the *bocage* country did not end just south of the city, but continued for several miles beyond.

While the U.S. V Corps took Hill 192, U.S. XIX Corps also began a major thrust toward the city, which lay barely four miles south of its front line. They struck out toward Hill 112,* the key position north of St. Lô and second only to Hill 192 in tactical importance. Unfortunately, attacking toward this hill meant that they would be confronted by dozens of hedgerows, defended by veteran soldiers. Six battalions of U.S. heavy artillery—155mm, 4.5-inch, and 8-inch guns—blasted Meindl's line. The attack did not begin until afternoon, when it was reasonably certain that Panzer Lehr would not renew its offensive. Had the Americans attacked here 24 hours earlier, before Bayerlein filled the gap, Rommel's center would have penetrated and the entire German front might have come unglued. There was no way they could have known this, however. Now a brutal fight ensued, and both sides suffered heavy losses. The battle became general all along the line. By nightfall the 3rd Parachute Division was reduced to 35 percent of its authorized strength. The 353rd Division's battle group had lost around 800 men: about 80 percent of its original force. Most of these losses were inflicted by the enemy's artillery. Meindl was forced to commit his last reserves to prevent a disaster.[120]

---

*Not to be confused with the other Hill 112, located near Caen.

Eugen Meindl called SS General Hausser at 7th Army HQ and requested reinforcements. Specifically, he wanted the regiment of the 5th Parachute Division which was just arriving from Brittany, but Hausser refused to turn it over. He believed that the defeat of Panzer Lehr's recent counterattack placed the LXXXIV Corps' sector west of St. Lô in even greater danger of collapse than Meindl's. The airborne commander did not argue, but tartly remarked that someone was going to have to come up with a brilliant plan very soon if the Americans were to be countered.[121]

The German resistance had also taken its toll. The American spearhead, the 29th Infantry Division, was unable to keep up the pressure the next day. They continued to attack on July 12–13, but gained little ground. Seeing that this tough outfit was temporarily exhausted, General Colbert shifted the burden of the attack to the 35th Infantry Division. They gained ground on the right flank of the German 352nd Division and soon threatened to cut it off in a bend of the Vire River. The 352nd, in battle since D-Day, had met 40 American attacks in the last three days. Now it finally wavered, but the Americans were again too slow. Meindl had finally received some reinforcements in the form of the remnants of the 30th Mobile Brigade and a battle group from the 266th Infantry Division, both of which he immediately committed to the threatened zone. This move again slowed the American momentum, but did not stop it entirely. The remnants of the 352nd escaped, but three days later, on the morning of July 16, the U.S. 1st Army captured Hill 122, just 3,000 yards north of St. Lô. The fall of the city was now just a matter of time.[122]

The next day, July 17, Hausser requested permission to abandon the city. His chief of staff, Major General Max Pemsel, telephoned Rommel's operations officer at Army Group B Headquarters. Pemsel wanted the request forwarded to OB West and then on to OKW, which meant Hitler. Colonel Tempelhoff thought this was impractical, for he knew what the reply would be. His answer to Pemsel is noteworthy. "You take whatever measures you think are necessary," Tempelhoff said. "If you have to withdraw, go ahead; just report to us afterwards that the enemy penetrated your main line of resistance in several places and that you barely succeeded in reestablishing a new line to the rear."[123] Rommel had chosen his staff well. The II Parachute Corps escaped annihilation, despite Hitler's order. The city fell on July 19. However, Meindl still occupied the heights a mile south of St. Lô. Bradley had captured only a large mass of ruins, at the cost of over 5,000 casualties in six days. Since its attacks began on July 3, the U.S.

1st Army had lost 40,000 men.[124] The Americans were still bogged down in hedgerow country, and the German front was still intact.

While the Americans slugged their way toward St. Lo, Rommel faced another threat on his right flank. With typical determination he pivoted to meet it. This turned out to be his last battle. Appropriately, it was against his old foe from North Africa, Sir Bernard Law Montgomery.

The fall of that part of the Caen urban area north of the Orne had improved Monty's overall position only a little. As long as the Germans held the southern suburbs, they still held the neck of the Caen bottle. The end of the hedgerow country was in sight, but Montgomery still could not get there. Therefore, in view of the overall deterioration of the Allies' strategic position, he decided to launch yet another offensive on July 15, with the big punch coming on July 17. It was code-named "Goodwood," and had the objective of breaking free into the tank country south of Caen.

The initial thrust came on the British right flank and was launched by their XXX and newly committed XII corps. It was aimed at the high ground south of Villers-Bocage but its real objectives was apparently to pin down the German reserves. The Allies gained a little ground against the XXXXVII Panzer Corps and were three miles west of Tilly when nightfall came.[125]

The offensive on the British left began on the night of July 16/17, when their 53rd Infantry Division took the village of Cahier north of the Orne. Fifth Panzer Army retook it the next day in heavy fighting, but another threat posed itself almost immediately: the British I Corps attacked Colombelles, and Eberbach had to throw the 21st Panzer Division back into the battle to prevent them from overrunning the suburbs south of Caen. Montgomery believed his attacks had left Rommel with only one panzer division uncommitted: the burnt-out 12th SS, which was licking its wounds in the woods south of Falaise. By dawn on July 18, Montgomery's attacks had pinned down the 10th SS Panzer Division near Esquay, the 9th SS Panzer near Evrecy and Maltot, as well as the 21st Panzer at Colombelles. Now Monty unleashed his main attack: it came from the Allied far left flank, out of the airborne bridgehead east of the Orne River.[126] This sector had huge drawbacks. First, its assembly areas were visible to the German positions at Bois de Bavent and Colombes. Second, it was constricted, with a narrow frontage. The armored divisions Montgomery committed from here would have to advance in file instead of on line, which would greatly reduce their effectiveness. Third, the Germans had a string of fortified villages and outposts all along the left flank of the route of advance. These were coordinated, prepared positions, with overlapping fields of fire. The British left flank would be exposed throughout the length of its initial advance. Fourth, the bridgehead was too small to allow for the maximum employment of artillery. Fifth, the road network was small and in poor condition, at least partially resulting from Allied shelling. Traffic congestion would be a major problem.[127]

Field Marshal Montgomery had three British armored divisions available for the attack: the 7th, 11th, and Guards, all under British VII Corps. In addition, 500 reserve tanks were already in Normandy and the Canadian 4th Armoured and Polish 1st Armored divisions, now in England, stood ready for embarkation to the continent. Heavy losses, therefore, would be acceptable if the decisive breakthrough could be made.[128]

As previously mentioned, the British armored divisions would have to advance in file (that is, one behind the other) instead of on line. Montgomery picked Major General "Pip" Roberts's veteran 11th Armoured to lead the way, followed by the Guards and 7th Armoured. The Canadian infantry would cover the left flank, the British the right.[129] This scheme of operations was not a very satisfactory arrangement, but Montgomery felt sure his spearheads would be able to reach the Orne Canal, bridge it, brush aside the remnants of the 12th SS Panzer Division, and capture Falaise to the south. If successful, the offensive would destroy three German divisions, unglue Rommel's whole front, and open the gates to Paris.[130]

The British counted on air power to pave the way. The bombardment represented the greatest air concentration in history to that date. A thousand British Lancaster and Halifax heavy bombers and 1,500 U.S. Fortress and Liberator heavy bombers, followed by 600 British and American medium bombers, would saturate an 8,000 yard sector with 12,000 tons of bombs—5,000 tons of which would fall in less than 45 minutes. They would be supported by more than 2,000 fighters. British Air Vice Marshal Broadhurst, commander of this vast armada, remarked: "I don't really know what bit of air will be left unoccupied when the show starts."[131] In addition to the aerial blitzkrieg, naval gunfire and 720 field artillery pieces, which had 250,000 rounds to fire, would blast the German strong points. The Canadian 2nd and 3rd Infantry divisions would attack into the gap thus created and secure its flanks. An entire armored corps would then attack through the hole in Rommel's line—into tank country! Paris and the destruction of Army Group B seemed within Montgomery's grasp.

Unfortunately, as Major General J. F. C. Fuller wrote, "The Germans ... had seen through these clumsy tactics."[132] Rommel met with Sepp Dietrich and Wilhelm Bittick, the commanders of the I SS and II SS Panzer corps, respectively. They concluded that the Allied offensive was imminent, and would come in the zone of the 16th Luftwaffe Field Division, the worst combat unit in the Army Group. They had already been routed once, it will be recalled, and there was no reason to believe that they would perform any better now.[133] Accordingly, Rommel brought up two fresh formations to meet the Allied thrust. These were the newly arrived 272nd Infantry and 1st SS Panzer Division "Leibstandarte Adolf Hitler."[134] Montgomery thought the SS panzer division was fully committed near Esquay, but he was mistaken.[135] Rommel also concentrated a few remaining Tiger tanks, 194 field guns, 272 of the six-barreled Nebelwerfer rocket launchers,[136] and 78 88mm antiaircraft guns at Bourguebus Ridge. This position was out of the range of British artillery, but in the Allies' suspected route of advance. The U.S. 8th Air Force was supposed to bomb this general area, but apparently Allied intelligence failed to detect the camouflaged positions of the 88s. In any event they were completely missed by the bombs, and were ready when Monty unleashed his tanks.[137]

The carpet bombing began at 5:00 A.M. on July 17. The 16th Luft-waffe Field Division was totally destroyed. The last 50 tanks of the 22nd Panzer Regiment, 21st Panzer Division, were bombed in their positions near Emieville. All of them were hit, and most of them were destroyed. To the shock of the Allies, however, the Desert Fox had estab-lished not one but five defensive zones to deal with the offensive. They consisted of a line of infantry to absorb the initial shock, a supporting line of tanks immediately behind them, a line of strong points with antitank guns, strong artillery concentrations in concealed positions, and a second line of strong points with mobile reserves (including panzers) some miles behind. "Twelve thousand tons of bombs did not succeed in cracking this formida-ble obstacle," Admiral Ruge wrote.[138]

The main attack ran right into Rommel's flak nest at Bourguebus Ridge, where it immediately bogged down.[139] The II SS Panzer Corps quickly committed its Tiger companies, along with elements of the newly attached 1st SS Panzer Division. The British armored spearhead, which expected only scattered resistance, was halted in confusion. At nightfall, SS Major General Wisch, the commander of the Leibstandarte, launched a counter-attack with his Panthers. They alone shot up 80 British tanks. The British 11st Armoured Division lost 126 tanks that day—over half its total strength. The Guards Armoured Division lost another 60 on the Caen-Vimont road, all victims of the flak nest. In all, Montgomery lost 200 tanks on the first day of the offensive.[140] "Goodwood" had been stopped in its tracks, its back broken. There was even some talk of relieving Field Marshal Montgomery of his command for the abject failure of this offensive.[141] Erwin Rommel had won a major victory. He did not know it, however, for he was lying unconscious in a field hospital, and was not expected to live.

"A Pitiless Destiny"

At 4:00 P.M. on July 17, 1944, Field Marshal Erwin Rommel left the headquarters of the II SS Panzer Corps, on his way back to La Roche-Guyon. He never reached it. What happened to him was not unusual: it happened to thousands of German soldiers on the Western Front in 1944 and 1945. Captain Helmuth Lang, his aide, was with him at the time. He later told the story of Rommel's last hours as a military commander.

"All along the roads we could see transport in flames: from time to time enemy bombers forced us to take to second-class roads. About 6:00 P.M. the Marshal's car was in the neighborhood of Livarot. Transport which had just been attacked was piled up along the road and strong groups of enemy dive-bombers were still at work close by. That is why we turned off along a sheltered road, to join the main road again two and a half miles from Vimoutiers.

"When we reached it we saw above Livarot about eight enemy dive-bombers. We learnt later that they had been interfering with traffic on the main road from Livarot to Vimoutiers. Suddenly Sergeant Holke, our spotter, warned us that two aircraft were flying in our direction. The driver, Daniel, was told to put on speed and turn off on a little side road to the right, about 300 yards ahead of us, which would give us some shelter.

"Before we could reach it, the enemy aircraft, flying at great speed only a few feet above the road, came up to within 500 yards of us and the first one opened fire. Marshal Rommel was looking back at this moment. The left-hand side of the car was hit by the first burst. A cannon-shell shattered Daniel's left shoulder and left arm. Marshal Rommel was wounded in the face by broken glass and received a blow on the left temple and cheekbone which caused a triple fracture of the skull and made him lose consciousness immediately. Major Neuhaus was struck on the holster of his revolver and the force of the blow broke his pelvis.

"As a result of his serious wounds, Daniel, the driver, lost control of the car. It struck the stump of a tree, skidded over to the left of the road, and then turned over in a ditch on the right. Captain Lang and Sergeant Holke jumped out of the car and took shelter on the right of the road. Marshal Rommel, who, at the start of the attack, had hold of the handle of the door, was thrown out, unconscious, when the car turned over and lay stretched out on the road about twenty yards behind it. A second aircraft flew over and tried to drop bombs on those who were lying on the ground."[1]

Rommel's left cheekbone was destroyed, he had numerous shell splinters and fragments in his head, his left eye was injured, his skull badly fractured, and his temple penetrated. It was 45 minutes before Captain Lang and Sergeant Holke could get him to a French religious hospital. At first it was thought that there was no chance of him living through such serious wounds.[2]

Later that night the Field Marshal, still unconscious, was transferred to the Luftwaffe hospital at Bernay, about 25 miles away. His driver, Corporal Daniel, also unconscious, was transported with him. That night, doctors operated on the driver but were unable to save his life. He never regained consciousness.[3]

The average 52-year-old man probably would have died from the wounds Rommel received on July 17. However, Field Marshal Rommel's years of physical training and his strong constitution worked for him, and within a few days he had recovered enough to be moved to the more sophisticated hospital of Professor Esch at Vesinet.[4] A few weeks later he went home to Germany. He did not realize it yet, but he was as good as dead.

Up until Adolf Hitler interfered with his conduct of the Battle of El Alamein on November 3, 1942, Erwin Rommel had been completely loyal to him. On that day, the Fuehrer issued a senseless "stand fast" order which led to the virtual destruction of Panzer Army Afrika. Rommel was never able to regain the initiative in North Africa after that. Even after El Alamein, the Marshal continued to accord Hitler the respect due him as chief of state, even if the dictator pursued a military policy that no longer made sense. Only gradually did his attitude begin to change. He was bitter about the loss of so many men in North Africa, where Germany lost 130,000 men when Tunisia fell. Rommel could have overrun Egypt and captured the Suez Canal if he had been given only a small fraction of this Army Group just a few months before.

Exactly when Rommel learned of the mass murders of Himmler's SS, or who told him, is not known. We do have some clues, however. In December 1943, his son Manfred asked his permission to join the Waffen-SS. Rommel curtly rejected this idea as "out of the question." He would not allow his son to serve under the command of a man who carried out mass killings.

"Do you mean Himmler?" Manfred asked.

"Yes," the Marshal replied. At this time Rommel did not know how deeply Hitler was involved in this mass slaughter, or even if he knew about it at all.[5]

It was only in the early months of 1944 that he learned of the magnitude of the Nazis' crimes, and of the extent of Hitler's involvement in them. His son wrote: "From that moment on, all my father's inner allegiance to Adolf Hitler, whom he had once admired, was destroyed, and he brought himself, from his knowledge of the Fuehrer's crimes, to act against him."[6]

Although he did not realize it at the time, Rommel first became connected with the conspiracy to assassinate Adolf Hitler in February 1944. At that time he was visited by Doctor Stroelin, the mayor of Stuttgart. Stroelin came to Rommel at the request of Doctor Goerdeler, the former mayor of Leipzig and a leading member of the conspiracy. They discussed the possibility of a legal change of government and the means to end the war.[7] Stroelin, however, moved too quickly for a man like Rommel, who was a straightforward soldier and really was out of his element in the realm of power politics. With Rommel's wife, son, and friend Hermann Aldinger present, the Stuttgart mayor made a speech on the subject of the criminality of Hitler and the Nazis. He even had documentary proof that they were systematically committing genocide against the Jews. Finally he said: "If Hitler does not die, then we are all lost." That was really too much for the professional soldier, who exclaimed, "Herr Stroelin, I would be grateful if you would refrain from speaking such opinions in the presence of my young son!"[8] Stroelin, realizing he had gone too far too fast, packed up and departed, but Rommel would have cause to think of their meeting again. In fact, from this day on Rommel inched nearer and nearer to the conspirator's orbit, although he never advocated actually killing Hitler. It would have no doubt surprised Rommel if the mayor had told him the whole truth: the conspirators' plans to assassinate the Fuehrer were already well advanced; Stroelin and several other members of the resistance intended to make Erwin Rommel President of the Reich!

Other powerful or important Germans had already joined or were soon to join the secret resistance movement. They all realized the war was lost, and hoped to rid Germany of the madman in Rastenburg before he went down to final defeat and dragged the whole nation with him. General of Infantry Alexander von Falkenhausen, the Military Governor of Belgium and Northern France, cast his lot with the plotters. Rommel's chief of staff, Doctor Hans Speidel, was a longtime advocate of the removal of Adolf Hitler, by whatever means necessary. General Heinrich von Stuelpnagel, the Military Governor of France, met Rommel at a country house near St. Germain early that spring. Von Stuelpnagel, his chief of staff, Lieutenant Colonel Caesar von Hofacker, and Rommel all agreed that the Nazi regime must be overthrown. Both Rommel and the military governor told Field Marshal von Rundstedt of their discussions.[9] The aging marshal's reaction was typical of the senior German commanders of the time. He would not help them, but he would do nothing to stop them either. "You are young. You know and love the people. *You* do it!" were his exact words to the Desert Fox. Like far too many men who could have made a difference, he acquiesced.[10] All too many generals in the top echelon, who showed great physical courage, lacked the moral fortitude to stand up against their supreme commander, even when it became obvious that he was a madman. This was the true tragedy of the German officer corps in World War II.

Rommel's interest in the conspiracy increased as the time for the Allied invasion approached. Sometime after May 15 he met with General of Artillery Eduard Wagner, the First Quartermaster General of the Army. For the first time he was informed of the active resistance, the planned revolt, and of the previous attempts on Hitler's life. He learned that a bomb once had been placed aboard Hitler's airplane, but had failed to explode. He learned that a certain Captain von dem Bussche had been prepared to blow himself up to kill the Fuehrer, but could not manage to get close enough to carry out his plan. Rommel, as always politically naive, objected to the idea of assassination. He wanted Hitler arrested and forced to stand trial for his crimes.[11] He did not want to create a great Nazi martyr. Wagner's comments concerning Rommel's rather idealistic views are not recorded. It is known, however, that Rommel did not change Wagner's mind, nor the minds of his associates. Men with greater political vision were in charge of the plot, and Rommel's notions could not divert them from their course. Coolly, with great courage and strength of character, they plotted to blow up Adolf Hitler.

The real leader of the conspiracy was Colonel Count Claus von Stauffenberg, the Chief of Staff to the Commander-in-Chief of the Replacement Army, headquartered in Berlin. Von Stauffenberg had served briefly in Rommel's Army Group Afrika and, although they had met only professionally, von Stauffenberg considered Rommel "a great leader."[12] While acting as Operations Officer of the 10th Panzer Division in April 1943, von Stauffenberg, like Rommel a year later, fell victim to an Allied fighter-bomber. His left arm was now useless, and one of his eyes was gone, but he soldiered on. This human dynamo became the catalytic agent for the conspiracy. Around himself he rallied the best men still alive in Nazi Germany. They included Colonel General Ludwig Beck, the former Chief of the General Staff and Prussia's last philosopher-in-uniform; Admiral Wilhelm Canaris, the Chief of the Bureau of Intelligence; and Julius Leber, the former Socialist member of the Reichstag, who was so tough that not even the Gestapo could get a single word out of him despite weeks of prolonged torture. Other members of the resistance included Count Helmuth von Moltke, a diplomat and a descendant of the field marshal who defeated and captured Napoleon III at Sedan; General Helmuth Stieff, the Chief of the Organization Branch at OKH; Albrecht Haushofer, the son of Professor Karl Haushofer and a noted geopolitical thinker in his own right; Field Marshal Erwin von Witzleben, the former C-in-C West, now retired; Count Wolf von Helldorf, Police President of Berlin; General Erich Hoepner, former commander of the 1st Panzer Army; Ulrich von Hassell, former German ambassador to Rome; Count Friedrich Werner von Schulenburg, former ambassador to Moscow; Father Alfred Delp, a Jesuit leader; Major General Henning von Treschow, the Chief of Staff of Army Group Center, now fighting for its life on the Eastern Front; and dozens of others.

The addition of Rommel as a sympathizer apparently provided new momentum to the conspirators. Colonel General Dollmann and Colonel General von Salmuth both told Rommel that they were prepared to obey his orders, even if they were in direct contradiction to those issued by Adolf Hitler. General Geyr von Schweppenburg also made a similar pronouncement. Lieutenant General Count Lutz von Schwerin of the 116th Panzer Division and Lieutenant General Baron Heinrich von Luettwitz of the 2nd Panzer Division declared to the Field Marshal that their units would be available for use against the Nazi regime.[13]

On July 9 Lieutenant Colonel von Hofacker visited Rommel at La Roche-Guyon. Von Hofacker had a great deal of personal influence with Rommel because his father had commanded Lieutenant Rommel on the Italian Front in World War I.[14] Also, the military situation had deteriorated considerably since von Hofacker and his chief, General von Stuelpnagel, had first met with Rommel early that spring. The Desert Fox would take to heart anything young Hofacker had to say.

The persuasive staff officer spoke of the growing German resistance to Nazism, and urged independent military action to end the war in the West. He asked Rommel how long the Normandy Front could be held. They needed to know in Berlin, he said, in order to know how to proceed against Hitler. "At the most 14 days to three weeks," Rommel replied, with typical candor. "Then a breakthrough may be expected. We have no additional forces to throw into the battle." Von Hofacker departed to visit von Kluge, but promised to meet with Rommel again on July 15.[15]

Before that date, Rommel conferred with all of hi top commanders. It is possible that he was sounding them out, to determine what they would do if Hitler was arrested. Even SS Generals Dietrich and Hausser disagreed with Hitler's conduct of the war. Dietrich went so far as to demand "independent action if the front is broken." Finally on July 17, just hours before he was wounded, the Desert Fox went so far as to ask Dietrich, "Would you always execute my orders, even if they contradicted the Fuehrer's orders?"

Dietrich extended his hand, and replied, "You're the boss, Herr Feldmarschall. I obey only you—whatever it is you're planning."[16] If Dietrich was to be believed, Rommel could expect no resistance from the Waffen-SS in Normandy if Hitler was removed.[17]

On July 12 Field Marshal von Kluge visited his most brilliant and most difficult subordinate at La Roche-Guyon. The two marshals discussed the deteriorating military situation and found themselves in complete agreement, for a change. Rommel suggested that the army and corps commanders forward an ultimatum to Hitler, and take bilateral action against him if he rejected it, as expected. Von Kluge listened attentively and agreed in principle to Rommel's statements. However, "Clever Hans" would not commit himself to the hilt. He said he would make his final decision after discussions with the army commanders. After von Kluge left, Rommel told his chief of staff that he would take independent action against the Nazi dictator, no matter what von Kluge decided.[18] Unlike Field Marshal von Kluge, Rommel was motivated solely by his sense of duty and morality, and by his love for Germany. As always, since the first day he put on the uniform as a private soldier, he stood ready to sacrifice himself for his country.

Three days later Rommel sent the following message to Adolf Hitler. History has since labeled it the ultimatum of July 15. It drove another nail into Rommel's coffin, and read:

HQ, 15 July

C-in-C, Army Group B

The situation on the Normandy front is growing worse every day and is now approaching a grave crisis.

Due to the severity of the fighting, the enemy's enormous use of material—above all, artillery and tanks—and the effect of his unrestricted command of the air over the battle area, our casualties are so high that the fighting power of our divisions is rapidly diminishing. Replacements from home are few in number and, with the difficult transport situation, take weeks to get to the front. As against 97,000 casualties (including 2,360 officers)—i.e., an average of 2,500 to 3,000 a day—replacements to date number 10,000, of whom about 6,000 have actually arrived at the front.

Material losses are also huge and have so far been replaced on a very small scale; in tanks, for example, only 17 replacements have arrived to date as compared with 225 losses.

The newly arrived infantry divisions are raw and, with their small establishment of artillery, antitank guns and close-combat anti-tank weapons, are in no state to make a lengthy stand against major enemy attacks coming after hours of drum-fire and heavy bombing. The fighting has shown that with this use of material by the enemy, even the bravest army will be smashed piece by piece, losing men, arms, and territory in the process.

Owing to the destruction of the railway system and the threat of the enemy air force to roads and tracks up to 90 miles behind the front, supply conditions are so bad that only the barest essentials can be brought to the front. It is consequently now necessary to exercise the greatest economy in all fields, and especially in artillery and mortar ammunition. These conditions are unlikely to improve, as enemy action is steadily reducing the transport capacity available. Moreover, this activity in the air is likely to become even more effective as the numerous air-strips in the bridgehead are taken into use.

No new forces of any consequence can be brought up to the Normandy front except by weakening Fifteenth Army's front on the Channel, or the Mediterranean front in southern France. Yet Seventh Army's front, taken over all, urgently requires two fresh divisions, as the troops in Normandy are exhausted.

On the enemy's side, fresh forces and great quantities of war material are flowing into his front every day. His supplies are undisturbed by our air force. Enemy pressure is growing steadily stronger.

In these circumstances we must expect that in the foreseeable future the enemy will succeed in breaking through our thin front, above all, Seventh Army's, and thrusting deep into France. Apart from the Panzer Group's sector reserves, which are at present tied down by the fighting on their own front and—due to the enemy's command of the air—can only move by night, we dispose of no mobile reserve for the defence against such a breakthrough. Action by our air force will, as in the past, have little effect.

The troops are everywhere fighting heroically, but the unequal struggle is approaching its end. It is urgently necessary for the proper political conclusions to be drawn from this situation. As C-in-C of the Army Group I feel myself in duty bound to speak plainly on this point.

(signed) ROMMEL[19]

In transmitting the message, the word "political" was omitted from the last paragraph. Field Marshal von Kluge endorsed Rommel's ultimatum and stated that he agreed with the Desert Fox's opinions and demands. "I have given him his last chance," Rommel snapped. "If he does not take it, we will act!"[20]

The next day, July 16, Rommel made a rare visit to 15th Army's sector, and looked up Lieutenant Colonel Elmar Warning, a former member of the operations staff of the Afrika Korps. The physically huge Warning, now Operations Officer of the 17th Luftwaffe Field Division at Le Havre, had been the one on whom Rommel had unburdened himself at El Alamein in early November 1942, when Hitler first sent him a senseless "stand-fast" order.

"Field Marshal von Kluge and I have sent the Fuehrer an ultimatum, telling him the war can't be won militarily and asking him to draw the consequences," Rommel said.

"What if the Fuehrer refuses?" Warning wanted to know.

"Then I'm going to open up the Western Front!" Rommel cried, "because there's only one thing that matters now—the British and Americans must get to Berlin before the Russians do!"[21]

As we have seen, Rommel did not have a chance to act. Two days after writing the ultimatum, and the day after his visit to Warning, an Allied fighter-bomber cut him down. Now it was up to Count von Stauffenberg. He would act, without Rommel's help.

Meanwhile, disaster struck Nazi Germany on the Eastern Front. On June 22 the Russians launched their summer offensive of 1944. They broke through the thinly held lines of Army Group Center with over a million men and could not be stopped. Hitler fired the Army Group commander, Field Marshal Ernest Busch, even though he was a loyal Nazi, and replaced him with Field Marshal Walther Model. This change in leadership did no good, however, because both the 4th and the 9th armies (and much of the weakened 3rd Panzer Army) were already destroyed. The Russians penetrated 150 miles in a week, and the front on both sides of the Pripet Marshes collapsed. Army Group Center was done for as an effective combat force. Army Group North was cut off in Courland, its back to the Baltic Sea. By the end of July the surviving German soldiers had been driven back to the Vistula, near Warsaw. As was the case in the West, there was very little left to stop the enemy from pushing all the way to Berlin.

On July 20, 1944, the one-armed Chief of Staff of the Replacement Army arrived at Hitler's headquarters in East Prussia with a bomb in his briefcase. He placed it under Hitler's table, barely six feet from the Fuehrer, and then left. Unfortunately, Colonel Heinz Brandt bumped into the count's briefcase. Annoyed by the inconvenience, he moved it. He shifted it only a few feet, but in doing so he placed it on the other side of a thick oaken table support. When he did that he changed history. Moments later this support deflected the force of the explosion away from Adolf Hitler. Brandt had saved Hitler's life, though not his own. General Korten, Chief of the Luftwaffe General Staff, and several other important officers were killed by the blast. Rommel's only real friend at Fuehrer Headquarters, General Rudolf Schmundt, was blinded and mortally wounded, dying in agony several weeks later. Colonel General Jodl was among those hurt; only Field Marshal Keitel was completely uninjured. The one for whom the exercise had been planned, however, escaped unscathed. Adolf Hitler emerged from the ruins of his bunker, stunned by the blast. It took him some time to recover enough to react, but when he did his reaction was murderous. "I will smash and destroy these criminals who have presumed to stand in the way of Providence and myself!" he screamed in rage. "They deserve nothing but ignominious death! And I shall give it to them! This time the full measure will be paid by all who are involved, and by their families."[22] Erwin Rommel's fate was sealed, along with that of von Stauffenberg, Beck, von Hofacker, and hundreds of others.

For several days after being wounded, the hero of North Africa lay in that gray world between life and death. He was not expected to survive his first night in the French hospital. Then he made some progress, slowly, as if by pure force of will. While he recovered, the Battle of Normandy reached its climax.

Despite his heavy losses in "Goodwood," Montgomery continued to slug it out in the Caen sector, pinning down the panzer reserves of Army Group B. Field Marshal von Kluge assumed personal command of the army group following Rommel's wounding, and also retained command of OB West. His consolidation of power in his own hands did nothing to improve Germany's position, however.

On July 19, the armored divisions of the British VIII Corps continued to be held up by I SS Panzer Corps and Rommel's deep defensive obstacles, while the British I Corps remained bogged down near Troarn. The Canadian II Corps, however, gained some ground and cleared the Caen suburbs of Faubourg de Vaucelles and Colombes. The 1st SS, 9th SS, 10th SS, and part of the 2nd Panzer divisions were decisively engaged. The battle finally ended the next day when it rained and the battlefield turned into "a sea of mud."[23] The British offensive on the German right flank had been halted; meanwhile, however, the Americans were preparing to deliver the decisive blow miles to the west.

Shortly after the attempt on Hitler's life, the scales fell from the eyes of the High Command, and it began to grasp the fact that Normandy was really the site of the Great Invasion. At last infantry divisions from 15th

Army started to march down to Normandy as fast as their feet or ruined transportation system would carry them.

"The decision was made too late," Field Marshal Montgomery wrote later. "The divisions arrived so slowly and so piecemeal that they were to find themselves reinforcing failure."[24]

On July 24 a force of some 1,600 heavy and medium bombers was scheduled to obliterate Lieutenant General Bayerlein's Panzer Lehr Division in the 7th Army's zone. They were called back at the last minute because of the weather, but almost 100 of them dropped their bombs anyway. Most of these bombs fell within American lines, killing more than 100 men, including Lieutenant General Leslie J. McNair, Chief of U.S. Army Ground Forces and commander of the fictitious 1st U.S. Army Group, which Berlin believed would deliver the real invasion blow at Pas de Calais. McNair was secretly buried and replaced by Lieutenant General John L. DeWitt.[25] Eisenhower, although upset by the premature bomb releases, decided to try again the next day.

On July 25, 1944, the heaviest tactical employment of strategic air power during World War II was concentrated against the Panzer Lehr Division, then defending a sector west of St. Lô. From 9:00 A.M. until noon, 1,600 Flying Fortresses dropped thousands of tons of high explosives on Bayerlein's units. Tanks were hurled into the air like so many plastic toys. Entire companies were buried alive and completely wiped out. The massive carpet bombing continued on an unprecedented scale until the entire area resembled the surface of the moon.[26] Montgomery, still the supreme Allied ground commander, wrote later: "Enemy troops who were not casualties were stunned and dazed, and weapons not destroyed had to be dug out and cleaned before they could be used; communications were almost completely severed."[27] By the end of the day the U.S. troops had gained two miles, even though the remnants of Panzer Lehr and nearby units were resisting as best they could.[28]

General Bayerlein himself was trapped in a regimental command post near La Chappelle-en-Juger. The CP was an old Norman château with walls 10 feet thick. Only this saved Rommel's former chief of staff from being killed, along with most of his men. Later he told of his adventure:

Again and again the bomb carpets rolled toward us, most of them passing only a few yards away. The ground shuddered. Quick glimpses outside showed the whole area shrouded by a pall of dust, with fountains of earth spewing high in the air. For many hours we were unable to leave the cellar and it was afternoon before I was able to get out of the chateau and ride back on my motorcycle to Division H.Q. (I had long since learned to prefer a motorcycle to a car, having had six cars shot up during the invasion battle and several drivers killed.) We were repeatedly troubled by fighter-bombers on the way back.

When I arrived at Division Headquarters the first reports were just coming in of enemy infiltrations into the bombed area. Resistance was offered by the surviving detachments of my division, but most of these groups were wiped out. . . . Some weak reserves from other sectors tried to halt the avalanche by counterattacks, but their attempts were smashed by the enemy artillery and air force in the forming-up stage and came to nothing. By the following morning, the American breakthrough was complete.[29]

On July 26 von Kluge sent a messenger to Bayerlein's headquarters, ordering him to hold his positions. The lieutenant general, whose division had been totally smashed, replied tartly and bitterly to von Kluge's staff officer: "Out in the front every one is holding out, Herr Oberstleutnant. Every one. My grenadiers and my engineers and my tank crews—they're all holding their ground. Not a single man is leaving his post. Not one! They're lying in their foxholes mute and silent, for they are dead. Dead! Do you understand? You may report to the Field Marshal that the Panzer Lehr Division is annihilated."[30]

Bayerlein's shocking report was quite accurate. The general himself was soon overtaken by the pursuing Americans, and lay pinned down in a farmhouse until nightfall. Then he escaped and walked southward, a commander without a command. Bayerlein was luckier than most. A fleeing German vehicle picked him up about midnight and took him to safety. "But," he wrote, "the Americans were now pouring through into open country with nobody to stop them—just as Rommel had predicted."[31]

Only one regiment of the decimated 275th Infantry Division and the battalion-size Battle Group Heinz (from the same division) were left intact; they were thrown forward to plug the hole, where they had to face the entire U.S. VII Corps (1st, 4th, and 30th Infantry and 2nd and 3rd Armored divisions). By nightfall Battle Group Heinz had been wiped out and the 275th's regiment was down to 200 men. "As of this moment," von Kluge reported, "the front has . . . burst."[32]

Within the week U.S. 3rd Army Headquarters under Lieutenant General

George S. Patton was activated and took command of the breakout forces.[33] Soon they were behind Hausser's German 7th Army—with nothing left to stop them. The headquarters of the 2nd SS Panzer Division was among the rear-area units which tried to delay them; it was overrun and its commander, SS Colonel Tychsen, was among those killed in the fighting.[34]

Patton's army surged southward, out of the confines of the Cotentin Peninsula. Von Kluge attempted to cut off Patton's spearheads by counterattacking at Avranches, but the U.S. and Royal air forces crippled his strike forces in their assembly areas. The Allies had broken free; the Battle of Normandy was lost.

Hitler kept the news of Rommel's wounds secret from the public, and made it appear that he was responsible for Patton's Avranches breakthrough, which took place on July 30 and 31. This aggravated Rommel, who was meanwhile transferred from the Luftwaffe hospital at Bernay to the LeVesinet Military Hospital because the Caen sector had also begun to collapse.[35] Rommel recovered rapidly. On July 24, one week after his injuries, he was able to write to his wife. He told her his left eye was still swollen shut, and that his head hurt him at night, but that he felt much better in the daytime.[36]

Rommel was an awful patient for the doctors and nurses to deal with. He was a man of action, and being confined made him cantankerous and short-tempered. Besides all this, he was too powerful for the medical personnel to give him orders, or to treat without his approval. Despite the seriousness of his wounds, the Desert Fox repeatedly climbed out of bed when it suited him, until one day a surgeon came in with a human skull, which he proceeded to shatter with a hammer. "That's how bad your skull has been crushed," he told Rommel. "We know that from the X-rays."[37] Even this demonstration kept the Field Marshal cooperative for only a few days.

About this same time Baron von Esebeck, the German war correspondent who frequently traveled with Rommel, visited him at the hospital. "I'm glad it's you," Rommel said when he saw the baron. "I was afraid it was the doctor. He won't allow me to sit up. I'm sure he thinks I'm going to die, but I haven't any intention of dying. You'd better take a picture of me," he said as he got out of bed and put on his uniform jacket. He made von Esebeck take a profile of the right (undamaged) side of his face. "The British will be able to see that they haven't managed to kill me yet," he remarked. Then he began discussing the military situation, and again remarked that the war was lost.

"He was especially bitter about the complete failure of the Luftwaffe," the journalist remembered. "He said nothing about the attempt on Hitler's life."[38]

Speidel and Ruge also visited Rommel at Le Vesinet a few days later. They found that he was now shaving himself. A surgeon major general tried to keep him from moving about, but only received a severe reprimand for his efforts. "Don't tell me what I must do or mustn't do," Rommel said. "I know what I can do."[39]

After this, Admiral Ruge visited him almost daily, and read to him from a book entitled *The Tunnel.* "It was about building a tunnel from Europe to the United States," Ruge recalled, "exactly the sort of thing he liked. We used to talk about 'after the war.' He had been very much impressed by the enormous rise and fall of tide on the coast of Brittany and said that he would like to be actively interested in a project for drawing power from the tides. Anyway, he wanted to do something technical and practical."[40]

Ruge and Rommel also discussed the assassination attempt. The Desert Fox felt that murder was the wrong way to go about it. "The Hitler legend will never be destroyed until the German people know the whole truth," he said.[41]

Ruge feared for his chief's life. He wanted Rommel to surrender himself to the British, but never quite worked up enough courage to suggest it.[42] For his part, all Rommel wanted to do was to go home, to his family at Herrlingen. On August 8 he returned there, and startled his wife, who was not prepared for the ugliness of his head wounds. Rommel grinned at her reaction and said, "So long as I don't have to carry my head under one arm, things can't be all bad."[43] He continued to receive constant medical care, for his condition was still not good. Upon examining Rommel, Doctor Albrecht, a noted German brain surgeon, declared, "No man can be alive with wounds like that."[44]

Rommel was not only alive but growing better each day. He arranged to have his son posted to his staff, so the entire family was again reunited by mid-August.[45] The wounded Desert Fox spoke to his 15-year-old son about the war, and the hopelessness of continuing the fighting. He told the young Luftwaffe antiaircraft gun crewman that Germany should allow the British and Americans to occupy all of Central Europe, to keep the Russians outside the borders of the Reich. Rommel grew angry when he heard that a panzer division was being transferred from Poland to Holland. "These fools!" he roared. "They think of nothing but their own skins. What good is it to them to prolong their miserable lives by a few more months? The Eastern Front will simply crack and the next Russian push will bring them into German territory. We all know what that means."[46]

Rommel never could believe that the British and Americans were seriously allied with the Russians, or were as fully committed to them as they, in fact, were. He believed that a Third World War, between the Russians and the Western Allies, was only a matter of time. This war, however, would come only after the defeat of Nazi Germany.

While Rommel continued to recover and engage in idle conversations with his family, the Gestapo inevitably closed in on him. True enough, he had opposed the actual assassination attempt, but he had been implicated in it and had advocated the arrest of Adolf Hitler and his henchmen on charges of high treason. He had planned to open independent negotiations with the Western powers after the overthrow of the Nazi regime. He was also on some of the conspirators' lists as the next President of the Reich.

Count von Stauffenberg and General Beck were executed just before midnight on July 20 by Colonel General Fritz Fromm, the Commander-in-Chief of the Replacement Army. Fromm was an unscrupulous man who played on both sides of the conspiracy question. As one who was privy to the attempt, Fromm felt that the firing squad was the best way to cover his tracks, so he summarily liquidated five of the top conspirators. Although this piece of treachery did not save him, it did remove the top potential witnesses against Erwin Rommel. Major General von Treschow, the Chief of Staff of Army Group Center and a leading member of the resistance, blew himself up with hand grenades on the Russian Front as soon as he was sure the attempt had failed. He realized the Gestapo would eventually torture him into revealing the names of his coconspirators and, true to his code, he preferred death to this dishonor. There were, however, other witnesses around who were less thorough than Treschow when it came to suicide.

On July 21 General Heinrich von Stuelpnagel was summoned to Berlin, to explain why he had arrested the SS and Gestapo members in Paris on the day of the assassination attempt. That night the Military Governor of France drank heavily and carried on loud, irrational conversations with himself. The next day the general set out by car for the German capital. At Verdun, where he had distinguished himself as a junior officer in the 1914–1918 war, he ordered his driver to stop. He waded into the Meuse Canal and shot himself in the head. Both of Stuelpnagel's eyes were destroyed by the bullet, but he lived. The driver found the badly wounded officer, dragged him out of the water before he could drown, and rushed him to the hospital at Verdun. This attempted suicide was tantamount to an admission of guilt. According to Dr. Speidel, the Gestapo agents were already beside von Stuelpnagel's bed when he woke up, crying "Rommel!" over and over again.

The blind soldier was taken to Berlin, where he was tortured by the Gestapo. Apparently they could get no further information out of him, but he had already said too much in his delirium: Rommel was incriminated. Eventually Stuelpnagel was hanged with piano wire, like hundreds of others.[47]

Doctor Goerdeler, the former mayor of Leipzig, was also captured and tortured by the Gestapo. Unfortunately he was not as tough as Stuelpnagel or Julius Leber, and soon incriminated everyone he knew. The brutal but efficient Nazi secret police learned of Rommel's involvement with the resistance, and closed in on him, as they did on so many others during those dangerous and violent years.

Others went down first. Helmuth von Moltke was executed by the SS without benefit of trial. Albrecht Haushofer was also killed, and his father, Professor Karl Haushofer, was sent to a concentration camp. Julius Leber was tried and executed, as was Field Marshal von Witzleben and General Stieff. On August 18 Field Marshal von Kluge was relieved of his commands, replaced by Walther Model, and summoned to Berlin. Realizing the implications of this order, von Kluge took poison near Verdun, and died almost within sight of the spot where Heinrich von Stuelpnagel had blinded himself.

On September 6 Hans Speidel visited his former chief at Herrlingen for what proved to be their last meeting. He had been suspended from his duties as Chief of Staff of Army Group B despite Model's objections. Nevertheless Hitler insisted, and Speidel was replaced by General Hans Krebs, a hard-bitten Nazi veteran of the Eastern Front.[48] Speidel found his ex-commander in good health and in fine spirits. Already his left eye was half open. Naturally the two men discussed the events of July 20. Speaking of Hitler, Rommel said, "That pathological liar has now gone completely mad. He is venting his sadism on the conspirators of July 20, and this won't be the end of it. I am afraid that this madman will sacrifice the last German before he meets his own end."[49]

At 6:00 A.M. the next morning the Gestapo arrested General Speidel.

Rommel tried to obtain his release, but in vain.[50] Remarkably, Doctor Speidel survived both his imprisonment and the war. He became a professor of philosophy at Tuebingen University, where Manfred Rommel later studied law.[51] Speidel eventually rose to a high-ranking position in the North Atlantic Treaty Organization (NATO) forces.

Erwin Rommel would not survive the war, and he knew it. After Speidel's arrest, old friends and acquaintances stopped coming around. "The rats are leaving the sinking ship," he said with a bitter smile.[52]

A few days later the local party chief, a man named Maier, visited the wounded Field Marshal. He asked Rommel if he could trust the servants, and warned him that the SS leader in Ulm suspected that he was a defeatist. Rommel replied to this comment with characteristic bluntness. "Victory!" he snapped. "Why don't you look at a map? The British are here, the Americans are here, the Russians are here. What is the use of talking about victory?" When Maier said something about Hitler, Rommel denounced the Fuehrer as a "damned fool." "You should not say things like that, Field Marshal," the party boss warned. "You will have the Gestapo after you—if they are not after you already."[53]

Rommel and his son had gotten into the habit of taking daily walks through the woods near their home. One day the Field Marshal told his boy: "Look here, Manfred, it's possible that there are certain people around here who would like to do away with me quietly and without too much fuss—by an ambush in the woods, for instance. But I don't intend to let it put me off my walk. So for the time being, we'll take pistols. You can have my 8mm. These individuals don't hit anything with their first shots. If the shooting does start, the thing to do is to fire blind toward where it's coming from, and they'll almost always go for cover or aim badly."[54]

Manfred did not completely grasp the implications of these remarks until a few days later, when Rommel said, "Tell me, Manfred, what do you young chaps think when Hitler suddenly hangs a whole lot of people who have persuaded themselves—not wholly without reason—that the war is lost and we should make an end of it at last?"

"I don't know," his son answered. "They're all pretty sick of the war up at the gun-site, but most of them still believe we can win it somehow or other."

"But it's already lost. What if I, too, had declared myself ready to end it, even against Hitler's will?"

"Why do you ask that?" the lad answered.

"Oh, let's leave it for now," the senior Rommel replied. "Anyway, one thing is quite clear. It's intolerable that the fate and welfare of a whole nation should depend on the whim of a small group. There must be some limit; otherwise the most fantastic things can happen without anyone noticing."

"From that day on," Manfred wrote later, "I, too, had the feeling of approaching disaster."[55]

Rommel took steps to provide for his family after his death. He visited his old comrade Oscar Farny at his Durren estate, near Wangen. They had served in the same regiment as lieutenants, and had been close friends for years. Farny had left the Army and had entered politics as a member of the Centrist Party. He was eventually elected to the Reichstag, where he opposed the rising party of Adolf Hitler.[56] Then he retired from the political arena and took up farming, which explains why he was still alive in 1944. Rommel said to Farny: "I am in grave danger. Hitler wants to do away with me. His reasons are my ultimatum to him on July 15th, the open and honest opinions I have always expressed, the events of July 20th, and the reports of the Party and the Secret Police. If anything should happen to me, I beg you to take care of my son."[57]

When Farny protested in disbelief, Rommel replied, "You will see. He will have me put to death. You are a politician and should understand this criminal better than I. He won't be afraid to do this."[58]

His anxiety about the future of Germany, the premonitions of his own death, the unhealed head wounds, and the inactivity combined to give Rommel sleepless nights and restless days. He wrote his former artillery advisor, Colonel Lattmann, on September 27: "I'm very dissatisfied with the slow progress my recovery is making. I'm suffering badly from insomnia and constant headaches, and I'm not up to very much at all. You can imagine how hard it is for me to have to remain idle at times like these."[59]

On October 7 the expected summons to Berlin came. Field Marshal Keitel talked with Rommel's aide, and requested Rommel's appearance at an important conference, to be held three days later. A special train would pick him up at Ulm. "I'm not that much of a fool," Rommel exclaimed. "We know these people now. I'd never get to Berlin alive."[60] Admiral Ruge, who was visiting him at the time, did not believe this at first, until Rommel said, "I know they would kill me on the way and stage an accident." Rommel phoned Keitel, but talked only to Schmundt's successor, Lieutenant General Wilhelm Burgdorf. He told the new personnel officer that he was still unfit to travel.[61] Professor Albrecht, the brain surgeon, immediately substantiated this assertion, and certified Rommel as unfit to travel. He apparently also believed that the Gestapo was out to murder the Desert Fox, for he tried to persuade him to go to his clinic, where it would be harder for the Secret Police to get at him. Rommel thanked Albrecht, and said that he would keep his offer in mind.[62] However, time was running out for the Desert Fox. His refusal to go to Berlin extended his life by less than a week.

On October 13 Rommel was out with his friend, Captain Hermann Aldinger. He was another one of Rommel's old comrades from World War I, who had also served as his aide in 1941, when Rommel commanded the Afrika Korps. Aldinger's health had broken down in the harsh desert environment, but now he was again back with his old friend.[63] Rommel told Aldinger that, in the event of his death, he wanted to be buried in one of three places: Heidenheim (his birthplace), Heidelberg, or Herrlingen.[64] While they were gone, a telegram arrived from Berlin. It told Rommel that Burgdorf and Major General Maisel would arrive from Berlin at noon the next day. Since July 20 Ernest Maisel, Chief of the Legal Section of the Army Personnel Branch, had been engaged in investigating officers suspected of being involved in the attempt on Hitler's life. Rommel commented to Aldinger that the two men were doubtless coming to talk to him about the invasion, or about a new assignment. However, he surely knew better, and was unusually quiet the rest of the day.[65]

On October 14, 1944, the last day of his life, Field Marshal Erwin Rommel rose early. His son received leave that day, almost certainly owing to the influence of his father. They ate breakfast together at 7:00 A.M., and later took a walk in the garden.

"At twelve o'clock today two generals are coming to see me to discuss my future employment," Rommel told Manfred. "So today will decide what is planned for me; whether a People's Court or a new command in the East."

"Would you accept such a command?" Manfred asked.

Rommel took his son by the arm and said: "My dear boy, our enemy in the East is so terrible that every other consideration has to give way before it. If he succeeds in overrunning Europe, even only temporarily, it will be the end of everything which has made life appear worth living. Of course I would go."[66]

Manfred knew his father was worried. They walked for some time. The conversation centered around Manfred and his future. Rommel wanted him to be a doctor, and not a soldier.[67] The Desert Fox probably would have been surprised to learn that his son would become a lawyer and eventually the mayor of Stuttgart, a city slightly larger than Milwaukee, in the late 1970s.

At about 11:00 A.M. they returned home. Shortly before noon Rommel changed from his civilian clothes to his old African outfit, his favorite uniform.[68] At precisely twelve o'clock the Army sedan arrived from Berlin. The two generals alighted, and, after exchanges of courtesies, asked to speak to the Field Marshal alone. They talked for nearly an hour. Then Rommel went upstairs to see his wife.[69]

Frau Rommel knew immediately that something was wrong. "There was so strange and terrible an expression on his face . . . ," she recalled later.

"What's the matter with you?" she exclaimed. "What has happened? Are you ill?"

"I have come to say good-bye," he replied. "In a quarter of an hour I shall be dead. . . . They suspect me of having taken part in the attempt to kill Hitler. It seems my name was on Goerdeler's list to be President of the Reich. . . . I have never seen Goerdeler in my life. . . . They say that von Stuelpnagel, General Speidel, and Colonel von Hofacker have denounced me. . . . It is the usual trick. . . . I have told them that I do not believe it and that it cannot be true. . . . The Fuehrer has given me the choice of taking poison or being dragged before the People's Court. They have brought the poison. They say it will take only three seconds to act."

Frau Rommel begged her husband to stand trial. "No," replied the Field Marshal. He realized what would happen to his family if he tried to take this course. "I would not be afraid to be tried in public, for I can defend everything I have done. But I know that I should never reach Berlin alive."[70]

Frau Rommel felt faint, but returned his last embrace. Then he left, and the tears came.[71]

After speaking to Lucie, Rommel saw his son for the last time. "I have just had to tell your mother that I shall be dead in a quarter of an hour," he said in a calm voice. "To die by the hand of one's own people is hard. But the house is surrounded and Hitler is charging me with high treason. 'In view of my services in Africa,'" he continued sarcastically, "I am to have the choice of dying by poison. The two generals have brought it with them. It's fatal in three seconds. If I accept, none of the usual steps will be taken against my family, that is against you. They will also leave my staff alone."

"Do you believe it?" Manfred asked.

"Yes, I believe it," replied his father. "It is very much in their interest to see that the affair does not come out into the open. By the way, I have been charged to put you under a promise of the strictest silence. If a single word of this comes out, they will no longer feel themselves bound by the agreement."

"Can't we defend ourselves . . . ," the teenager began, but was cut short.

"There's no point," Rommel broke in. "It's better for one to die than for all of us to be killed in a shooting affray. Anyway, we've practically no ammunition." This settled, they said their final good-byes.[72]

Last of all, Rommel said farewell to his old friend, Hermann Aldinger. They had fought side by side during World War I and in the first desperate and exciting days of the Afrika Korps. Like Manfred, Captain Aldinger wanted Rommel to shoot his way out. They had been in bad places before, he said, and had gotten out by this method.

"It's no good, my friend," Rommel answered. "This is it. All the streets are blocked with SS cars and the Gestapo are all around the house. We could never get back to the troops. They've taken over the telephone. I cannot even ring up my headquarters."

Aldinger wanted to at least shoot Maisel and Burgdorf. "No," Rommel said. "They have their orders. Besides, I have my wife and Manfred to think of." He explained that nothing would happen to them if he committed suicide. His family would receive a pension, and he would be buried in Herrlingen with full military honors.[73] "It's all been prepared to the last detail," he said. "I'm to be given a state funeral. I have asked that it should take place in Ulm. In a quarter of an hour you, Aldinger, will receive a telephone call from the Wagnerschule Reserve Hospital in Ulm to say that I've had a brain seizure on the way to a conference." The Field Marshal looked at his watch. "I must go," he said. "They've only given me ten minutes."[74]

Rommel, Aldinger, and Manfred walked down the stairs together. In the hall Rommel's dachshund puppy, Elbo, saw him, and threw himself into a fit of joy. This sight must have made it even harder on the Desert Fox, who always loved dogs. "Shut the dog in the study, Manfred," he said. When the young man returned, the three of them walked out of the house together. The crunch of the gravel beneath their shoes sounded unusually loud, Manfred later recalled.[75]

As they approached the gate Burgdorf and Maisel saluted and then stood to one side. The SS drive opened the back door and stood at attention. Rommel swung his marshal's baton under his left arm, and shook hands with Aldinger and Manfred one last time. His face was calm. Then he got into the car, followed by Burgdorf and Maisel. The car ascended the hill near the house and disappeared around a bend a bend in the road. Erwin Rommel never looked back.[76]

A few hundred yards beyond the hill the car stopped in an open space at the edge of the woods. Maisel and the driver got out, leaving Rommel alone with Burgdorf. Five minutes later Burgdorf got out, leaving the Field Marshal alone. The Nazi general paced up and down alongside the sedan. In another five minutes he waved to Maisel and the driver. When they arrived, the SS driver later testified, they found Rommel doubled up and sobbing. He was practically unconscious and obviously in his death throes.[77] Burgdorf himself was killed when the Russians overran Berlin in April 1945, so exactly what transpired in Rommel's last ten minutes is impossible to determine. One thing is certain: at 1:25 P.M. on October 14, 1944, Field Marshal Erwin Rommel was reported dead on arrival at the Wagnerschule Reserve Hospital in Ulm. The hospital doctors were obviously suspicious, but said nothing. No postmortem was allowed. The body was to be cremated—no evidence of what really happened was to be left behind. One feature, however, struck all who saw the body of Germany's great military leader: the expression of deep contempt on his dead face. "It was an expression we had never seen on it in life," his widow recalled later. The expression may still be seen on his death-mask.[78]

Soon the expressions of condolence came pouring in from the great and small. Among the most effusive came from members of the Nazi hierarchy who were responsible for, or at least privy to, the cause of his death. On October 16, Hitler sent a message to Frau Rommel: "Accept my sincerest sympathy for the heavy loss you have suffered with the death of your husband. The name of Field Marshal Rommel will be ever linked with the heroic battles in North Africa."[79] Hitler did not mention the Battle of Normandy in his wire.

Seven months later the former house painter was finished. Almost completely mad, he shot himself in the head. The Russians were a few hundred yards from his bunker. He had gambled everything and lost, becoming, at last, not the originator of a Thousand Year Reich, but one of the most despised figures in the history of man.

Reichsmarschal Hermann Goering wrote that his bitter enemy ". . . has died a hero's death as the result of his wounds. . . . I send you, my dear Frau Rommel, the heartfelt sympathy of myself and the German people."[80]

Like the more honorable Rommel, "Fat Hermann" died of poison by his own hand. He committed suicide in the Nuremberg prison on October 16, 1946, two hours before he would have been hanged.

Minister of Propaganda Dr. Joseph Goebbels sent a telegram to Lucie Rommel: "In Field Marshal Rommel the German Army loses one of its most successful commanders, whose name will be forever linked with the heroic two-year struggle of the Afrika Korps. Please be assured of our deepest sympathy in your grief."[81]

A few months later, as Berlin fell, Goebbels and his wife murdered their six young children while they slept, and then committed suicide themselves. They survived their Fuehrer by a few hours.

Field Marshal Model, who now commanded Rommel's old Army Group B as well as OB West, published an Order of the Day. In it he called Rommel "one of the greatest German commanders . . . with a lightning power of decision, a soldier of the greatest bravery and of unequalled dash. . . . Always in the front line, he inspired his men to new deeds of heroism by his example. . . ."[82]

Of all the top Nazis who privately or publicly expressed sympathy, Model was probably the only one who was sincere. It is reasonably certain that he never knew Rommel's death was, in fact, murder. In the months ahead Walther Model led Rommel's old command to its final defeats. Then, surrounded in the Ruhr Pocket, he dissolved Army Group B and, on April 18, 1945, hopelessly surrounded by the Americans, he shot himself in a wooded area north of Dusseldorf.

At least two of Rommel's worst enemies refused to take part in the farce. Field Marshal Keitel and Colonel General Jodl sent no letters of condolence. They might have been accomplices to murder, but, in this case at least, they were not hypocrites.

On October 16, 1946, both of these men were hanged by the Allies as major war criminals. They outlived Rommel two years, almost to the day. They were the last of his enemies to die, except perhaps for Martin Bormann, Hitler's party chief, who has variously been reported as killed in Berlin in April 1945 and as alive in South America in the 1970s. The truth may never be known.

Heinrich Himmler sent a personal representative to Frau Rommel's home, to express his regrets. The person he chose was none other than Captain Alfred Berndt, one of Rommel's aides from North Africa and now a member of the SS. Berndt had been an official in the Ministry of

Propaganda but had been dismissed for repeating something Rommel had told him: that the war was lost. Now he was one of Himmler's personal assistants. According to Berndt, neither Hitler nor Himmler ordered Rommel's murder. The responsibility lay solely with Keitel and Jodl. This statement must be considered a lie. The two military lackeys would never have dared to perform such an audacious act without Hitler's permission.[83]

As an SS major, Berndt was killed in action on the Eastern Front in the last days of the Third Reich. Himmler poisoned himself after being captured by the British in May 1945.

Erwin Rommel's body lay in state at the Ulm town hall for two days. He was buried on October 18, 1944, with full military honors. Thousands of common people from miles around came to mourn the dead leader, and many of his surviving friends also attended the funeral. Admiral Ruge represented the German Navy. Stroelin, von Neurath, and Frau Speidel were also present, as no doubt were Farny and Aldinger. Many others who certainly would have attended could not do so. Bayerlein, for instance, was leading the remnants of Panzer Lehr out of France, while Walther Nehring, the former Afrika Korps commander, was leading the battered XXIV Panzer Corps out of Russia. Ludwig Cruewell, Rommel's deputy commander in Africa, was in an Allied prisoner-of-war camp, as were a host of his lieutenants: Gustav von Vaerst, Baron Johannes von Ravenstein, Reverend Wilhelm Bach, Ritter von Thoma, and dozens of others. Speidel was in a Gestapo cell; Caesar von Hofacker, Dollmann, Marcks, Daniel, Georg von Bismarck, von Stauffenberg, and dozens of others were already dead.[84]

Field Marshal von Rundstedt, now greatly aged, unwittingly performed the last act in the tragic farce. In his funeral oration he spoke of Rommel as one whose "heart belonged to the Fuehrer," and claimed that the Desert Fox was "imbued with the National-Socialist spirit."[85]

As ironic as von Rundstedt's address was, it had one saving phrase: "A pitiless destiny," he said, "has snatched him from us, just at the moment when the fighting has come to its crisis."[86] A pitiless destiny indeed!

Rommel's coffin, draped in a huge swastika flag, was carried to the crematorium. He was escorted by two companies of infantry, a Luftwaffe company, and a company of Waffen-SS. Later his ashes were interred in a corner of the graveyard of the village church of Herrlingen, the pretty little village near Ulm. A small stream flows nearby, and the cemetery is said to be quite peaceful.[87] Erwin Rommel was at rest at last.

Notes

1

1. Erwin Rommel, *The Rommel Papers*, ed. B. H. Liddell Hart (New York: Harcourt, Brace & Company, 1953), pp. 446-47.
2. Ibid., p. 426.
3. Glenn Infield, *The Big Week* (Los Angeles: Pinnacle Books, 1974), p. 86.
4. David Irving, *The Trail of the Fox* (New York: E. P. Dutton and Company, 1977), p. 314 (hereafter cited as "Irving").
5. Gordon A. Harrison, *Cross-Channel Attack*, U.S. Army in World War II, The European Theater of Operations, Office of the Chief of Military History, U.S. Department of the Army (Washington, D.C.: United States Government Printing Office, 1951), p. 149.
6. Irving, p. 313.
7. Christopher Chant, Richard Humble, William Fowler, and Jenny Shaw, *Hitler's Generals and Their Battles* (New York: Chartwell Books, Inc., 1976), p. 60.
8. Cornelius Ryan, *The Longest Day* (New York: Popular Library, 1959) (by arrangement with Simon and Schuster, Inc.), pp. 22-23.
9. Irving, p. 315.
10. Harrison, p. 131.
11. Alan F. Wilt, *The Atlantic Wall: Hitler's Defense in the West, 1941–1945* (Ames, IA: Iowa State University Press, 1975), p. 46; Hilpert was transferred to the Russian Front, where he distinguished himself as commander of XXIII Corps and later I Corps. In May 1945 he was a Colonel General and commander of Army Group Courland (formerly North), which he surrendered to the Red Army. He died in a Soviet prison camp in the mid-1950s.
12. Ibid., pp. 58-59.
13. Ibid., p. 59.
14. Harrison, p. 137.
15. Wilt, p. 3.
16. Harrison, p. 138.
17. Ibid., p. 142; also see United States Army Military Intelligence Service, "Order of Battle of the German Army," (Washington, D.C.: Military Intelligence Service, October 1942, April 1943, and January 1945) (hereafter cited as "OB").
18. Friedrich Ruge, "The Invasion of Normandy," in H. A. Jacobsen and J. Rohwer, *Decisive Battles of World War II: The German View* (New York: G. P. Putnam's Sons, 1965), p. 321.
19. Ryan, p. 23.
20. Ibid., p. 26.

21. Rommel, p. 461.
22. Irving, p. 313.
23. Ruge, p. 323; Colonel General Alfred Jodl, the Chief of Operations of OKW, conducted his own tour of the Atlantic Wall in January 1944, and agreed with Rommel's conclusions wholeheartedly. Jodl was especially peeved at the Luftwaffe, which was not planning ahead for the invasion at all (David Irving, *Hitler's War*. New York: The Viking Press, 1977, p. 603) (hereafter cited as "Irving, 1977").
24. Rommel, p. 453.
25. Ibid., pp. 454-55.
26. Harrison, pp. 246-47.
27. Irving, p. 316.
28. Harrison, p. 450-51.
29. Hans Speidel, *Invasion 1944* (New York: Paperback Library, Inc., 1950), p. 41 (originally published as *Invasion 1944. Ein Beitrag zu Rommels und des Reiches Schicksal*. Tubingen and Stuttgart: Rainer Wunderlich Verlag Hermann Leins, 1949) (originally published in U.S. by Henry Regnery Company, Chicago, 1950); Joseph Goebbels, *The Goebbels Diaries*. ed. Louis P. Lochner, New York: Universal-Award House, Inc., 1971 (originally published by Doubleday and Company, Inc., Garden City, N.Y., 1948), pp. 391-92; *Kriegstagebuch des Oberkommando der Wehrmacht (Wehrmachtfuehrungsstab)*. Book IV: 1 Januar 1944–22 Mai 1945 (Frankfurt-am-Main: Bernard and Graefe Verlag für Wehrwesen, 1961), p. 414.
30. Speidel, p. 41; *Kriegstagebuch des OKW*. Volume IV, Part 1 (1944), pp. 279-80.
31. Speidel, pp. 41-42.
32. Ibid., p. 41.
33. Ibid., p. 43.
34. Ibid.; 17th SS Panzer Grenadier Division and the remnants of the 352nd Infantry Division were later attached to II Parachute Corps (*Kriegstagebuch des OKW*. IV, Part 1 (1944), pp. 279-80).
35. Harrison, pp. 247-48; Leo von Schweppenburg had distinguished himself as commander of the XXIV Panzer Corps in Russia in 1941; later he commanded XXXX Panzer Corps in the Caucasus campaign of 1942-1943 (see Paul Carell, *Hitler Moves East. 1941-1943* New York: Bantam Books, 1966), pp. 519-23, 549 (originally published by Little, Brown and Company, Boston, 1965).
36. Speidel, p. 42.
37. Ibid., p. 43.
38. Wilt, p. 128.
39. Harrison, p. 238.
40. Ibid., p. 147.
41. Rommel, p. 481.
42. Harrison, p. 146.
43. Ibid., p. 144; also see John Toland, *Adolf Hitler* (New York: Ballantine Books, 1977), p. 1065 (originally published by Random House, 1976).
44. Toland, p. 1072.
45. Harrison, p. 242.
46. Ibid.
47. Ibid., p. 241.
48. Peter Neumann, *The Black March: The Personal Story of an SS Man* (New York: Bantam Books, Inc., 1960), p. 225 (originally published by Editions France-Empire, Paris, under the title *SS!*, 1958).
49. Paul Carell, *Invasion: They're Coming!* (New York: E. P. Dutton, 1963), p. 14.

50. Ryan, p. 15.
51. Gause had been Rommel's Chief of Staff in Libya, where he was seriously wounded in May, 1942. In 1943 he became Chief of Staff of Panzer Army Afrika (see Samuel W. Mitcham, Jr., *Rommel's Desert War*. Briarcliff Manor, N.Y.: Stein and Day, 1982).
52. Irving, p. 340.
53. Speidel, p. 10.
54. For the whole story of the German resistance movement against Hitler, see Allen W. Dulles, *Germany's Underground* (Westport, CT: Greenwood Press, 1978); Constantine FitzGibbon, *20 July*. (New York: W. W. Norton and Co., Inc., 1956); James Forman, *Code Name Valkyrie: Count von Stauffenberg and the Plot to Kill Hitler*(New York: Laurel-Leaf Library, 1975); Peter Hoffman, *The History of the German Resistance, 1933-1945* (Cambridge, MA: M.I.T. Press, 1977); and Erich Zimmermann and Hans-Adolf Jacobsen, *Germans Against Hitler, July 20, 1944* (Bonn: Federal German Government Press and Information Office, 1960).
55. Speidel, p. 39.
56. Rommel, pp. 462-64.
57. Ibid., p. 461.
58. Harrison, p. 247.
59. Irving, 1977, p. 604.
60. Irving, pp. 317-18; 324.
61. Speidel, pp. 50-51.
62. Harrison, p. 141.
63. Carell, p. 10.
64. Ruge, p. 326.
65. Rommel, p. 455.
66. Ibid.
67. Irving, p. 323.
68. Vincent J. Esposito (ed.), *A Concise History of World War II* (New York: Frederick A. Praeger, Publishers, 1964).
69. Irving, p. 323.
70. Rommel, p. 457.
71. Irving, p. 323.
72. Rommel, pp. 458-59.
73. Ibid., p. 459.
74. Ibid.
75. Ibid., p. 460.
76. Ibid.
77. Ruge, p. 328.
78. Harrison, pp. 250-52.
79. Ryan, p. 29.
80. Ibid.
81. Carell, p. 9.
82. Ryan, p. 22.
83. Desmond Young, *Rommel: The Desert Fox* (New York: Harper & Row, 1950), pp. 192-93 of the 1965 paperback edition.
84. Speidel, p. 40.
85. Ibid.
86. Irving, p. 325.
87. Ibid., p. 320.
88. Ibid.

89. *Kriegstagebuch des OKW*. Volume IV, Part 1 (1944), p. 312.
90. Irving, p. 327.
91. Ibid., p. 333.
92. Speidel, p. 40.
93. Ibid., p. 21.
94. Harrison, p. 243.
95. Speidel, pp. 36-37.
96. Ibid., pp. 57-59.
97. Mitcham, pp. 127-59.
98. Heinz Guderian, *Panzer Leader* (New York: Ballantine Books, 1967), pp. 262-63 (originally published by E. P. Dutton, New York, 1957).
99. Ibid., p. 263.
100. Harrison, p. 253. Sodenstern had been Chief of Staff of Army Group A (1939-40) in Poland and France and Chief of Staff of Army Group South (under various designations) on the Russian Front (1941-early 1944) (OB 1945: 627).
101. Rommel, p. 467.
102. Harrison, p. 155.
103. Ibid., p. 258.
104. Rommel, p. 466.
105. Irving, pp. 336-37.
106. Ibid., p. 336.
107. Rommel, p. 466, and Harrison, p. 248.
108. Blaskowitz (age 61) commanded the 8th Army in Poland (1939) and the 1st Army in occupied France from early 1941 until he assumed command of Army Group G. He was quite unpopular with Adolf Hitler, which is why he was never promoted to Field Marshal.
109. Harrison, p. 248.
110. Wilt, p. 110.
111. Ruge, p. 330.
112. Harrison, p. 248.
113. Speidel, p. 52.
114. Ibid., p. 33.
115. B. H. Liddell Hart, *History of the Second World War* (New York: G. P. Putnam's Sons, 1972), Volume II, p. 549.
116. Rommel, pp. 468-69.
117. Ibid., p. 470.
118. Harrison, p. 257.
119. Ruge, p. 330.
120. Speidel, pp. 33-34.
121. Harrison, p. 138.
122. Liddell Hart, II, pp. 548-49.
123. Ruge. p. 322.
124. Harrison, p. 138.
125. Ibid., pp. 259-60.
126. Neumann, p. 225.
127. Rumania in particular was bitterly resentful of the 18 divisions she lost between the Don and the Volga (Toland, p. 1065).
128. Harrison, p. 234.
129. Ibid., pp. 234-35.
130. Ibid., p. 235; Baron von Funck had commanded the 7th Panzer Division in Russia for two years;

this was the same unit which Rommel had led with such dash in France in 1940. Funck was reportedly killed in action in France in August, 1944 (OB 1945: 552).

131. Speidel, pp. 44-45.
132. Harrison, pp. 210-11; also see Infield, pp. 45-48.
133. Harrison, p. 266.
134. Speidel, p. 46-47.
135. Ibid.
136. Ibid., p. 87.
137. See Harrison, p. 267.
138. Ruge, pp. 323-29.
139. Harrison, p. 225.
140. Esposito, p. 80.
141. Speidel, pp. 46-47.
142. Harrison, p. 225.
143. Ibid., pp. 228-30.
144. J. F. C. Fuller, *The Second World War, 1939-45: A Strategical and Tactical History* (New York: Duell, Sloan and Pearce, 1949), p. 294 (hereafter referred to as "Fuller, 1949").
145. Harrison, pp. 228-30.
146. Fuller, 1949, p. 294.
147. Harrison, pp. 228-30.
148. Esposito, p. 80.
149. Toland, p. 1071.
150. Irving, pp. 346-49.
151. Irving, 1977, p. 625.
152. Irving, p. 351.

2

1. Harrison, p. 248.
2. Ibid., p. 236.
3. Ibid., p. 240.
4. Ibid.
5. Wilt, p. 127.
6. Speidel, p. 29.
7. Esposito, p. 85.
8. Speidel, p. 29.
9. Harrison, pp. 255-57.
10. Carell, p. 84.
11. Harrison, pp. 257, 263; Ruge, p. 329.
12. Ruge, p. 329.
13. Rommel, p. 460.
14. Alexander McKee, *Last Round Against Rommel* (New York: Signet Books, 1966), pp. 26-27.
15. Harrison, p. 231.
16. Carell, p. 14; Toland, p. 1073.
17. Ryan, p. 21.
18. Bernard Law Montgomery, The Viscount of Alamein, *Normandy to the Baltic* (London: Hutchinson and Company, Publishers, Ltd., 1958), p. 43.
19. Ryan, p. 82.

20. Carell, p. 22.
21. Ryan, pp. 82-83.
22. Harrison, p. 206.
23. Ibid., pp. 283-89.
24. Ryan, pp. 30-34.
25. Ibid., p. 113.
26. Ibid., p. 145; Carell, pp. 31-32.
27. Ryan, pp. 145-49.
28. Montgomery, p. 22.
29. Harrison, p. 278.
30. Fuller, 1949, p. 295.
31. Carell, p. 39.
32. Harrison, pp 300-1.
33. Ibid.
34. Carell, pp. 50-51.
35. Ryan, pp. 30-34.
36. Carell, p. 74.
37. Ibid., pp. 40-42.
38. Ibid., pp. 43-44.
39. Ibid., p. 55.
40. Ibid., pp. 56-57.
41. Harrison, pp. 300-1; Carell, pp. 55-56.
42. Carell, p. 56.
43. Ibid., pp. 33-34.
44. Ibid., pp. 57-58.
45. Harrison, pp. 295-97.
46. Ibid.
47. Carell, pp. 63-64.
48. Carell, pp. 65-68; Harrison, pp. 303-4.
49. Carell, pp. 79-80.
50. Esposito, p. 87.
51. OB 1945, p. 238.
52. Ryan, p. 199.
53. Harrison, p. 313.
54. Carell, p. 82.
55. Harrison, p. 313.
56. Carell, p. 83.
57. Ibid.
58. Ibid., pp. 84-85.
59. Ibid., p. 86.
60. Ibid.
61. Ibid., p. 87.
62. Ibid., pp. 87-88.
63. Harrison, p. 320.
64. Ibid., p. 322.
65. Ibid., pp. 326-28.
66. Ryan, p. 256.
67. Ibid., pp. 256-57.
68. Ibid., p. 257.

69. Liddell Hart, II, p. 550.
70. Ryan, pp. 284-85.
71. Ibid., p. 285.
72. Ibid.
73. Toland, p. 1074.
74. Ryan, p. 279.
75. Ryan, pp. 283-84; Toland, p. 1074.
76. Toland, p. 1075.
77. McKee, p. 34.
78. Ibid., p. 35.
79. Ibid., p. 51.
80. Carell, p. 89.
81. Ibid., p. 90; Montgomery, p. 45.
82. Carell, p. 91.
83. Esposito, p. 88.
84. Carell, pp. 91-92; Hart blames the British failure on the "excessive caution of the commanders on the spot" (Hart, II, p. 546).
85. Carell, p. 92.
86. McKee, p. 66.
87. Carell, pp. 24-25; the original 21st Panzer Division was part of the Afrika Korps from 1941 to 1943 and was destroyed in Tunisia. It was reconstituted in 1943.
88. Carrel, pp. 24-25.
89. Ibid., p. 25.
90. Ibid., pp. 98-100.
91. Ibid., p. 97.
92. Ibid.
93. Ibid., pp. 99-100.
94. Ryan, p. 296; Carell, p. 101.
95. Ryan, p. 297.
96. Ryan, pp. 297-98.
97. McKee, pp. 58-59; Carell, pp. 102-4.
98. Irving, p. 374.
99. Ryan, pp. 298-99.
100. Ibid., pp. 285, 294.
101. Ibid., p. 296.
102. Ibid., p. 297.
103. Ruge, 336.
104. Ryan, 301.
105. Irving, p. 374.

3

1. Esposito, p. 88.
2. Ruge, p. 336; Esposito, p. 85.
3. Esposito, pp. 85-88.
4. Ryan, p. 303; estimates of German casualties are so varied as to be useless. They probably lost 5,000 to 6,000 men.

5. Carell, p. 66.
6. Ibid., p. 85.
7. Ibid., p. 95-96.
8. Ibid., p. 96.
9. Liddell Hart, II, p. 550; Toland, p. 1076.
10. Ryan, p. 296.
11. Carell, pp. 105-7.
12. Ibid., p. 116.
13. Harrison, p. 333.
14. Carell, pp. 114-15. Besides Pickert and Rommel, a number of other key German officers were absent all or part of D-Day, including Sepp Dietrich, who was in Belgium. Three divisional commanders whose troops were in the Cotentin Peninsula (Lieutenant General Heinz Hellmich of the 243rd Infantry, Major General Wilhelm Falley of the 91st Air Landing, and Lieutenant General Karl Wilhelm von Schlieben of the 709th Infantry) were en route to the war game at Rennes. Colonel Hans Georg von Tempelhof, Rommel's Operations Officer, and Colonel Wilhelm Meyer-Detring of OB West's Operations Staff were on leave. Admiral Theodor Krancke, the chief naval officer in the West, was in Bordeaux on an inspection trip. So many key officers were absent from their posts that Hitler ordered an investigation to see if the British Military Intelligence had anything to do with it.
15. Irving, p. 323.
16. Harrison, p. 338.
17. Ibid.,
18. Ibid., pp. 343-45.
19. McKee, pp. 70-71.
20. Ruge, p. 332.
21. Montgomery, pp. 58-60.
22. See Speidel, pp. 80-81.
23. Carell, p. 23.
24. McKee, p. 76.
25. Carell, p. 136.
26. Ibid., p. 136.
27. Harrison, pp. 351-53.
28. Ibid., pp. 352-53.
29. Harrison, p. 356; Carell, pp. 132-33.
30. Harrison, pp. 347-49.
31. McKee, pp. 76-77.
32. Ibid., p. 77.
33. Ibid., p. 78.
34. Ibid., pp. 78-80.
35. Ibid., pp. 80-81.
36. Carell, pp. 137-38.
37. Ruge, p. 337.
38. Speidel, pp. 85-86; Irving, p. 381.
39. Rommel, pp. 476-77.
40. Irving, p. 379.
41. Ibid., pp. 375-79.
42. Rommel, p. 476.
43. Speidel, pp. 82-83.
44. Ruge, p. 337.

45. Liddell Hart, II, p. 551.
46. Irving, 1977, p. 640.
47. Ruge, p. 337.
48. Harrison, p. 360.
49. Harrison, pp. 360-61; Carell, p. 133.
50. Carell, pp. 133-34.
51. Ibid., p. 134.
52. Harrison, pp. 364-66.
53. McKee, pp. 82-83.
54. Ibid., p. 87.
55. Carell, p. 154.
56. McKee, p. 94.
57. Carell, pp. 157-58.
58. Ibid., pp. 158-59.
59. Ibid., p. 158.
60. Ibid., pp. 161-62.
61. Ibid., pp. 162-63.
62. Ibid., p. 164.
63. Ibid., p. 159.
64. Irving, p. 385.
65. Speidel, p. 89.
66. Ibid.
67. Ibid., pp. 91-92.
68. Ibid., p. 92.
69. Rommel, p. 479.
70. Carell, p. 162.
71. Speidel, pp. 92-93.
72. Ibid., p. 93.
73. Ibid.
74. Ibid., pp. 93-94.
75. Ibid., p. 94.
76. Rommel, p. 479.

4

1. Harrison, p. 387.
2. Carell, p. 167.
3. Harrison, pp. 385-95; Carrel, p. 167.
4. Harrison, pp. 385-95.
5. Ibid., p. 402.
6. Ibid., p. 404.
7. Ibid., pp. 402-3.
8. Ibid., p. 404.
9. Carell, pp. 184, 167-68.
10. Montgomery, p. 54.
11. Harrison, pp. 413-14.
12. Carell, p. 170.

13. Harrison, p. 415.
14. Carell, p. 169-70.
15. Ibid., pp. 170-72.
16. Ibid., p. 173.
17. Irving, p. 392.
18. Carell, pp. 172-74; Montgomery, p. 62.
19. McKee, p. 126.
20. Ibid., p. 126.
21. Harrison, p. 426.
22. McKee, p. 126.
23. Ibid., p. 128.
24. Ruge, p. 342.
25. McKee, pp. 128-29.
26. Harrison, p. 430; Carell, p. 181.
27. Harrison, p. 431.
28. Carell, p. 179.
29. Ibid.
30. Irving, p. 391.
31. Carell, pp. 185-86.
32. Ibid., p. 188.
33. Ibid., pp. 189-91, 209-11.
34. Speidel, p. 88; Montgomery, p. 63.
35. Harrison, p. 441.
36. Ibid.
37. Ibid., pp. 441, 447.
38. Montgomery, p. 63.

5

1. Ruge, p. 343.
2. Carell, pp. 200-1.
3. Ibid., pp. 201-2.
4. Ruge, p. 342.
5. Carell, pp. 201-2.
6. Ruge, p. 340.
7. Harrison, pp. 442-43.
8. B. H. Liddell Hart, *The Other Side of the Hill* (London: Cassell, 1951), p. 409.
9. McKee, p. 123.
10. Ibid., p. 122; Montgomery, p. 64.
11. Carell, pp. 203-4.
12. Ibid., pp. 204-5.
13. Ibid., p. 207.
14. Harrison, pp. 443-44.
15. McKee, p. 133.
16. Montgomery, p. 64.
17. McKee, p. 133.
18. Ibid., p. 136.

19. Ibid., pp. 133-34; 141.
20. Ibid., pp. 134-35.
21. Ibid., p. 138.
22. Harrison, p. 444.
23. McKee, pp. 144-45.
24. Ibid., p. 148; Montgomery, pp. 64-65.
25. Carell, p. 207.
26. McKee, pp. 154-58.
27. Ibid., pp. 161-63.
28. Carell, p. 209.
29. Ruge, p. 341.
30. Ibid.
31. Harrison, p. 444.
32. Ibid., p. 445.
33. Speidel, pp. 103-4.
34. OB 1945, pp. 529, 597.
35. Carell, pp. 209-10; 7th Mortar Brigade included the 83rd and 84th Mortar Regiments and was
    commanded by Colonel Tzschoekell.
36. Speidel, pp. 88-89.
37. See McKee, pp. 158-62.
38. Speidel, p. 89.
39. Irving, p. 397.
40. Ibid., p. 398.
41. Ibid., pp. 398-99.
42. Speidel, p. 89.
43. Toland, pp. 1080-81.
44. Irving, 1977, pp. 649-50.
45. Toland, p. 1081.
46. Rommel, p. 480.
47. Irving, p. 399.
48. Speidel, pp. 101-2.
49. Ibid.
50. Harrison, p. 447; Irving, 1977, p. 650.
51. Speidel, pp. 103-4.
52. Irving, 1977, p. 651.
53. Harrison, p. 447.
54. Rommel, p. 467.
55. Chant et al., p. 86.
56. Rommel, pp. 467-68.
57. Speidel, p. 105.
58. Ibid., pp. 105-6.
59. Irving, p. 403.
60. Speidel, pp. 105-6.
61. Irving, p. 403.
62. Rommel, p. 481.
63. Ibid.
64. Ibid., pp. 482-83.
65. Hart, 1951, p. 413.
66. Ibid., p. 485.

67. Irving, pp. 401-2.
68. Carell, p. 217.
69. Martin Blumenson, *Breakout and Pursuit*. U.S. Army in World War II, The European Theater of Operations, Office of the Chief of Military History (Washington, D.C.: United States Government Printing Office, 1961), p. 148.
70. Ibid., pp. 53, 78, 119.
71. Blumenson, pp. 78-84; Montgomery, p. 71.
72. Blumenson, p. 57.
73. Ibid.,
74. Ibid., p. 58.
75. Carell, p. 170-72.
76. Blumenson, p. 63.
77. Ibid., pp. 55-57.
78. Ibid., pp. 72-76.
79. Ibid., pp. 78-80.
80. Ibid., pp. 78-84.
81. Ibid., p. 86.
82. Ibid., pp. 86-90.
83. Ibid., pp. 90-92.
84. Ibid., pp. 95-101.
85. Ibid., pp. 95-101.
86. Carell, p. 215.
87. McKee, pp. 175-79.
88. Ibid., p. 179.
89. Montgomery, pp. 73-74.
90. McKee, p. 179.
91. Ibid., pp. 179-81.
92. Blumenson, pp. 123-27.
93. Ibid., pp. 128-33.
94. Ibid., pp. 102-9.
95. Ibid., pp. 103, 113-15.
96. Ibid., pp. 116-17.
97. Carell, pp. 218-19.
98. McKee, pp. 191-92.
99. In his memoirs, Montgomery stated that the preparatory air strikes were launched from 9:50 P.M. to 10:30 P.M. on July 7 and the ground attack began at 4:20 A.M. on July 8. He explained that the bombers struck this far in advance of the ground attack because weather conditions were forecasted as unfavorable for air activity on the morning of July 8 (Montgomery, pp. 72-73).
100. McKee, pp. 197-201; Montgomery, pp. 72-73.
101. Carell, pp. 215-16.
102. Ibid.
103. McKee, p. 201.
104. Montgomery, pp. 74-75.
105. Carell, pp. 216-17.
106. Montgomery, p. 75.
107. Mitcham, p. 53.
108. Irving, pp. 339-340.
109. Ibid., p. 406.
110. McKee, pp. 205-11.

111. Ibid., pp. 212-17.
112. Montgomery, p. 78.
113. McKee, pp. 212-17.
114. Ibid., p. 227.
115. Ibid., pp. 227-28.
116. Montgomery, pp. 74-75.
117. Blumenson, pp. 147-49.
118. Ibid., pp. 149-52.
119. Ibid., pp. 152-53.
120. Ibid., pp. 152-57.
121. Ibid., pp. 157.
122. Ibid., pp. 159-162.
123. Ibid., pp. 168-69.
124. Esposito, p. 90.
125. Montgomery, p. 78.
126. Ibid., p. 79.
127. McKee, pp. 230-32.
128. Ibid., pp. 229-30.
129. Ibid., pp. 231-32.
130. Fuller, 1949, p. 300.
131. Ibid.
132. Ibid.
133. McKee, p. 235; Carell, p. 225.
134. Irving, p. 420.
135. Montgomery, p. 79.
136. Irving, p. 420.
137. McKee, pp. 240-46.
138. Ruge, p. 344.
139. Carell, pp. 226-28.
140. McKee, p. 256.
141. The suggestion that Montgomery be relieved was allegedly made by the Deputy Supreme Commander, British Air Chief Marshal Sir Arthur Tedder, Eisenhower's second-in-command. Tedder later denied that he made the suggestion (Liddell Hart, II, pp. 553, 556).

6

1. Young, pp. 170-71.
2. Speidel, p. 140; Young, p. 171.
3. Young, p. 171.
4. Ibid.
5. Rommel, p. 429.
6. Ibid.
7. Speidel, p. 65.
8. Irving, p. 328.
9. Speidel, p. 67.
10. Toland, p. 1084.
11. Speidel, pp. 67-68.

12. Forman, p. 72.
13. Speidel, p. 100.
14. Ibid., p. 106.
15. Ibid., pp. 106-7.
16. Irving, pp. 417-18.
17. Speidel, pp. 108-9.
18. Ibid., p. 108.
19. Rommel, pp. 486-87.
20. Speidel, p. 111.
21. Irving, pp. 413-14.
22. Forman, p. 216.
23. Montgomery, p. 82.
24. Ibid., p. 85.
25. Blumenson, p. 236.
26. Rommel, p. 489.
27. Montgomery, p. 86.
28. Ibid.
29. Rommel, pp. 489-90.
30. Carell, p. 235.
31. Rommel, p. 490.
32. Blumenson, p. 240.
33. Third U.S. Army was under Lieutenant General Omar Bradley's U.S. 12th Army Group. Both were activated on August 1, 1944. Lieutenant General Courtney Hodges replaced Bradley as commander of the U.S. 1st Army. The Canadian 1st Army under Lieutenant General Sir Henry D. G. Crerar was activated on July 23 as part of Montgomery's 21st Army Group.
34. Blumenson, p. 273. Tychsen had recently replaced SS Lieutenant General Heinz Lammerding, who had been wounded in an air attack. The 2nd SS Panzer lost two-thirds of its men during the Normandy fighting (Max Hastings, Das Reich, New York: Holt, Rinehart and Winston, 1981, pp. 217-18).
35. Speidel, p. 140.
36. Rommel, p. 493.
37. Irving, p. 427.
38. Young, p. 184.
39. Ibid.
40. Ibid.
41. Ibid., pp. 184-85.
42. Ibid., p. 185.
43. Irving, pp. 431-32.
44. Young, p. 185.
45. Rommel, p. 495.
46. Ibid., p. 497.
47. Young, p. 186.
48. Irving, p. 430. Krebs was the last Chief of the German General Staff. He committed suicide in May 1945.
49. Speidel, p. 141.
50. Young, p. 187.
51. Ibid., pp. 174-75.
52. Rommel, p. 500.
53. Young, p. 188.

54. Rommel, p. 497.
55. Ibid.
56. Ibid., p. 502.
57. Speidel, p. 142.
58. Ibid.
59. Irving, pp. 435-36.
60. Rommel, pp. 501-2.
61. Young, p. 190.
62. Rommel, p. 502.
63. Young, p. 190.
64. Irving, p. 439.
65. Young, p. 190.
66. Rommel, p. 502.
67. Young, pp. 190-91.
68. Rommel, p. 502.
69. Young, pp. 190-91.
70. Ibid., p. 191.
71. Irving, p. 443.
72. Rommel, p. 503.
73. Young, p. 191.
74. Rommel, pp. 503-4.
75. Ibid.
76. Ibid., p. 504.
77. Young, p. 194.
78. Ibid., p. 193.
79. Rommel, p. 505.
80. Ibid.
81. Ibid., pp. 505-6.
82. Young, p. 195.
83. Ibid., pp. 195-96.
84. Georg von Bismarck commanded the 21st Panzer Division in the Afrika Korps in the Gazala Line battles, the Second Battle of Tobruk, and the Egyptian Campaign of 1942. He was killed in action on the night of August 31/September 1, 1942, while he was leading his division through a British mine field in the first stage of what became the Battle of Alma Halfa Ridge.
85. Young, p. 197.
86. Ibid.
87. Ibid., pp. 198-99.

Bibliography

Blumenson, Martin. *Breakout and Pursuit,* U.S. Army in World War II, The European Theater of Operations, Office of the Chief of Military History, U.S. Department of the Army. Washington, D.C.: United States Government Printing Office, 1961.

Carell, Paul. *The Foxes of the Desert.* New York: Bantam Books, Inc., 1972 (originally published by E. P. Dutton, New York: 1960).

———. *Hitler Moves East, 1941–1943.* New York: Bantam Books, 1966 (originally published by Little, Brown and Company, Boston: 1965).

———. *Invasion: They're Coming!* Translated by E. Osers. New York: E. P. Dutton, New York, 1963).

Chant, Christopher, Richard Humble, William Fowler, and Jenny Shaw. *Hitler's Generals and Their Battles.* New York: Chartwell Books, Inc., 1976.

Dulles, Allen W. *Germany's Underground.* Westport, Conn.: Greenwood Press, 1978.

Edwards, Roger. *German Airborne Troops, 1936–1945.* Garden City, New York: Doubleday and Company, Inc., 1974.

Eisenhower, Dwight D. *Crusade in Europe.* Garden City, New York: Doubleday and Company, Inc., 1949.

Esposito, Vincent J., ed. *A Concise History of World War II.* New York: Frederick A. Praeger, Publishers, 1964 (copyrighted by The Americana Corporation, 1964).

FitzGibbon, Constantine. *20 July.* New York: W. W. Norton and Company, Inc., 1956.

Forman, James. *Code Name Valkyrie: Count von Stauffenberg and the Plot to Kill Hitler.* New York: Laurel-Leaf Library, 1975.

Fuller, J. F. C., *A Military History of the Western World.* (3 volumes). New York: Minerva Press, 1956.

————. *The Second World War, 1939–45: A Strategical and Tactical History*. New York: Duell, Sloan and Pearce, 1949.

Galland, Adolf. *The First and the Last*. New York: Henry Holt & Company, Inc., 1954.

Goebbels, Joseph. *The Goebbels Diaries*. Louis P. Lochner, ed. New York: Universal-Award House, Inc., 1971 (originally published by Doubleday and Company, Inc., Garden City, New York: 1948).

Guderian, Heinz. *Panzer Leader*. New York: Ballantine Books, 1967 (originally published by E. P. Dutton, New York: 1957).

Harrison, Gordon A. *Cross-Channel Attack*. U.S. Army in World War II, The European Theater of Operations, Office of the Chief of Military History, U.S. Department of the Army. Washington, D.C.: United States Government Printing Office, 1951.

Hastings, Max. *Das Reich*. New York: Holt, Rinehart and Winston, 1981.

Hoffman, Peter. *The History of the German Resistance, 1933–1945*. Cambridge, Mass.: M.I.T. Press, 1977.

Infield, Glenn. *Big Week*. Los Angeles: Pinnacle Books, 1974.

Irving, David. *Hitler's War*. New York: The Viking Press, 1977.

————. *The Trail of the Fox*. New York: E. P. Dutton, Thomas Congdon Books, 1977.

Jacobsen, Hans-Adolf, ed. *July 20, 1944*. Bonn: Federal German Government Press and Information Office, 1969.

———— and J. Rohwer, ed. *Decisive Battles of World War II: The German View*. New York: G. P. Putnam's Sons, 1965.

Keitel, Wilhelm. *In the Service of the Reich*. Briarcliff Manor, N.Y.: Stein and Day, Publishers, 1979.

Kriestagebuch des Oberkommando des Wehrmacht (Wehrmachfuehrungsstab), Bauk IV: 1 Januar 1944–22 Mai 1945. Frankfurt-am-Main: Bernard and Graefe Verlag fur Wehrwesen, 1961.

Lewin, Ronald. *Rommel as a Military Commander*. New York: Ballantine Books, Inc., 1970 (originally published by D. Van Nostrand Company, Inc., 1968).

Liddell Hart, B. H. *History of the Second World War*. (2 Volumes). New York: G. P. Putnam's Sons, 1972.

————. *The Other Side of the Hill*. London: Cassell, 1951.

McKee, Alexander. *Last Round Against Rommel*. New York: Signet Books, 1966.

Mellenthin, Frederick Wilhelm von. *Panzer Battles: A Study in the Em-

ployment of Armor in the Second World War. New York: Ballantine Books, 1976 (originally published by the University of Oklahoma Press, 1956).

Mitcham, Samuel W., Jr. *Rommel's Desert War.* Briarcliff Manor, New York: Stein and Day, Publishers, 1982.

Montgomery, Bernard Law, The Viscount of Alamein. *Normandy to the Baltic.* London: Hutchinson and Company, Publishers, Ltd., 1958.

Neumann, Peter. *The Black March: The Personal Story of an SS Man.* New York: Bantam Books, Inc., 1960 (originally published by Editions France-Empire, Paris, 1958, under the title *SS!*).

Rommel, Erwin. *The Rommel Papers.* B. H. Liddell Hart, ed. New York: Harcourt, Brace and Company, 1953.

Ruge, Friedrich. "The Invasion of Normandy," in H. A. Jacobsen and J. Rohwer (eds.), *The Decisive Battles of World War II: The German View.* New York: G. P. Putnam's Sons, 1965: pp. 317-49.

Ryan, Cornelius. *The Longest Day.* Popular Library (by arrangement with Simon and Schuster, Inc., New York: 1959).

Seaton, Albert. *The Russo-German War, 1941-45.* New York: Frederick A. Praeger, 1971.

Shirer, William L. *The Rise and Fall of the Third Reich.* New York: Simon and Schuster, 1960.

Speidel, Hans. *Invasion 1944.* New York: Paperback Library, Inc., 1950 (originally published by Henry Regnery Company, 1950).

Toland, John. *Adolf Hitler.* New York: Ballantine Books, 1977 (originally published by Random House, 1976).

United States Army Military Intelligence Service. "Order of Battle of the German Army. Editions of October 1942, April 1943, and January 1945. Washington, D.C.: Military Intelligence Service, 1942, 1943, and 1945, respectively.

Wilt, Alan F. *The Atlantic Wall: Hitler's Defense in the West, 1941-45.* Ames, Iowa: Iowa State University Press, 1975.

Young, Desmond. *Rommel: The Desert Fox.* New York: Harper & Row, 1965.

Zimmermann, Erich and Hans-Adolf Jacobsen. *Germans Against Hitler, July 20, 1944.* Bonn: Federal German Government Press and Information Office, 1960.

APPENDIX I

Tables of Equivalent Ranks

U.S. Army	German Army
General of the Army	Field Marshal (Generalfeldmarschall)
General	Colonel General (Generaloberst)
Lieutenant General	General (General)
Major General	Lieutenant General (Generalleutnant)
Brigadier General	Major General (Generalmajor)
Colonel	Colonel (Oberst)
Lieutenant Colonel	Lieutenant Colonel (Oberstleutnant)
Major	Major (Major)
Captain	Captain (Hauptmann)
First Lieutenant	Lieutenant (Oberleutnant)
Second Lieutenant	Lieutenant (Leutnant)

SS Rank	German Army Equivalent
Reichsfuehrer SS (Himmler)	Commander-in-Chief of the Army*
None	Field Marshal
Oberstgruppenfuehrer	Colonel General
Obergruppenfuehrer	General
Gruppenfuehrer	Lieutenant General
Brigadefuehrer	Major General
Oberfuehrer	None
Standartenfuehrer	Colonel
Obersturmbannfuehrer	Lieutenant Colonel
Sturmbannfuehrer	Major
Hauptsturmfuehrer	Captain
Obersturmfuehrer	First Lieutenant
Untersturmfuehrer	Second Lieutenant

---

*This post was held by Adolf Hitler from December 1941 until the end of the war.

APPENDIX II

German Units, Ranks, and Strengths

Unit	Rank of Commander*	Strength†
Army Group	Field Marshal	2 or more armies
Army	Colonel General	2 or more corps
Corps	General	2 or more divisions
Division	Lieutenant General/ Major General	10,000–18,000 men 200–350 tanks (if panzer)
Brigade‡	Major General/ Colonel	2 or more regiments
Regiment	Colonel	2–7 battalions
Battalion	Lieutenant Colonel/ Major/Captain	2 or more companies (approximately 500 men per infantry battalion; usually 50–80 tanks per panzer battalion)
Company§	Captain/Lieutenant	3–5 platoons
Platoon	Lieutenant/ Sergeant Major	Infantry: 30–40 men Panzer: 4 or 5 tanks
Section	Warrant Officer/ Sergeant Major	2 squads (more or less)
Squad	Sergeant	Infantry: 7–10 men Armor: 1 tank

*Frequently, units were commanded by lower-ranking men as the war went on.

†As the war progressed, the number of men and tanks in most units declined accordingly. SS units usually had more men and tanks than Army units.

‡Rarely used in the German Army.

§Called batteries in the artillery (4 or 5 guns per battery).

APPENDIX III

German Staff Abbreviations

1a—Staff Officer, Operations
    (equivalent to S-3 in the U.S. Army)
1b—Staff Officer, Supplies
    (equivalent to S-4 in the U.S. Army)
1c—Staff Officer, Intelligence
    (equivalent to S-2 in the U.S. Army)
11a—Staff Officer, Personnel
    (equivalent to S-1 in the U.S. Army)

The U.S. staff position S-5 (Civil Affairs Section) had no equivalent in the German Army during World War II.

APPENDIX IV

Characteristics of Opposing Tanks

Model	Weight (in tons)	Speed (mph)	Range (miles)	Armament	Crew
		BRITISH			
Mark IV "Churchill"	43.1	15	120	1 6-pounder	5
Mark VI "Crusader"	22.1	27	200	1 2-pounder	5
Mark VIII "Cromwell"	30.8	38	174	1 75mm	5
		AMERICAN			
M3A1 "Stuart"*	14.3	36	60	1 37mm	4
M4A3 "Sherman"	37.1	30	120	1 76mm 3 MGs	5
		GERMAN			
PzKw II	9.3	25	118	1 20mm 1 MG	3
PzKw III	24.5	25	160	1 50mm 2 MGs	5
PzKw IV	19.7	26	125	1 75mm 2 MGs	5
PzKw V "Panther"	49.3	25	125	1 75mm 2 MGs	5
PzKw VI "Tiger"	62.0	23	73	1 88mm 2 MGs	5

*Reconnaissance tank

GENERAL INDEX

SUBJECT INDEX